Prophetic Women
of Bold Love

Shaun

Madigan

Prophetic Women of Bold Love

Spiritualities of Non-Violence

Shawn Madigan, PhD, CSJ

To order additional copies of this book, contact:
Xlibris Corporation
1-888-795-4274
www.Xlibris.com
Orders@Xlibris.com
77604

Contents

Acknowledgments

People

Lisa Barelli
Bill Campbell
Rosemarie Cerminaro
Noemi Chazan
Patricia Crockford
Lianna Gilman
Terry Greenblatt
Mairead Corrigan Maguire
Judy Mayotte
Judy Miller, CSJ
Julie Noordhoek
Mercy Amba Oduyoye
Mrs. Sadako Ogata
Ann Pace, CSJ
Jehan Sadat (Mrs. Anwar Sadat)
Sisters of St. Joseph: Japan, St. Louis, St. Paul
Victoria Stansky
Alicia Torello
St. Catherine University Theology Faculty
Mary Lynn Windsor
Linda Woolridge

Publishing Houses/ Groups

Augsburg-Fortress, Minneapolis, MN
Chosen Books, LLC, Chappaqua, NY
Context Institute, Langley, WA
Food First: Institute for Food & Development Policy, Oakland, CA
Gill and Macmillan, Dublin, Ireland
Harper-Collins, New York, NY
Hay House, Carlsbad, CA
Houghton Mifflin Harcourt Publication, New York, NY
Hunt Alternatives Fund, Washington, DC
Hyperion, Buena Vista Books, New York, NY
INCORE, University of Ulster, Londonderry, North Ireland
Mainstream Publishers, Edinburgh, Ltd.
Norton and Co., New York, NY
Peace People, Belfast, North Ireland
Random House, New York, NY
Simon and Schuster, New York, NY
University of Pennsylvania Press, Philadelphia, PA
University Press of New England, Lebanon, NH
Urgent Action Fund for Women's Human Rights
Wesleyan University Press, Middletown, CT
Wisdom Publications, Somerville, MA

Introduction

In the Jewish scriptures the prophet Daniel acknowledged that the God of the chosen people was a God whose justice and forgiveness were placed in the mystery of compassion (Dan. 9:7-9). In the Christian scriptures, the evangelists present Jesus Christ as one who is just but also encourages his followers to "Be merciful just as your Father is merciful" (Luke 6:36). Compassionate justice and mercy are themes that are also found in Buddhism's Noble Eightfold Path, Muslim sutras and Hinduism. In these and many other religious traditions, forgiveness and mercy are strengths that ground the inner and outer peace of the holy ones or saints. Such strengths can transform a world of enemies into a world of peace.

The women in this volume embody the transforming strengths of justice and compassion that their respective religious traditions teach. Each manifests the Sacred in her own life and has affected the life of many others. Insofar as prophets manifest the living presence of the Sacred in word and deed, each of the women in this work could be called a prophet of bold love. Some of the women are living still and continue to affect the world of this relatively new century. A spirituality of nonviolence grounds the lives of these women who have known violence in various forms throughout their lives.

The women in this volume are not preaching sermons. They have lived or are living with justice and compassion for all. They represent a diversity of cultures, of religious traditions, of personalities and of experiences of violence. The form of violence each knows varies in number and kind: physical, economic, military, social, ethnic, religious, ecological, racist, sexist, psychological. Regardless of the form or combination of forms of violence, none of these women responded in kind. Instead, each one responded with a strong sense of active reconciliation, compassion and forgiveness providing hope for a new future of peace.

Like holy people of any age, each woman has been an active participant in shaping her own meanings out of a faith tradition. The interactive blend of action and contemplation varies with the uniqueness of the spirituality in each woman. Yet, in spite of the uniqueness of each one's life journey, there is a formative spirituality of prophetic living and bold love that unites these women in a sisterhood of communion for a better world. The walls of "I" separated from "they" have dissolved into a larger "we." Each of the women had dreams and visions of a better world and each labored to make at least some of the dreams and visions come true.

A brief biographical sketch and the reflections of each woman require no commentary on my part, for the lives and words of the women demonstrate clearly their prophetic strengths of compassion and bold love. The reflective reader will learn new faces of the strengths of women whose lives transform their respective parts of the world and perhaps hear a challenge to do the same. It is no easy task at this point in history to respond to the challenge to form a global community of peace and justice. The women in this work have set forth a vision of the possible. May those who bring these visions and hopes into reality continue to increase and may we be in that number in the days ahead.

> Dark and cold we may be, but this
> Is no winter now. The frozen misery
> Of centuries breaks, cracks, begins to move;
> The thunder is the thunder of the floes,
> The thaw, the flood, the Upstart Spring.
> Thank God, our time is now when wrong
> Comes up to face us everywhere,
> Never to leave us till we take

The longest stride of soul men (and women) ever took.
Affairs are now soul size:
The enterprise
Is exploration into God![1]

Professor Shawn Madigan, CSJ
Pentecost, 2010

NOTE

[1] Christopher Fry, *A Sleep of Prisoners: Three Plays* (New York: Oxford Univ. Press, 1965). 209.

1

Corrie ten Boom, Holland

Corrie ten Boom was born in Haarlem, Amsterdam, Nederlands, on April 15, 1892. An older brother, Willem, a sister, Betsie, her father, mother, two aunts and eventually a little sister Nolle had happy memories of the house. Corrie's father was a master watchmaker. Each Monday Corrie's father took a train to the Naval Observatory in Amsterdam to get the exact time. In summers Corrie accompanied him and had special time alone with him.

One of the most vivid memories Corrie recalled from her childhood was the first experience of death. At age six Corrie went with her mother to an upper room in their town where a young couple mourned the death of their baby. Corrie went to the baby's room and touched its cold little fingers. For the first time she realized that death would happen to all whom she loved. That night when she started to cry about this, her father assured her that death wouldn't happen until she was ready and God would then give her the strength to live with it.

At sixteen Corrie fell in love with Karel, a friend of her brother Willem. Karel was in his twenties. Corrie looked forward to Karel visiting them, for she and Karel were able to talk about anything. They became the closest of friends even if they did not see each other that often. Willem married his friend Tine and was ordained in the Dutch Reform Church. The ten Boom family made the trip to Brabant as did Karel, Willem and Corrie's friend. Karel and Corrie picked up their friendship quickly as if they had not been apart. As he left Karel asked Corrie to write to him often. She was delighted and felt marriage to her was not too far off.

Willem noticed Corrie's love for Karel, so he felt he must tell her why Karel could never marry her. Karel was from a very wealthy prominent family, and the ten Boom family was common. Willem assured Corrie that Karel did love her but marriage was out of the picture. Corrie was heart broken. Once again it was her father who gave her good advice.

> Love is the strongest force in the world. When it is blocked, it means pain. There are two things we can do when this happens. We can kill the love so that it stops hurting . . . . Or we can ask God to open up another route for that love to travel.[1]

In time, Corrie found many other routes for love to travel. When she finished secondary school she did not go to the university because her mother was ill. Corrie and her sister Betsie took over as much of their mother's work as they could. Corrie also took over some of the work in the watchmaker's shop. Her mother's ongoing concern for all suffering people taught Corrie that " . . . love is larger than the walls which shut it in."[2]

After Mrs. ten Boom died Corrie and Betsie agreed to stay in the ten Boom house to help their father so that Nolle could leave to get married. Betsie cooked and cleaned while Corrie became her father's first apprentice as a watchmaker and was the first woman to be granted a watchmaker's license in Holland.

The growing Nazi movement did not really touch the ten Boom family until an older family friend named Christolph was physically beaten by Otto, a German apprentice to Mr. ten Boom. Mr. ten Boom couldn't believe that his courteous German apprentice would ever beat old Christolph. However, Willem reminded his father that the Nazis had no respect for deformed or old and weak people. When Mr. ten Boom asked Otto about the physical mistreatment of Christolph, Otto looked at him with contempt and left the shop.

In 1937 Mr. ten Boom, Corrie, Betsie, Willem and Nollie along with many others celebrated the 100th birthday of the watchmaker's shop. This shop had the reputation of being one of the finest watchmaking establishments in Europe. At the celebration the family learned that Willem was assisting Jews to escape death through the underground. The family was not really involved with the underground until 1939 when Willem brought an elderly German watchmaker to meet his father. The elderly Jewish businessman had escaped on a milk truck after some German youth lit his beard on fire. The man fled with nothing. Graciously Mr. ten Boom, Corrie and Betsie put him up in the ten Boom house.

The Nazis invaded Holland and occupied it in 1940. They considered the Dutch to be fellow Aryans, so for a time no Dutch were executed. That changed in May, 1942. Restrictions were imposed. More fearful Jews began knocking at the ten Boom door for asylum because Willem had spread the word that the ten Booms could give them safe housing. The biggest problem was getting enough food cards, for each household was restricted to using only its own card.

Willem told Corrie she had to use her own ingenuity to get more cards. She didn't know how that would work, but one evening the light dawned. Corrie remembered a friend, Fred, who now worked with ration cards. After curfew she bicycled to his place. Fred said the cards were counted every day by the Nazis, so the only way to get cards was for him to be robbed. Corrie needed a hundred cards. Fred said to come back in a week which she did. His face was swollen and bruised and his lower lip was cut. He smiled as he told her the news. "My friend took very naturally to the part," was all he said as he now issued one hundred cards.[3]

Corrie's next challenge came when she was summoned to a meeting by one of Willem's sons. After curfew she and her nephew rode on bike rims to a mansion hidden in the trees in the countryside. Corrie was introduced to a very distinguished group of people. Each person had the name "Smit," the common name given to everyone in the underground.

To her utter surprise Corrie was introduced as the head of the underground in the city of Haarlem! Each "Smit" came froward to tell Corrie what talents that Smit could use for the good of all. These talents ranged from paper forgery, false license plates, fake identifications, house safety reconstructions and multiple other talents. One Smit said that he would visit the ten Boom house in the morning to see about improvements. Corrie told her father that a builder would stop by to inspect the house.

When Smit came he tapped on walls and located a lot of wasted space. He told Corrie and her father that some men would come to tear down walls and set up false spaces for hiding. This simple procedure would save many more lives and give the family safety too. Smit told Corrie and Betsie to keep their room at the top of the stairs. While searches were going on below they would have time to make their space seem normal. The rooms would have new walls that were rolled into the hidden spaces and rolled out as people hid in the spaces. It took six days for the sliding walls, false bookcases and additional safety items to be installed.

When all was ready Smit had the family and their guests run drills. The drills got progressively better, and each person learned what to do. Corrie's job would be to detain the Nazi searchers in the shop below while Mr. ten Boom and Betsie would push evidence of additional plates or other items used by guest diners behind the moving panels. Quietly the guests would slip into their hiding places in the false spaces. Smit reminded everyone that meal time was a favorite time for Nazi raids. After many dry runs the fear did not disappear, but the ten Boom family felt more secure in their ability to hide the Jews and not get caught.[4]

For more than a year the family and guests were not caught. Ostensibly this family was simply an older watchmaker living with his two spinster daughters above his tiny shop. Actually this house called the Beje was the center of an underground ring that spread to the farthest corners of Holland. Corrie became frightened after her sister Nolle was sent to jail in Haarlem for harboring Jews. After ten days, Nolle was sent to a federal prison in Amsterdam.

The Nazis started barging into homes more frequently. They came at night, woke people up and interrogated them about any Jews they might be hiding. The resistance workers decided Corrie and Betsie should receive further training in being non-committal. In time Corrie got quite good at stating that there were no Jews in hiding as soon as she was awakened.

Corrie and Willem's wife Tine became increasingly concerned about Willem. Because he was an ordained minister the Nazis had been content to follow him but not to put him in jail unless they actually caught him in the process of hiding or transporting Jews. Corrie's father remained as calm and steadfast as ever. For him being Christian meant they must help.

One evening the three ten Booms, their seven permanent guests and two additional Jews who were temporary residents were eating. Corrie heard a knock at the door and went to answer it. It was the former German apprentice, Otto, now in uniform and looking officious. He demanded to be let in, his eyes searching the environment. He invited himself upstairs to discuss old times, all the while knocking on walls to discover any hollow sounds. Corrie detained him as long as she could but he pushed his way to the stairs. Father and Betsie looked up from their meal. The table was now set for three with Corrie's unfinished plate on the far side. There had been twelve people eating at the table minutes before. Otto lingered for 15 minutes more to boast about being an officer. After another half hour, the all clear was given to the cramped and shaky guests.[5]

As Christmas approached in 1943 many families the ten Booms knew had someone either in jail or at a work camp. As was their custom with their Jewish guests the ten Booms celebrated the days of Hanukkah with them. Close to Christmas the police chief sent a messenger to tell Corrie he had to see her immediately. After sending his other workers from the room he informed Corrie that he knew what she was doing, was in sympathy with the effort, but wanted her to know that there was someone she trusted who was an informant. The chief wanted this informant assassinated. Corrie said no although she was saddened by the news. Then she and the chief said a prayer for the Dutch informants who were turning against their own people.

After this night Corrie had a sense of dread that soon her family would be caught. This sense of dread increased when a young courier for the partisans was arrested. Everyone knew this young man would tell everything during the days of interrogation. The resistance group met and agreed that the ten Booms should turn out their guests for their own safety. The family talked and prayed about it but decided they had to continue helping others until they could do it no longer. "Perhaps only when human effort had done its best and failed would God's power alone be free to work."[6]

On the morning of February 28, 1944, Corrie was in bed with a high fever and flu. She awoke to loud pounding and then the opening of the front door. She heard feet scurrying quickly past her bed and familiar sounds of walls and panels moving. This was the day she had dreaded. Things moved quickly from interrogation to being slapped in the face numerous times, being knocked to the floor for consistently saying she did not know what the man was talking about and eventually being dragged down the stairs. Men with hammers started pounding out the walls to discover the hiding spaces.

Betsie and her father were beaten during the harsh questioning. When the phone rang a soldier picked it up to hear a partisan telling the family they were in danger because someone had informed on them. This was all the proof the Gestapo needed that the family had been providing safe haven for the Jews. The ten Booms were told to dress warmly, get into the street and do as directed. On the street they saw Nolle, some of their hidden Jews, Willem, some neighbors and many others being led toward a large gym. Here with many other people, some badly beaten, the group was told they were in a holding place. They could go out to a latrine one at a time with a guard, but otherwise they were not to leave the space. People from Haarlem had gathered behind police barricades to catch a glimpse of relatives or friends from the gym who would be bused to a new destination, the Hague, which was Gestapo headquarters for Holland.

After more interrogation at the Hague, the group was marched to the federal penitentiary of Scheveningen until further notice. Here Corrie and others were placed in overcrowded cells with no way to check on other members of the family. The world now consisted of this cubicle. Corrie got used to the straw "bed" on the floor once she was tired enough. When she was placed in solitary confinement she tried to console herself by recalling some basic faith beliefs about victory coming through suffering. "I would look around at the bare little cell and wonder what conceivable victory could come from a place like this."[7]

In spring while all the guards were at a party to celebrate Hitler's birthday, the women in prison finally shouted their names to each other. Corrie learned that her sister Betsie was in this same prison, that her brother Willem had been released and that her father had died.

In June Corrie, Betsie and a trainload of other women were transferred to Vught, another camp in Holland. Upon arrival guards took whatever small possessions the women had carried in their pillowcases. Betsie and Corrie were assigned to work stations. Those who didn't meet quotas were punished. It was here that both Corrie and Betsy found out that a family friend had betrayed them. Corrie was furious, but Betsie said their friend must be feeling even worse so they should pray for him. In mid-November Betsie began to cough up blood. Corrie knew she had to help Betsie do her work or they would not be leaving this camp together.

The Nazis decided to move some of the women to the dreaded Ravensbruck in Germany where thousands had already died. Corrie and Betsie were among those loaded on a train for the four-day trip. Betsie became more ill with each passing day. At Ravensbruck, the women were in overcrowded barracks. Corrie and others would gather secretly to pray when their guards were elsewhere. With her deep faith Betsie experienced a peaceful death.[8]

Three mornings after Betsie's death Corrie's name was called. She was to be released! The prison doctor sent her to the hospital to get rid of the severe edema that had swollen her leg. Corrie was shocked at the lack of compassion she witnessed in this hospital. She saw women survivors who were horribly burned and mutilated on a prison train which had been bombed. Two nurses did nothing but mimic the burned women's cries of pain.

Corrie understood that the most fatal disease of the concentration camp was to stop feeling anything for anybody. For many it was the only way to survive. There was little reaction to the women who were paralyzed or unconscious. That first night four women fell from upper bunks and died on the floor. No one really cared since it seemed better to narrow the mind to one's own needs and not see or think about others' needs. Corrie could not live with that mentality. She brought bed pans to the women who were so severely injured they could not walk to a latrine. The deep gratitude of the patients was heart-wrenching. They expected only cruelty as a response to pain.

On New Year's Day 1945 Corrie was discharged after signing a form that stated she had never been ill at Ravensbruck and that the treatment had been good. She was dropped at a train station, waited for hours, rode many trains, got off at a Dutch border city, Gromingen, and limped to a hospital near the station. Here a nurse listened to the story of horror and gave her the care she had been denied. Such kindness moved Corrie to tears.

After 10 days hospital authorities arranged a ride for Corrie to get to her brother Willem's old place. The whole trip was illegal and took place at night without headlights. In the gray early morning the truck pulled up to Willem's big brick nursing home. Willem arrived slowly, limping down the corridor with the help of a cane. He embraced Corrie for a long time while she told him the details of Betsy's illness and death.

Willem arranged for Corrie to go to the family home in Haarlam. Corrie sensed that Willem was dying and this was to be their final good-bye. Upon arrival at the family home in Haarlem Corrie saw that her sister Nolle and her girls had been there cleaning up everything as best they could. She remembered her father's words to the Gestapo chief in the Hague, "I will open my door to anyone in need."[9] That memory gave her an idea.

Corrie knew the trials of being a war or prison victim and the time it took to heal. There had to be some place and space for others to come to terms with the sufferings of war. In thanksgiving for a son who returned safely from the war, Mrs. Bierens de Haan gave Corrie a fifty-two room mansion to provide housing for victims of war who had no place to go. The mansion was slowly restored and called the Bloemendaal. In 1947 the first Dutch people to arrive and live there were former prisoners of the Japanese in Indonesia.

This place of peace assisted the occupants to slowly heal from their suffering. Corrie noticed that one key to healing was learning to forgive. She saw that it was not the Germans or the Japanese people the occupants had the most trouble forgiving. It was the Dutch betrayers These former collaborators had to keep the head shaved. They were unable to find jobs and were objects of cruelty as they roamed the streets. Corrie turned over the ten Boom house to these former collaborators who had no place to go.[10]

In their own time people worked out the deep pain within them. It most often started in the garden as people planted and watched things grow. Corrie would tell these people about the suffering of the former collaborators who never had a visitor or a piece of mail. Gradually the people offered carrots or flowers or other produce to the former betrayers as a token of forgiveness.[11]

Corrie got contributions for Bloemendaal from speaking to groups all over the world. After speaking in a church in Munich, Germany, a former guard from Ravensbruck came up to her. He thanked her for the message that God could forgive even the worst sins. She recognized him and was so filled with anger that she could not extend her hand. She prayed for Jesus to give her some of his compassion for the world's people.

> Into my heart a love appeared for this stranger that almost overwhelmed me. I discovered it is not on our forgiveness anymore than on our goodness that the world's healing hinges. When Christ tells us to love our enemies, he gives us the love itself.[12]

Her preaching about forgiveness and love for all people raised enough funds to start many houses all over Europe for war victims on all sides of the former conflict. She never considered herself a heroine in spite of what many others claimed.[13]

Corrie was honored by the State of Israel for her work of aiding the Jewish people. Rabbi Daniel Lapin has lamented how little Corrie ten Boom is known among American Jews and how she has been ignored by the Holocaust Memorial Museum. Corrie was knighted by the Queen of Holland in recognition of her work during the war. A museum in Haarlem is dedicated to her and her family. In 1977 Corrie moved to Orange, California. Successive strokes in 1978 left her an invalid. She died on April 15, 1983, her 91st birthday.[14]

Even after her death the life of Corrie ten Boom remains a model of bold love that conquers fear. Her willingness to live with strong compassion for the victims of hatred provided a clear answer to a basic Christian question for every age: "Who do you say that I am?" (Mark 8:32)

NOTES

[1] *The Hiding Place* by Corrie ten Boom with John and Elizabeth Sherill. Copyright 1971. (Chappaqua, NY: Chosen Books LLC, 1971) *65*. The prior story is detailed on 30-65.

[2] 68; 69-78.

3   97-98; 81-98.

4   99-120.

5   129-30.

6   134; 130-34.

7   150. Further details about the raid and the times in prison can be found on 135-58.

8   159-218.

9   228; 220-28.

10   230-33.

11   232.

12   233.

13   236-37.

14   www.wikipedia.org/wiki/ Corrie_ten_Boom

2

Sophie Scholl, Germany

Sophie Scholl was born on May 9, 1921, in Forchtenburg on the Kocher River in Baden-Wurtenberg, Gemany. Water and woods provided a beautiful and peaceful environment for the five Scholl children, Inge, Hans, Elizabeth, Werner and Sophie. Their father Robert was a well-educated man and a loved mayor of Forchtenberg. Their mother Magdalene Miller had been an active deaconess whose loving, strong and peaceful nature was well known.

All the Scholl children loved art and music. Sophie excelled in writing as well. For business reasons Robert and his family moved to Ulm where the five Scholl children enrolled in secondary school. Hitler had seized power and many believed that this meant there would be more prosperous times for Germany. Hans was fifteen and Sophie was twelve when this happened and like other children were swept into the excitement of the Youth Movement with its marching youth and banners waving to drumbeat and song. They were surprised when their father disapproved by insisting that the Nazis were abusing and misusing the hopes of the German people. The Scholl teenagers ignored the voice of their father.[1]

Sophie and Hans eventually witnessed some restrictive and vindictive acts of their respective Youth Group leaders. Other group members could ignore the incidents, but the Scholl children could not. They objected and then dropped out of the groups because they saw the wisdom of their father's objections to Nazi philosophy and behaviors.

The children noticed teachers disappearing if they criticized Hitler, deformed, weak or elderly Germans being exterminated or sent to concentration camps and even young children being driven off by SS men and never returning. In spring 1942 the Bishop of Munich and other leaders began to publicly denounce the Gestapo and their tactics.

Stories were shared behind closed doors about weak or elderly Germans, physically deformed and mentally unhealthy children who needed care, and simply disappeared. Nurse friends of Mrs. Scholl stopped by to talk to her about their pain over what was happening. One of the nurses told about her patients who were young children in the hospital for the mentally ill. Black vans driven by SS men appeared at intervals; the SS told the children they were going on a secret journey so they excitedly raced into the vans and never returned.

Some nurses told Mrs. Scholl that they told the fearful children the SS vans were taking them to heaven so they would not be afraid. The nurses cried as they recounted how the little children ran to the vans singing, never suspecting they were soon to be exterminated.

The Scholl teenagers were infuriated by these stories. Sophie unsuccessfully tried to avoid the mandatory War Auxiliary Service that was required before anyone could go to university. She endured it so she could get to Munich University in May, 1942. She had now seen enough to begin to search for the meaning of her life and the role of her faith in that search. She saw German society changing. "It was a time of social constrictions . . . She began to raise questions about God, and her eyes opened to see the surrounding world."[2]

Sophie felt at home with Hans' friends at university who discussed everything about the present situation in Germany. This close knit group decided to lead various secret resistance movements against the Gestapo and along with other students at Munich University refused to support the war effort with their money. They collected stale bread from bakers and saw that it reached people in concentration camps who were starving. Some of them joined the Christian underground. They examined the teachings of Soren Kirkegaard, Theodore Haecker and other authors the Nazis condemned. Sophie and her friends at Munich shared concerns about these injustices and their faith grew into activism for the oppressed. Sophie felt she had at last come to know the heart of Christianity.[3]

In May, June and July of 1942 the student group and a group of German war veterans who had witnessed terrible abuses of their "enemies" in Russia and elsewhere began *The White Rose* movement. They carefully worded informative pamphlets that told the German people of the abuses the Nazis were committing and the right of the German people to end these abuses. The first leaflet of *The White Rose* pointed to the goodness of most

German people and the shame that all Germans would feel for decades over the terrible inhumanity imposed by the Nazi regime. They asked, "Is the German people, in their innermost soul, so corrupt and decayed?"[4]

When the university term ended in the summer, Hans and some other students were forced to perform obligatory military service in Russia. Sophie decided to go back to Ulm for vacation. In August her father was tried and sentenced to four months in prison for making a critical comment about Hitler. Sophie decided to play her flute outside the prison walls, hoping her father would hear the freedom song they both loved that proclaimed "Thoughts are free and these free thoughts can tear down many walls."

Hans and friends returned from the Russian front. The genocide they witnessed there made them even more adamant about *The White Rose* movement. Sophie also became more adamant since her father was suffering even after his release from prison. Due to his criticism of Hitler he could not return to his former executive job. His punishment was to become a low-level subordinate worker whose pay would barely support the family.

In November Sophie visited her sister Inge on her way to spread the leaflets of *The White Rose*. Sophie told Inge that she had committed herself to the resistance with full awareness that if she or the others were caught, they all would be executed. Inge never joined the movement but she supported and agreed with the work of Hans and Sophie. Meanwhile, the Gestapo in Munich was sure that Munich was the center of *The White Rose* operation but had difficulty catching the students and professors who directed it.

When December recess came Hans and Sophie returned to Ulm for the holidays. Their commitment to *The White Rose* movement made their father uneasy. When he was given one of *The White Rose* leaflets by Sophie, she wanted him to say how proud he was. However, he couldn't say it because he was afraid for their lives.

Sophie's life at the university was a far cry from the peace she always felt when she was back home in Ulm. In a final letter to a young man she loved who was convinced of Nazi righteousness Sophie described the change in her that always happened when she left the security of the Scholl home in Ulm and took the train back to the University of Munich. The love in the Scholl house was free of charge and always there. "I feel truly safe and at peace, for I sense an unselfish love and that is comparatively rare."[5]

Upon their return to Munich Sophie, Hans and others in *The White Rose* printed a fourth leaflet that called the German people to take a stand against the lies and brutality of a regime that caused untold suffering to the German people. The defeat of the Germans at Stalingrad had been glossed over by the regime. *The White Rose* notified the people about that defeat as the last of a long succession of lies and cover-ups. If there was to be a rebirth of Germany's people, the people had to admit their guilt and make a choice to turn the tide against the regime. "For Hitler and his followers there is no punishment on this earth commensurate with their crimes . . . We will not be silent. We are your conscience. *The White Rose* will not leave you in peace."[6]

Thursday, February 18, was the day to distribute these pamphlets in Germany. Sophie and Hans walked to the university. Since classes were in session, they began scattering leaflets with little fear of being seen. When they got outside, they saw a few leaflets left in the valise each carried so went back inside to drop off the remaining leaflets. The lecture hall doors opened, and students and a janitor saw them drop the leaflets. The university president called the Gestapo who arrived in minutes and interrogated Hans and Sophie in the courtyard of the university. Hans and Sophie claimed they had nothing to do with the leaflets that were blowing around. However, members of the Gestapo searched their dorm rooms and found evidence of the leaflets as well as several hundred postage stamps which was enough to incriminate them, so they were quickly ushered off to the prison.

Sophie and Hans took full responsibility for the leaflets to protect others in the group. They were especially worried about Christolph Probst who now was married and had young children. The interrogation of the Scholls took place in Wittelsbach Palais, Gestapo headquarters with Robert Mohr as the chief interrogator. He wondered if these two young people could really be resistance leaders. As the interrogation proceeded, Robert Mohr became secretly impressed with the young Hans and Sophie. Their principles were something even he had to respect in spite of his Gestapo position.

The interrogation of the Scholls went on through much of the night and much of the next day. Robert Mohr could get little satisfaction from his interrogations. Finally, a trial date was set for the following Monday. Hans and Sophie would be tried by the People's Court in Munich. Christolph Probst was caught and brought in. He would also be tried at the same time, even though the Scholls claimed Christolph did not assist them. Word reached the Scholl parents who then requested and were granted permission to be at the trial and to visit their children.[7]

Sophie had a sense that the trial would be quick and that a death sentence would come. She asked her cell mate Else Goebel to write recollections of their last days and give this to Sophie's parents. Else befriended Sophie and agreed to do as she asked. In time she got the writings of their final four days to Sophie's parents.

Else introduces herself as a worker in the reception area of the prison whose job was to keep card files on each person who was incarcerated or came to visit others in prison. Else recalls her first impression of Sophie as a highly principled young woman. As they shared stories in their cell in the evening hours, Else had a premonition of the cruel fate that would befall Sophie, her brother and Christolph. She knew they would be put to death.

February 18 was the first day Else met Sophie who seemed quite calm and almost cheerful in spite of the surroundings. When Else and Sophie were in the cell alone, Else encouraged Sophie to destroy any leaflets she might still have. Else looked at Sophie and felt the Gestapo must be thoroughly mistaken. How could the attractive and kind-faced young woman have taken part in such daring activities?

Sophie and Else exchanged information about themselves. Sophie said she was in jail for being caught with leaflets so did not expect any release or anything else that was good. Else told Sophie she should admit nothing because if there was no proof, the only conviction could come from her own words.

Footsteps approached and both Hans and Sophie were taken for interrogation in another building without any food for supper. The interrogation that should have been thirty minutes went on into the night. Else recalls praying for the two young people as the night dragged on. She noted that hours passed and even the guards wondered what was taking so long. Secretly Else hoped that the Scholls might have been released during the night. However, when she went to her morning job. she learned that the Scholls had been interrogated all through the night.

Early in the morning, under the impact of incriminating evidence, after hours of denying everything, Sophie had made a careful confession of her role. Else did not see Sophie until the following night in the cell. She was in wonder at how Sophie could be so calm after such an ordeal. Sophie told Else that the Gestapo informers had thoroughly searched her university rooms. There was a torn up leaflet that they had now pasted together. This kind of evidence meant that Sophie had no hope of being released. So Sophie and Hans saw that the only thing they could now do was claim guilt so that no other friends would be endangered.

Else remembers how impressed she was by the deep faith Sophie showed during the days of little sleep and much interrogation. The willingness to sacrifice one's life for others was rare in such a young person. Meanwhile

Sophie kept assuring Else in their alone moments that the Allies would soon be coming. Once the Allies came there would be freedom from the tyranny of Nazism. Else was not heartened by Sophie's hope. She felt deep sadness because she was quite certain Sophie would be dead by the time the Allies invaded.

On both Friday and Saturday the hours of interrogation lasted for much of the day. Else found out that there wouldn't be interrogations on Sunday which she considered good news. She recalled that Sophie was not particularly pleased by the news. There was an intellectual challenge for Sophie as she took on to the people doing the interrogation. She enjoyed being a debater and liked provocative discussions. Robert Mohr also enjoyed being an interrogator. He had come to respect Sophie's clear philosophical mind and was taken with her goodness.

He tried to find some reason for Sophie to not be convicted. He kept asking her to admit that she did not realize the significance of her activities. If she only knew the glories of the National Socialism teachings, she would never have gotten involved with *The White Rose*. It seemed evident that Mohr wanted to do whatever he could to get mercy for Sophie from the court.

Sophie informed Mohr that she would do everything again exactly the same way. It was not Sophie but rather Mohr and the Gestapo who had the wrong philosophy of life. On Sunday morning Else was at her reception area and saw that the recent arrivals included Christolph Probst. In spite of their greatest efforts Sophie and Hans could not spare their friends. Else pulled out the index card and saw that Christolph Provost was there to be convicted of high treason.

Else did not want to tell Sophie, but she felt she had to. She remembers how horrified Sophie was when she heard the news. Christolph was not only a good friend but also the father of three small children. He had actually not done much after becoming a father since the students did not want him to get dragged into any punishments when and if they were caught.

Sometime on Sunday Mohr came by with some fruit, cookies and a few cigarettes for Sophie. He asked Else about Sophie and seemed to feel genuinely bad about the black clouds that were hanging over Sophie and her friends. He had a daughter close to Sophie's age.

It was close to three o'clock in the afternoon when Sophie was summoned to formally receive a bill of indictment. Else had already been told that the next day would be the trial. The dreaded "People's Court" was sitting in Munich, and everyone knew that whoever they tried received maximum punishment. Else knew in her heart that Sophie was doomed long before Sophie returned.

Sophie came back a short time later. She was pale and her hand shook as she started to read the long bill of indictment. As Sophie read it her face became calm and by the time she finished calm had returned to her. Else was moved at Sophie's concern for her friends. She was still hoping that at least some of them would continue their work. Else grew even more fond of Sophie as their time together was clearly coming to an end.

Sophie's last days were spent reflecting on the small difference one death makes. She was hoping that news of her death might stir more students to take up the cause of justice. She hoped that if her brother was condemned to death she also would be since she was every bit as guilty as he was.

The defense attorney appointed by the court was a committed Nazi who really did not want to defend Sophie. Else remembered the attorney as a fearful puppet who did not even ask proper questions. Sophie also sensed this, so she simply informed the lawyer that her brother was entitled to death by firing squad since he was a war veteran. The lawyer would not promise anything. When Sophie inquired whether she would be hanged in public or die under the guillotine, he was shocked and claimed not to know. Questions like that were not routinely asked by a young woman with such calm.

Then Sophie told Else about her parents and that she felt badly about their suffering. For her mother to lose two children at the same time would cause terrible suffering even though there was another son somewhere in Russia with the German army. Sophie was sure that her father would understand why they had to do what they were doing.

All that night the light was on and every half-hour an officer looked in to make sure that everything was alright. Sophie slept well all night; shortly before seven Else woke her for the trial day. Sophie woke up quickly and told Else about a dream she had during the night.

The dream pictured a fine sunny day. Sophie was carrying a baby in a long white gown to be baptized. The road to the church went up the steep mountainside but Sophie held the baby firmly. Without warning a glacier crevice suddenly opened. She barely had time to lay the baby down on the safe side before she plunged down into the abyss. Sophie felt that the baby in the white gown was the ideal that would last, but first Sophie had to die for that ideal.

The conversation stopped when Else was summoned to her job. Else recalls the pain she felt assuring Sophie she was with her in these final hours and she promised to tell Sophie's parents about their last four days together.

They shook hands one last time. "May God be with you, Sophie." No sooner had they parted than two officers took Sophie to trial.[8]

Sophie's parents attended the trial of the People's Court in Munich. The three young people on trial spoke bravely and movingly of their love for Germany and the reasons for their attempts to stand as authentic Germans of integrity and honor. Sophie's father was distraught at the lack of defense so he himself got up and tried to defend his children. However, he was ushered out as was his wife. It did not take the judge long to deliberate on what the sentence would be.

The banished parents could not hear the final sentencing. However, as the doors opened and people poured out, they heard that their children and Christolph would be guillotined that evening. The parents visited Sophie and Hans one last time. Hans bent lovingly over the bar that separated him from his parents and said, "I have no hatred." He embraced his father who assured Hans that both he and Sophie would be enshrined in history. Sophie walked in with dignity ushered by a woman warden. Sophie's mother brought Sophie her favorite candy which she took gratefully and then thanked both her parents for their strong love. Like Hans Sophie displayed a strength in the last hours that made her parents marvel.

Like her brother Hans, Sophie was sure that their deaths would fan the flames in the hearts of others who believed that justice must come. The parents were not sure given the fears of the people. Then Sophie's mother said calmly that Sophie should simply remember Jesus. Sophie took her mother's hand and told her that she too should remember Jesus who would be her strength in the days ahead. Sophie embraced her mother for the last time.

The parents left, and the prison wardens allowed Sophie, Hans and Christolph to see each other one final time. They smoked a last cigarette together. Christolph said, "I didn't realize that dying could be so easy . . . in a few minutes we'll meet again in eternity." The warden's report affirms how bravely each young person walked to the execution and the successful quickness with which they were guillotined.[9]

Inge took the train to Munich on Tuesday morning and went to Sophie's room in Munich where she found a diary overlooked by the Gestapo. She and her parents arranged for burial next to the prison where Christolph, Hans and Sophie had been executed. Inge recalls that her mother had gathered together her rations and said they should have a good meal in the restaurant because Sophie would have wanted that.

Other members of *The White Rose* were caught and beheaded. Alexander Schmorell and Kurt Huber were beheaded on July 13, 1943, and Willi

Graf on October 12, 1943. Others were given prison terms ranging from six months to ten years.

The text of the sixth *White Rose* leaflet was smuggled out of Germany through Scandinavia to England. In mid 1943 millions of propaganda copies were dropped over Germany by Allied planes. The leaflet was retitled "The Manifesto of the Students of Munich" to honor the brave students of Munich University whose lives were given for freedom.

When the war finally ended the bravery of the professors and students of Munich University was not forgotten. The square of the central hall of Munich University has been named "Geschwister-Scholl-Platz" after Hans and Sophie Scholl. The square next to this one has been named "Professor-Huber-Platz." Many schools, streets and places all over Germany were renamed in memory of the members of *The White Rose*.

In an extended German national TV competition held in 2004 to choose "the ten greatest Germans of all time" (ZDF TV), Germans under the age of 40 catapulted Hans and Sophie Scholl of *The White Rose* to fourth place, selecting them over Bach, Goethe, Gutenberg, Willy Brandt, Bismarck, and Albert Einstein.[10] On February 22, 2003 a bust of Sophie Scholl was placed by the government of Bavaria in the Walhalla temple. In February 2005, *Sophie Scholl-Die letzten Tage*" previewed *(Sophie Scholl: The Final Days)*. Drawing on interviews with survivors and transcripts that had remained hidden in East German archives until 1990, this film was nominated for an Academy Award for Best Foreign Language Film in January, 2006.[11]

NOTES

[1]   A DVD titled *Sophie Scholl: the Final Days* is a German film with English sub titles. Inge Scholl has written a book about *The White Rose* movement in Germany and the part her sister and brother played in it. This is *The White Rose* (Hanover, NH: Univ. Press of New England, 1973). A second edition of the popular work was published in 1983 by Wesleyan Univ. Press. *The White Rose*, 6.

[2]   This is part of Inge's assessment of Sophie. Herman Vinke interviewed Inge about Sophie for his work, *The Short Life of Sophie Scholl* (New York: Harper and Row, 1984), 93.

[3]   *The Short Life of Sophie Scholl*, 112.

[4]   *The Short Life of Sophie Scholl*, 112-116.

5   *The Short Life of Sophie Scholl.* 153.
6   *The White Rose,* 87-88.
7   The story is told in detail in *The Short Life of Sophie Scholl,* 159-65.
8   The complete text can be found in *The Short Life of Sophie Scholl,* 167-78.
9   The events are described between 179-189, *The Short Life of Sophie Scholl.*
10   The White Rose organization has many sources on the web where more can be read about this group. Typing in "The White Rose" will yield abundant information. Two sources for these paragraphs are Wikipedia or www.wikipedia.org/wiki/White_Rose
11   Two earlier film accounts of *The White Rose* resistance were Percy Adlon's *Fünf letzte Tage* ((The) Last Five Days) and Michael Verhoeven's *Die Weisse Rose* (The White Rose) in 1982.

3

Naomi Chazan and Terry Greenblatt, Israel

In 1917 the British government's Balfour Declaration established a national home for the Jewish people in Palestine. In 1922 the League of Nations formally agreed that the land east of the Jordan River belonged to the Emirate of Jordan. Arabs resented this externally enforced division of their lands. Palestinian and Arab resentment against British rule and Palestinian resentment about the growing number of Jewish immigrants contributed to the riots of 1929 and 1936. Many Jews were murdered.

During World War II the British tried to gain Arab Support by forbidding European Jews entry into Palestine. On June 29, 1946, British authorities arrested about 2700 Jewish activists and fighters in Palestine. July 22, 1946, an extremist Zionist group responded by bombing the King David Hotel in Jerusalem which was a base for the British Secretariat, the military command and the police. Ninety-one people were killed, mostly Arab civilians.

Between 1946 and 1947 the Zionist leadership began an illegal immigration of about 70,000 Jews. An additional 70,000 Jews were captured at sea by the British and imprisoned in camps on Cyprus. The deaths of approximately six million European Jews during the Holocaust increased world support for settling Jewish refugees in Palestine. Israel declared itself an independent Jewish state on May 14, 1948.

A 1949 Armistice Agreement signed by Israel and its neighbors left 78% of Palestine in Jewish hands. The remaining territories, the Gaza Strip and the West Bank were occupied by Egypt. Additionally the war created about 750,000 Palestinian refugees who lived inside Israel's borders. Thousands of exiled Jews also sought refuge in Israel. Differences and violence over territory continued between Palestinians and Jews. Many Palestinians and their offspring continued to live in refugee camps. In 1964 the Palestine Liberation Organization (PLO) was founded to work for the rights of Palestinian refugees. In 1974 the Arab League recognized the PLO as the sole legitimate representative of the Palestinian people. The PLO was ousted from Jordan and took refuge in Lebanon. From here it carried out its violent attacks on Israel, which in turn caused retaliation on Lebanon in 1982. The PLO relocated in Tunisia.

In 1987 Palestinians revolted against abuses by Israel in the First Intifada. The Israeli army retaliated. The UN Security Council condemned Israel's brutality. In 2005 the withdrawal of Israel from the Gaza Strip was an attempt toward conciliation but peace never came.

Within the complicated history of conflict between Palestinians and Israelis there is another less heralded story about the peace movements of Israeli and Palestinian women.[1] The United Nations Security Council resolution 1325 that calls on member states to include women in all peace and security matters has acknowledged in word the importance of women peacemakers. Two of many Israeli women working for peace within the complicated history of Palestinian and Israel peoples are Naomi Chazan and Terry Greenblatt.

Naomi and Terry have committed themselves to non-violence and peace in spite of strong opposition. Their passion for peace and their initiatives have influenced global groups to help wage peace between the people. Some of their insights follow.[2]

Naomi Chazan (1946-)

Naomi Chazan has been a steady voice for social and political justice in the State of Israel. Her father, Abe Haman, was Israeli ambassador to the United States and a president of Hebrew University. Naomi earned her BA and MA at Barnard College (Columbia University). While in the United State, Naomi came to know Golda Meir who took great interest in Naomi and visited her when Golda was attending meetings at the United Nations. After finishing her studies in the United States Naomi returned to Hebrew University where she earned her doctorate in comparative politics and joined the political science faculty.

One of Naomi's major interests has been advancing the status of women in Israel. In 1984 she co-founded the Israel Women's Network. In 1989 she founded the Israel Women's Peace Net. She is particularly concerned with the impact of persistent militarism that blocks the advancement of women in Israel. She became one of the most visible leaders of the Women's Peace Movement. After election to the Knesset in 1992 she served as Deputy Speaker of the Knesset, as Chairperson of the Committee to Combat Drug Abuse, as a member of the committees on Foreign Affairs and Defense, Economics, the Advancement of the Status of Woman and Immigration and Absorption. She is Professor Emerita of Political Science at the Hebrew University of Jerusalem, chaired the Harry S. Truman Research Institute for the Advancement of Peace, been visiting professor at Harvard University, and was a member of the Israeli Delegation to UN Conference on Women in Nairobi in 1985 and in Beijing in 1995.

Since 2005 she has been head of the School of Government and Society at the Academic College of Tel Aviv in Yaffro. She continues to lecture and pursue justice and equality for all in spite of opposition. A few of her insights follow.

April 10, 2000. Political Leadership in Divided Societies: The Case of Israel and Palestine. Stormont, Northern Ireland Parliament Buildings[3]

Four Fs are going to spell success if handled properly . . . The first is *fear*. Why? I think fear governs all our successes in Israel/Palestine, what I know and experienced in South Africa, Cyprus and Northern Ireland . . . What pushes us to reconcile the fear of prolonging an impossible situation? What pushes us to stop negotiating? The fear of something we don't know and the fear of the future. So factor number 1 is fear and it works both ways and against the grain. When there is improvement we let fear of the future begin. When there is no improvement we let fear of the future permit change . . . we have to recognize this (fear) and have to make it work for us.

Factor number two is *fatigue*. But fatigue is not just physical, it's mental fatigue, it's historical fatigue, it's emotional fatigue, it's fatigue in every sense of the term. Fatigue is a tremendous capital for making things happen. Why? When things are really bad we forget we are tired, and one of the things that frightens me the most, I must admit, is that when things here keep moving forward we allow fatigue to overtake us. Because the nuts and bolts of implementing agreements are a task of drudgery in the extreme and drudgery allows us to get tired and when we are tired we are no good. So the second factor is fatigue.

A third factor is *friction*, personal friction . . . but friction also between external influences which tend to bring out the best in us not the worse.

Most Americans and South Koreans don't love the US, but when President Clinton intervenes it actually moves the process forward. So the friction between the externals creates domestic pressures . . . Leaders like to do what we think . . . We will have the friction between external influence which moves us forward and the domestic internal prosaic pressure which helps to hold us back. We need the balance.

The fourth factor is *failure*, and in order to answer what failure is one has to know that power measures success. I can say to you today with the greatest belief of certainty that success for us is the completion and implementation of a full peace treaty with the Palestinians and Syrians and the Lebanese. What do I mean by that? Success by us is the creation of a Palestinian state along side Israel. A full peace treaty along with Syria will involve a full withdrawal from the Golan Heights and a comprehensive peace. If that is success then why does failure happen? Failure means that we have not achieved our goal, our specific detailed concrete goal that I just described. These four factors are key to success.

Washington, DC. Oct. 8, 2002. The Foundation for Middle East Peace lecture [4] I start with two caveats: I am a voice of the opposition in Israel to the left of the national unity government. We are trying very hard to promote an alternative approach to extricate ourselves from the present situation. That is the first caveat. The second is that I will only allude to the connection between the Palestinian-Israeli conflict and the Iraqi situation . . . I want to focus on the situation on the ground in Israel and suggest where there is some flexibility and where there are difficulties . . .

I do not share the notion that the situation is impossible, but it has become even more complicated, and requires a great deal of creativity, ingenuity, and finesse. We have a stalemate because terrorism, which Israelis fear most, is continuing, and occupation, which Palestinians fear the most, is continuing . . . One word summarizes the situation on the ground: deadlock. The Palestinians cannot defeat Israel militarily, and Israel cannot defeat the Palestinians politically. These are the facts of life . . . But this deadlock has its own dynamic which is escalation. In the absence of positive movement there is negative movement. This negative spiral is extremely worrisome because it revolves almost entirely around violence . . . .

If I had to bet Israel's future on what happens in the Knesset I would be in grave trouble. Good politicians have their values very firm in their minds and their ears very close to the ground. Often the positions that are taken or expressed by elected officials are what they think their constituencies want to hear . . . Let me say something else. I am sick and tired of everybody telling me and other Israeli spokespersons that if you're pro-Israeli you cannot understand the just Palestinian demand for self-determination, and if you're pro-Palestinian you can't understand the Israeli demand for security . . . We should not talk about being pro-Palestinian or pro-Israeli. We should talk about how to secure a reasonable agreement that will stop the violence and let the people in the region live normal lives. You can't achieve that without joining hands with both Israelis and Palestinians. If you're not willing to do that you're contributing directly or indirectly to the perpetuation of the situation. That is unacceptable

Oct. 15, 2004. The Inaugural Conference of the Union of Progressive Zionists[5]

I want to suggest that we are in an incredibly difficult moment with one glimmer of light. There may be opportunities opening now that we haven't had for the past four years since the beginning of the second Intifada . . . In case you haven't noticed the problem is not getting moderate Israelis and moderate Palestinians to agree . . . The problem today is getting to the negotiating table. And therefore, ninety percent of the work of peacemakers on both sides is within our own communities. The peace forces in Israel have to work in Israel . . . .

. . . A viable Palestinian state along side Israel is in Israel's uppermost interest, and that is the only way to achieve justice and security for both Palestinians and Israelis. A two state solution is imperative . . . a two state solution today is the only way to fulfill the Zionist dream . . .

The current situation is the worst situation on the ground that we have known since 1987 and possibly since 1948 . . . The violence is unspeakable. The terrorism is out of hand, and things are being done in our name which are equally unspeakable . . . The killing of over a hundred Palestinians, many of whom were women and children, the daily humiliation of checkpoints are things that we have to search our consciences about very carefully . . . .

All around us is a lack of confidence and growing animosity. It is so deep it is going to take generations to overcome . . . The far right has introduced religion into the equation. Why can you not withdraw from territory, even Gaza? Because it is sacred. And if in any way you question the biblical roots, then essentially what you're doing is sinning: it is a sin. It has to be answered . . . I suggest that knowing the Biblical source is imperative in dealing with this issue and the answer is profound, but I'll just put it in simple terms. If the land is really sacred then it is a sin to try and possess it because you cannot possess sanctity. Therefore, those who claim that because the land was given by God, and therefore we must possess it, are profaning God and profaning our heritage.

. . . The time has come to repossess the symbols of universal humanism and Jewish humanity and to look people in the eye and say, "You know what? Don't call me a bad Jew because what you are doing (who incite violent attacks in the name of God) is even worse than indescribable."

Terry Greenblatt

Terry Greenblatt was born in New York but has lived and worked in Israel for more than three decades. She has been a local, national and international spokesperson for both Israeli and Palestinian women who are committed to peaceful resolution of the Israeli-Palestinian conflicts. For six years, Terry directed Bat Shalom (Daughter for Peace), the Israeli women's organization for promoting peace. Bat Shalom was instrumental in networking nine organizations under the umbrella of "the Coalition of Women for Peace." This coalition is a mix of Palestinian and Jewish women living in Israel who call for a two state solution to the conflicts between Palestinians and Jews, use of the 1967 borders, the restoration of human rights, the ending of the occupation of Palestinian territories and recognition of Jerusalem as a shared capital.[6]

Terry has initiated a global network of women peace activists, government officials, grassroots organizations and a host of non-government sponsored groups so that the work for peace throughout the world might improve through multiple connections. She is a co-founder and a director of The Women's Voice (Kol Ha-Isha). She is a cofounder of Israeli Women Against the Occupation (Shani). Terry is also a co-founder of a school without walls which focuses on Women's Studies and Economic Empowerment.

Terry with other women in multiple peace groups has initiated lobbies that demand the enforcement of equality for all women who are Israeli citizens whether Jew, Muslim or Christian. When official talks between Israelis and Palestinian leaders have broken down Bat Shalom and the Jerusalem Link have stayed in the process of peace building. The women oppose the building of more walls as a means of peace. Dialogue will foster more sustainable peace than high walls can provide.

Terry has spoken to the UN Security Council, to US representatives on Capitol Hill, to the European Parliament and to most of the parliaments of

Europe. All of Terry's presentations are made with a Palestinian woman ally to present a basic model that says people with differences can be united in their hopes for peace and strategies to achieve it.

Terry has worked with NGOs for peace and helped to institutionalize the Jerusalem Link. The structure and mode of operation of the Jerusalem Link is a model for peace making. The Board is made up of people representing different perspectives on the Israeli-Palestinian tensions. Yet the hope for peace draws the members together sufficiently to "stay at the table" until a plan is acceptable to diverse groups so they can all move forward together. The members take these agreements to their respective publics for further dialogue and perhaps future peace.

Terry spent 2007 as Activist in Residence in San Francisco. She attended a global peace conference sponsored by the Women Nobel Peace Prize laureates in Ireland in summer, 2007. Her passion for peace and a resolution of the Israeli-Palestinian conflict make her a strong candidate for the Nobel Peace Prize in the years to come. Two of her many addresses follow.

July, 2001. The San Francisco Jewish Film Festival[7]

I live in Jerusalem, and I have spent much of the past 10 months being scared. In hopes of generating a discussion that might take us beyond attacking and delegitimizing each other I want to talk about the fear we share these days and the questions I believe we should consider together.

I am the director of Bat Shalom, the national Israeli women's peace organization and a core member organization of the Women's Coalition for Peace. For the past 10 months Jewish and Palestinian Israeli women have been relentlessly, creatively and courageously opposing the escalating violence and human rights violations in our region.

We are scared as we protest in the streets of Tel Aviv and in Palestinian villages under siege. We have stood huddled in small groups of six or seven, as well as with the over 10,000 women and men in 150 cities and towns around the world who stood in solidarity with us this past June 8. [June 8 marks the anniversary of Israel's occupation of the Palestinian Territories. On June 8, 2001 Women In Black held a vigil and marched in concert with other organizations around the world calling for peace.] We are harassed and cursed, harassed and arrested. And again I am scared as we raise our voices for a peace born in justice—the only kind of peace that will ensure long-term security for our two peoples—and scared again as we demand a mutually negotiated agreement that provides each side with the land, historical narrative, resources, and dignity it deserves . . .

[I am] anxious as I sit across from a Palestinian peace and liberation colleague before an Israeli-Palestinian woman's political dialogue, and she opens with a smile and then a tear and looks over and says, "Terry, my soul is overwhelmed with sorrow to the point of death." I am frightened again that I am not large enough to hold her pain, scared that I could potentially drown in her well of desperation.

And on the days that I stand witness as part of the Israeli women's checkpoint watch, monitoring and documenting human rights abuses at Israeli checkpoints around Jerusalem, the three women who are on duty with me tentatively exchange emergency phone numbers with each other in case something should happen while on duty. I find that my stomach only calms down when I have crossed back into West Jerusalem, and all that I am left to deal with is the normal level of anxiety that accompanies us as we make our individual ways home traveling on the public buses and in taxis that do not always make it to their destinations without blowing up.

But the more profoundly scary situations for me oftentimes have little to do with my own physical safety. In recent months Israeli, American, and Palestinian participants in the Oslo and Camp David negotiating teams have been publishing opinion papers on the collapse of the peace process. We now have documentation that reveals the original spirit and intention of Oslo—which was based on the understanding that the imbalance of power between the occupier and the occupied and the negative history between our two peoples—represented almost insurmountable obstacles for conventional-type negotiations.

As Israeli negotiator Dr. Ron Pundak noted, "Our goal was to work towards a conceptual change which would lead to a dialogue based as much as possible on fairness, equality, and common objectives. For many years our two peoples had tried to attain achievements at the expense of the other side. Every victory won by one side was considered a defeat for the other. In contrast Oslo was from the start guided by efforts to abandon this approach and to achieve as many win-win situations as possible . . ."

The spirit of Oslo was never tested and therefore it is unacceptable to say that a negotiated settlement is impossible. Oslo didn't fail; we did. I am terrified to know that our leadership was aware of the profound shift in consciousness and public education for peace that were necessary to attempt a negotiated agreement and was unable to, or chose not to, risk authentically acknowledging the other side as an integral partner for our own success. We never sat down together on the same side of the table and TOGETHER LOOKED at our common and complex joint history with the commitment and intention of not getting up until—in respect and reciprocity—we could get up together and begin our new history as good neighbors . . .

People often ask me what I have learned living and doing peace work with Israeli and Palestinian women living in a conflict zone. "What I can tell you is that women learn from women's lives. Women's characteristic life experience gives them the potential for two things: a very special kind of intelligence, social intelligence, and a very special kind of courage, social courage: the courage to cross the lines drawn between us which are also the lines drawn inside our heads. And the intelligence to do it safely without a gun and to do it productively." [Cynthia Cockburn, 2001, City University, London, England]

I believe that existing borders are not necessarily an obstacle for women. Led by our feelings and instincts women will cross them. Nothing will stop us. It is scary to me that as bad as the current situation is no one is asking us what we—the women—think or have to offer; no one has yet realized how critical our contribution is to the process. As women we want to be able to look our children in the eyes without shame and tell them that injustice was committed in our name, and we did our best to stop it. Even when we are women whose very existence contradicts each other we will talk—we will not shoot.

I am suggesting that it is imperative and constructive for us, all of us, to individually and communally examine our fears. There is much that informs our political positions and passions that has its roots in those fears. In that process of examination lies much of the potential for the genuine unity and identity we might one day be able to reclaim—together. For though we promise and envision according to our hopes, we perform only according to our fears.

May 7, 2002. Address to the Security Council of the United Nations[8]

I represent Bat Shalom (Daughter of Peace), an Israeli feminist peace organization. I also represent Israeli women and mothers who are famished for peace. We are women working for a genuine peace grounded in the just resolution of the Israeli-Palestinian conflict, respect for human rights and an equal voice for Jewish and Arab women within Israeli society. Since 1994 Bat Shalom has been part of a bi-national institution called the Jerusalem Link, and the joint declaration that I will read at the conclusion of my talk was developed with our sister partner, a Palestinian women's NGO, the Jerusalem Center for Women. We work in coalition with more than one hundred women's peace and anti-occupation initiatives around the world that have mobilized in response to the insufferable situation in our region.

I stand before you this afternoon in the presence of the enormous power you represent and with the terrible awareness of how dangerous that power can be. As a woman I know that anyone with even the smallest advantage over another is capable of abusing or misusing that power. I stand here as an ally and advocate of those women in Israel, Jewish and Arab, who ask of you to use your power wisely and with a moral compass whose needle is uncompromisingly pointed toward justice.

We ask that you fulfill your responsibility as set out in the United Nations Charter. You are mandated to save succeeding generations from the scourge of war—for until you do, we women living in a militaristic society are destined to continue raising our children to perpetrate war and become messengers of hatred, of racism, and of destruction.

You are mandated to reaffirm faith in fundamental human rights. For until you do, the soul of our society will never heal, neither from our fear of global anti-Semitism, nor from the inhumanity of our subjugation and dehumanization of the Palestinian people. For until you do, the extremists on both sides will rejoice, both those who talk of the transfer of indigenous populations and an eternal occupation, as well as those who walk into a coffeehouse or a supermarket and blow themselves and others up leaving our joint future smoldering in the rubble. For until you do, those of us who are struggling to promote a human rights agenda inextricably embedded in an effective political solution cannot possibly further our mission.

You are mandated to establish conditions under which justice and respect for international law can be maintained. This includes ensuring the security and well being of Israelis. But it also includes insisting on a standard of behavior and compliance to international law on the part of Israel be it a fact-finding mission to Jenin or the dismantlement of illegal settlements in the West Bank and Gaza. For until you do, we Israelis will continue to be driven by our fear and mistrust and insist that this war we are waging is for our very survival as a nation, even though it is not.

And lastly you are mandated to promote social progress and better standards of life, for until you do, until there is the degree of humanitarian aid for the rehabilitation and reconstruction of the devastation of Palestine and her people, until the Israeli people can fully trust that international bodies are committed to ensuring our survival, neither nation will be able to begin to address the ultimate challenge of creating a culture of peace in our region.

Next year we will commemorate the 10th anniversary of the Oslo Accords. Few remember anymore the exhilaration of daring to believe that we could possibly be nearing the end of this hundred-year conflict. For us Israeli and Palestinian women and the international community of hundreds of thousands of women who along with us have remained steadfast in their solidarity for and commitment to a just, comprehensive and lasting peace in the Middle East there will be no celebration of this anniversary. There will be no candles lit in jubilation—rather, a collective global mourning for a region that is burning, wreaking destruction on a magnificent land and her two peoples, and leaving the most dangerous ashes in its wake—ashes of profound fear, hopelessness and despair.

This month Israeli and Palestinian women have once again jointly declared what a just and sustainable peace must look like. I look around this room and but for ourselves I do not see any women/see too few women. And I cannot but be aware of the failure of both our local leadership as well as you, the international community, to productively navigate our peoples on a path towards peace. How much of the reason for this is the absence of women in this room, in the countless rooms where decisions are made that affect the daily lives of Israeli and Palestinian men, women and children? I cannot help but be aware that the slim glimmers of hope in this terrible situation have consistently been provided by the grassroots women's peace activists on both sides. Given this dismal history of past performance, it is unthinkable not to include women, large numbers of women, in the upcoming peace process.

You need us because if the goal is not simply the absence of war, but the creation of a sustainable peace by fostering fundamental societal changes, we are crucial to everyone's security concerns. You need us, because wars are no longer fought on battlefields. You have brought the war home to us. Many more civilians than soldiers are being killed in ours and other conflicts around the world. The wars are being waged now on our doorsteps and in our living rooms and in our sacred houses and ceremonies of religious worship, and women have a vested interest in keeping families and communities safe.

You need us because to honorably comply with your own legislation, Resolution 1325, we must be included. You need us because we continue to hold human rights and the sanctity of life as paramount values, and unfortunately today, they are too easily being bartered away as either obstacles to security policies or as incongruent with national liberation aspirations.

You need us because we have developed a process and socio-political fluency that keep authentic and productive dialogue moving forward even as the violence escalates and both sides continue to terrorize one another. Women's characteristic life experience gives us the potential for two things: a very special kind of intelligence, social intelligence, and a very special kind of courage, social courage.

We have developed the courage to cross the lines of difference drawn between us which are also the lines drawn inside our heads. And the intelligence to do it safely without a gun or a bomb and to do it productively. And most importantly we are learning to shift our positions, finding ourselves moving towards each other without tearing out our roots in the process. Even when we are women whose very existence and narrative contradicts each other, we will talk—we will not shoot.

You need us because we women are willing to sit together on the same side of the table and together look at our complex joint history with the commitment and intention of not getting up until—in respect and reciprocity—we can get up together and begin our new history and fulfill our joint destiny.

There is much talk now about an International Peace Conference. Colin Powell has already prepared us for the outcome when he said this week that no one should have high expectations from the conference. Women in the peace and anti-occupation movement in Israel are recommending that expectations must remain higher than ever before because we cannot afford them not to be. We suggest now just might be the moment to realize how critical our contribution is. We have never had a voice or power at these tables and quite possibly we will get it wrong the first few times. But we would come with what we believe are innovative and creative strategies grounded in democratic and feminist ideology and experience and exemplified by what women have managed to accomplish in civil society with little resources and insignificant power.

We would change the discourse from the 'for or against' model, the called pro-Israeli/anti-Palestinian or pro-Palestinian/anti-Israeli. This kind of inadequate and restricted thinking would be appropriate if we were rooting for a football team, but we are not playing a game any more. More than 2000 people have been killed during the past 20 months and countless more disabled. Positions, conditions, policies, and decisions must be evaluated as being pro-justice, pro-life and pro-dignity. Participating partners must be challenged to conduct a moral impact analysis of their positions, and a new and critical dimension of transparency must be introduced into the negotiation process. What gets said and decided upon in the sessions gets documented and what gets documented gets disseminated to both peoples to be discussed and debated in uni-nationally town meetings, and then to serve as a the basis for civil society bi-national dialogue.

The upcoming peace conference, if it is to be held, must be international, not regional. The international community shares responsibility for the deterioration of the situation, and must be our partners in fashioning and implementing a solution. My country, Israel, has a long-standing fear of international intervention because we Jews have had a long and bitter experience of suffering as the world stood by not noticing. Now the Palestinians, unfortunately, have come to share that kind of experience. My government fears that international intervention will prevent it from carrying out its agenda. We the peace activists of Israel are insisting that you do just that.

We women would determine that the ultimate goal of the peace conference is a final status agreement and an end to the Palestinian-Israeli conflict. A long-term intermediate agreement can translate into only one thing—continued occupation and prolonging the status quo. Both sides must commit to a series of meetings with the understanding that while 100 years of conflict cannot be satisfactorily resolved immediately, each stage of the agreement gets implemented without delay. Changes in the realities on the ground will serve as "acts of honor" with each side demonstrating to the other that while each is most certainly paying a "price" for peace, each also most certainly has a trustworthy partner for peace. These "peace facts" on the ground are a necessary condition for re-building trust, for creating the climate in which the people on both sides will choose and support leaders who can bring them to peace and not to war.

We in the Jerusalem Link don't have all the answers. In fact, all we have is the next step, a step that might potentially move us forward rather than backward, one that comes with demonstrated efficacy, durability, and integrity. But at this point that does seem to be a lot more than your various governments have. So if this body is genuinely committed to bringing some sort of peace and security to the Middle East, you need to bring us women to the center of all your deliberations.

Should we continue to be ignored (which is quite different than ignorance, because one really has to work at it), we shall all be held responsible for the evil we may have prevented. I thank you for your time and your attention. I would like to leave you with the Bat Shalom/Jerusalem Center for Women Joint Declaration published three weeks ago in Israel and in Palestine:

Palestinian and Israeli Women Demand Immediate End to Occupation. Israel has launched a war against defenseless Palestinian communities. The terrorization of innocent civilians, the unlawful killings and arrests, the siege imposed upon President Arafat, and the destruction of property, infrastructures and institutions, can only lead to further escalation, prolonging the sufferings of both nations and destroying any prospects for peace. The climate of fear and the obsession with reprisals that grips our two peoples obscure the true cause of this cycle of violence—the continued and unlawful Israeli occupation of the Palestinian people and their land.

It is our role as women on both sides to speak out loudly against the humanitarian crimes committed in order to permanently subjugate an entire nation. Right now in the face of uncontrolled military turmoil we jointly ask the international community of states to accept its duty and mandate by international humanitarian law to prevent abuses of an occupying power by officially intervening to protect the Palestinian people. Beyond the immediate crisis we know that there is one future for us both. The deliberate harming of innocent civilians, Palestinian or Israeli, must not be condoned. By working together we improve our chances for a better future. We believe that women can develop an alternative voice promoting effective peace initiatives and sound approaches. We undertake to work for this goal together.

Women have already begun to give substance to the recognition that a just peace is a peace between equals. When we call for a Palestinian state (on the territories occupied on 4th of June 1967) alongside the state of Israel, we envision true sovereignty for each state including control over land and natural resources. We envision a settlement based on international law which would endorse sharing the whole city of Jerusalem, the dismantling of the settlements and a just solution to the question of refugees according to relevant UN resolutions. In continuing our joint work together we want not only to achieve an end to the occupation; we want to help create the conditions for a life of security and dignity for both peoples.

We call upon all women and men, young and old, to join us in our sincere quest to preserve life, human dignity and freedom in our region. Dehumanization, hatred, revenge and oppression contribute nothing to the resolution of a century of conflict. Mutual recognition and respect of each other's individual and collective rights will pave the way for peace making.

NOTES

[1]   An exception to this is the Women Waging Peace Organization. Their web site lists women from around the world who are contributing to the peace effort. www.womenwagingpeace.net

[2]   The following works are but a few of many that can deepen insight into the multiple issues and people active in working toward peace between Palestinians and Jews. John Wallach and Janet Wallach, *The New Palestinians: The Emerging Generation of Leaders* (Rocklin, CA: Prima Publishing, 1992); Marguerite Guzman Bouvard, *Women Reshaping Human Rights* (Wilmington, DE: Scholarly Resources, 1996).

[3]   The University of Ulster in Londonderry houses The International Center of Excellence for the Study of Peace and Conflict Resolution (INCORE). This website is the source of the excerpt *www.incore.ulst.ac.uk/research/projects/ptp/chazan.html*

[4]   The entire address can be found on the website of The Foundation for Middle East Peace www.fmep.org/analysis/articles/search_for_peace.html

[5]   *www.habonimdror.org/peacepossible/gresource/Naomi* Chazan transcript.pdf. This web site of Habonim Dror in North America contains the entire lecture and many peace resources.

[6]   Janet M. Powers, *Blossoms on the Olive Tree: Israeli and Palestinian Women Working for Peace* (Westport, CT: Praeger, 2006).

[7]   The Initiative for Inclusive Security from Women Waging Peace is the source of this address. www.womenwagingpeace.net/content/articles/0050a.html

[8]   The Coalition of Women for Peace has integrated ten groups of women for peace and has multiple resources for peace. Terry gave permission to use this speech which is also on the website *www.coalitionofwomen.org/home/english/contents.*

4

Patricia Crockford, Malta, Palestine

Patricia Crockford arrived to work with the Palestinian people in the aftermath of the 1948 Israeli-Palestinian war. After the war the official State of Israel expelled Palestinians from the land to create the largest refugee problem the world had ever seen. Today there are still more than five million Palestinian refugees living in camps.

In 1948 the Democratic Women's Movement organized to assist Palestinians and to encourage Israelis and Palestinians to work together. Christian, Jewish and Muslim women joined together in the effort. The Women Against the Occupation and Women for Co-Existence are two contemporary groups that cross racial, political and religious lines in their efforts for reconciliation and a lasting peace between Israelis and Palestinians.

Yassir Arafat founded Fatah or the Palestinian Liberation Movement in 1957. The 1967 Six Day War saw Israel capturing the Golan Heights from Syria, the West Bank from Jordan, and Gaza and most of the Sinai Peninsula from Egypt. In 1969 Arafat was appointed the PLO's leader and commander in chief of the Palestinian Revolutionary Forces.

In 1973 the Yom Kippur War occurred with Israel claiming Arafat was responsible for the terrorist attacks against Israel. Arafat claimed the Zionists were blocking peaceful progress desired by Palestinians. In 1974 Arab heads of state recognized Arafat as the legitimate spokesperson for the Palestinian people. He addressed the United Nations in New York to plead for just action for the Palestinian people. In 1976 the Palestine Liberation Organization was admitted to full membership in the Arab League.

Now Women's Peace Movements emerged in force. The Four Mothers Movement, founded by four women whose sons were serving in the Israeli Army in Lebanon, had a direct impact on ending the war with Lebanon. The Jerusalem Link from the Palestinian side and 'Bat Shalom' on the Israeli side were groups of women waging peace. They fostered the two state theory for Israeli and Palestinian people with Jerusalem as a shared capital 'Markaz al Quds la l-Nissah' on the Palestinian side is also effective in protesting violence.

In December, 1988, Arafat accepted UN Resolution 242 of the Security Council which promised a recognition of Israel as a legitimate state and a future that would see the two state solution. By the end of 1988, 70 countries recognized the Palestine Liberation Organization as a legitimate group for negotiation and agreed to a Palestinian State. Violence continued.

Women in Black started demonstrating for peace every Friday in one of the main squares of Jerusalem. Some Fridays saw as many as 1000 Israeli women wearing black and mourning all victims of violence. In 1993 the Oslo Agreement stated that the West Bank and Gaza would have political autonomy and the Israeli government would not build new settlements on occupied land. The Palestine Liberation Organization officially recognized Israel. In 1994 Yassir Arafat together with Prime Minister Yitzhak Rabin and Shimon Peres of Israel shared the Nobel Peace Prize. The hope for peace was short-lived as a second Intifada occurred in 2000.

Amneh Badran, a Director of the Jerusalem Center for Women, claims that the second Intifada was not supported by Palestinians due to the degree of violence. The aftermath has been long term retaliation against Palestinians. Food and other necessities often do not reach the Palestinians who are also humiliated by curfews and border checks.[1]

Yassir Arafat died in 2004 and was succeeded by Mahmud Abbas as the PLO General Secretary. Tensions continue to divide the people but groups like 'Women for Peace' unite the people by rebuilding demolished homes and stopping destruction of the food and support source for Palestinians, the olive trees. Extremists regard the women's cooperative efforts for peace as contact with an enemy who should not be talked to but rather destroyed.[2] Patricia Crockford is one of the women for peace. Her summary of her life and work for peace follows in her own voice.

Life as a Peacemaker[3]

I have spent most of my life with the Palestinian people although I am not Palestinian. I was born in Malta and am now a Maltese nun who lives in Bethlehem. I have been teaching at Bethlehem University for the past 20 years.

As I sit writing I can hear the Muezzin at the Mosque nearby inviting the Muslims to start the fast of the Holy Month of Ramadan. It happens this year, 2006, that the Jews in the nearby settlement are simultaneously commemorating the yearly fast day of Atonement, Yom Kippur, the holiest day of the year. Only a few days ago the Orthodox Catholic Christians were celebrating a holy feast for them, the Feast of the Cross. This holy land is home to three Monotheistic Religions whose shared holy sites include the area in or around Jerusalem.

This land is about 10,000 square miles. Jews, Muslims, Druze and Christians live together here. Approximately 18% of the 800.000 people of Israel are Israeli Arabs. Israeli Arabs are the Palestinians who did not leave the part of Palestine occupied by Israel when many others were forced out or left for safety in 1948. Of these 800,000 Israeli Arabs about 100,000 are Christians. Until the middle of the 20th Century the Arabs lived in harmony with the small Jewish Community in Palestine.

When I was born Europe's War spilled over into Malta which was under British rule. Malta is in the middle of the Mediterranean, 60 miles from Italy and 90 miles from North Africa. Malta is a Republic in the British Commonwealth and part of the European Union. My earliest memories of Malta are of an underground shelter and huge explosions. It was wartime.

As a child I did not realize that my parents were using the sounds to make out where the bombs had fallen. I remember the night that our street received a direct hit. All of the houses opposite ours were burned to the ground. Our house had its doors and windows blown out and was so damaged that my little sister refused to go in, saying that it was not her home!

Because life in that shelter dominated experiences of life for five years I thought war was normal. I remember asking my Mother if there was a place on earth where bombs didn't fall. She said Switzerland was a neutral country. I kept asking my parents to take us to live in Switzerland. Of course we did not move. I lived through many more terrifying days and nights.

When the war was over prisoner-of-war camps were established all over the Island of Malta. One of my father's favorite outings every Sunday morning after Mass was a visit to these Camps. My father took us to meet and talk to the prisoners. We would take mother's bakery. As soon as I was old enough I asked to have a German pen-friend. I wanted to learn more about these people who bombed us and were imprisoned. I and a German pen friend corresponded for many years. Normal living returned after the war for us but wars were not over.

In 1948 a big event took place and my father called us all to listen to Ben Gurion. He was declaring the birth of the State of Israel. As children, we asked many questions about why this was important. My father replied that it was right for the Jews to get a homeland. I sensed this was a good thing but my own music making seemed more important than Ben Gurion.

I had been born into a family of musicians. Everyone in the family played or sang. My first teacher was a white Russian woman whose son was an accomplished violinist. He was my sister's first teacher. In addition to being musically gifted, my family was also very religious. Faith could grow easily in my family's life of love and service for others.

At twenty-five I decided to go to France to join a group of Sisters of St. Joseph who had been founded by Saint Emilie de Vialar. This community was the first group of women religious who went to serve in Jerusalem. I was asked to go to Jerusalem to help compose music for the Hebrew-Christian Church after my vows. I was excited to go.

I arrived in Jerusalem in 1966 and began to study Hebrew and Eastern Music. I lived in one of our houses which had been a boarding school for girls. This particular house was the famous Hadassah Hospital which serviced so many people during the 1948 war. I was thrilled to live among Jews because of the love for them that my parents instilled. Being in Jerusalem was a wonderful adventure and everything amazed me. I made many friends through the variety of things I did. During my first year I met primarily Jews and some so called "foreigners." During the Feast of Easter in 1967 I went to visit the Holy Sepulchre. This place was situated in the Jordanian part of Jerusalem. It was only a stone's throw from where I lived, but we had to have a legitimate Visa to enter Jordan.

I had told my Jewish classmates from Hebrew-language class that I was going to Jordan to see the Holy Sepulchre since I was a Christian. They all made it a point to give me their 'Petitions' to place in the cracks of the Wailing Wall. I was pleased to do this for my friends. My stay in Jordan was an eye-opener! This was my first time to visit an Arab country. It was only a short visit but I heard a lot from the Sisters and all their Arab friends about the situation. I returned to my home in Jewish Jerusalem with a very different view of Jews and Arabs.

On June 6, 1967, the Six-Day War began. Many Israeli Arabs and Jews knocked on the door of our convent to ask for asylum. Of course we accepted them! They felt that it was safer to stay with foreigners like us than to remain in their own homes. The numbers grew and we were indeed fortunate that the war only lasted six days! We were almost out of supplies of rice, flour, water and dry bread!

In those days in our convent shelter Arab-Jewish tensions were obvious. I was able to observe first-hand how the Jews and the Arabs who were there mistrusted each other. I tried to understand their diverse opinions and perceptions. However, as a Christian and a foreigner we did not take sides. I came to the conclusion that in order to keep a balanced view we would have to maintain friends on both sides and simply listen. Listening was the best way for me to understand the long history of perceived injustices on both sides.

As the Six-Day War ended I sensed we were all part of an important historical event. The Jews were elated at their victory and temporarily I sensed some joy too. It was short lived. As I went out in the street the aftermath of this war became painfully obvious. I went to the hospital our sisters ran so that I could see what had been the Arab side of Jerusalem. The sisters were trying to treat the wounded but many of these wounded people were being dragged from their beds to be imprisoned. Israeli soldiers were beating injured boys and young men, probably because it was assumed they were part of the war effort. I tried to stop the cruelty but couldn't.

As time went on Israel took more and more Palestinian space by force. The Palestinians were forced out of homes and land they had lived on for a long time. The number of refugees kept expanding. The people were more oppressed and there was little that we could do to stop it. While this was going on I was told to go to Europe to study Arabic and the religion of Islam. I was secretly thrilled to get away from the violence and suffering of this land; I knew a different environment would provide some time to think about the meaning of the whole experience. The ongoing tensions were so different from anything I had ever known. Four years later I decided to return to work in the same place and live in the same convent. The difference now was that this time I would be working with the Palestinians. The sisters had just opened the top floor of our convent to house 60 young Palestinian men from Galilee. They were studying at the Hebrew University in Jerusalem and could not find housing with the Jews because they were Arabs. The young men living with us were mostly Christian and Muslim. However, we also had a small number of Jews, Druze, and some foreigners who simply wanted to live among Arabs.

Two of us took care of the 60 young men. My helper was a Belgian lady. Together with our young male students we worked to create an atmosphere of peace and mutual respect for one another. New students continued to replace those in that first group for more than ten years. The diversity of young men and ourselves who ran the operation became a sign that people of different races, creeds and ideals could live together in harmony.

We were highly encouraged in this work by all our Israeli and Arab friends. They too saw that people could live in harmony in spite of differences. This wasn't by accident. We also planned events to further appreciation and understanding among the different ethnic and religious groups. We had lectures given on a regular basis by both Arab and Israeli intellectuals for the benefit of our house guests. Many of these students often invited their friends to come as well.

The whole living experience of different races and cultures living together in peace and respect was a wonderful experience. That particular ministry of mine ended when I was invited to teach music at the Catholic University of Bethlehem. That university had a wonderful history. It was a group of women who handed Pope Paul VI a proposal to start a university in Palestine when he came on a visit to the Holy Land. At the time, young Christian men and women who wanted to continue their studies left the country to study. Most never came back. Beginning a Catholic University in Bethlehem was one way to educate and liberate for justice and peace. Pope Paul VI acted and the Catholic University of Bethlehem opened its gates in 1973 under the auspices of the Vatican. Today the 2,500 students are about 70% Muslim and 30% Christian. All of us consciously work together in our diversity of religious, political and personal beliefs to further the peace that has been so long in coming!

Because Bethlehem was occupied by Israel since the Six-Day War the university was put under a military governor with soldiers everywhere. Palestinian students routinely were and still are stopped, searched, and mistreated by the soldiers. I could tell that this teaching experience in these conditions was going to be quite a different experience from my previous days of teaching in Jerusalem!

In 1983 I was asked to be a full-time teacher of music and to use that discipline to help the students not only to excel in music but to find some solace in the difficult life they were living. I became the first fulltime teacher of music at Bethlehem University. Students came from all over the West Bank and Gaza with approximately 79% of them from the Palestinian refugee camps. The refugee Palestinian students had attended the basic government or camp schools prior to this. Most had never had the opportunity of reading music before!

This was such a novel teaching environment! A quote from the Constitutions of our Congregation made sense of it. "The Sisters are called to announce the Good News of the Kingdom to the poor, to fight in the spirit of the Gospel against distinction and every kind of injustice and to be especially attentive to appeals . . . . from people whose fundamental rights are ignored." Well, that is what I was trying to do here.

There is no doubt that living under occupation with the fear it engenders is a terrible way to live. What could I do to help the students continue to be safe and to believe and hope that ultimately God's justice would prevail? It's one thing to believe peace will prevail when one is in a situation of basic equality and peace. But when daily violence and potential death are always in the shadows the challenge to work and hope for peace becomes a new challenge every day.

I met the challenge through use of music. Music is always a great inspiration for those who love it and I thought of a plan. The situation between Israelis and Palestinians kept getting more tense and dangerous but both Israeli and Palestinian students wanted to get along. I could help Palestinian students to look at the Jews in new ways by talking about my friendship with gifted Jewish musicians. Then in the brief peaceful times these gifted Jewish musicians could invite us to concerts as guests. They did that and also would come to give free concerts at the University so all students had the opportunity to see and hear accomplished musicians.

I told my students that I had seen the numbers that had been burned on the arms of these gifted musicians who had been in concentration camps. Palestinians have a great heart and these kinds of human stories opened student hearts to the suffering that many Jewish people knew.

The similarities in the history of suffering of the peoples could be a means for better understanding in the present. Israelis have suffered through the centuries, particularly with the atrocities of the Holocaust. The Palestinians have also suffered through the fifty years of Israeli occupation because their land has been taken away. Could this be a means for understanding?

Peace starts within oneself. In this land three monotheistic religions believe the Holy One has said not to kill. Yet people in all religions continue to suffer and sometimes to cause death. The suicide bombers on one side cause havoc on Israeli society and the Israeli Army's retaliation on the Palestinians causes terrible suffering on the other side. Until there is an inner peace in the heart of each person, outer peace will be fragile at best. I and others with me are trying to work for peace through our students at Bethlehem University.

From the beginning of my stay in Bethlehem Israelis have harassed and oppressed our students. The faculty taught through the three years of 1988-1991 when our University was closed by Israeli Military Orders. We also taught through the First Intifada which started in 1988. After that the situation for students and our university became worse. Check points were created at every entrance into Israel. Curfews, closures and collective punishment were imposed. Property was destroyed, trees were uprooted and targeted assassinations were occurring almost every day in the occupied territories. At the same time Jewish Settlements sprouted up all over the Arab Lands against all agreements.

During these times of turmoil our classes of 10 to 12 students took place wherever we could find a space. Sometimes this was in old people's homes, in hospital dining rooms, in hotel rooms or even in parks. Since it was forbidden by the Israelis to teach those of us who were faculty avoided going where soldiers would discover us. Maybe it was now time to get musicians from both sides to play together for an experience of cooperation.

So I opened the first music 'conservatoire' and with some friends gathered all the musicians in Bethlehem to play music together. We met every Saturday afternoon in our convent and played our instruments together. There were pianists, flutists, a viola player, an Arab lyre ('ud, in Arabic) player and a number of recorder players. This precious time spent playing music helped us to overcome the difficulties and the tensions between our peoples.

During the first Intifada one of my music students also used music to build a bridge. Khalid was from Dheisheh Refugee Camp. It was also a stronghold of resistance throughout the first Intifada and so it remained under Israeli watch. Khalid was in his room on the first floor of his house studying when a soldier kicked open the door as Khalid listened to *The Jupiter Symphony* by Mozart. The soldier asked Khalid how it was possible that an inhabitant of a refugee camp could be listening to Mozart! Khalid showed the soldier his collection of classical music and said he was a student at Bethlehem University. The soldier called the other soldiers who appreciated music. They came in as enemies and went out as friends.

Yassir Arafat and the Palestinian Authority made life in the territories more peaceful. Once again, Palestinians were allowed to move freely all over Israel and the Israelis were free to visit the territories. Many Palestinians living abroad came back to invest their money and create jobs for their fellow countrymen. Life was full of hope once again and the people looked forward to a new millennium in 2000.

Hope was high as many of my musician friends invited me and my students to concerts in Israeli Jerusalem or came over to give concerts in our university chapel or in the music room. These concerts were very well attended by the larger community of Bethlehem as well as by the students and their families. Our students learned to appreciate the Israelis and their goodness in new ways. In the Millennium Year the "little town of Bethlehem" received a face-lift! The houses were given a new coat of paint, the roads were repaired and asphalted, trees and flowers were planted in the squares and Bethlehem was ready to receive visitors again

People from all over the world started coming on pilgrimage including musicians, dancers, singers and jugglers. There were daily activities in the streets and new life came to the city center which was close to the Church of the Nativity. Every week was dedicated to a different country. These festivities abruptly ended in September when Ariel Sharon visited the Al-Aqsa Mosque in Jerusalem, the third holiest space for the Muslims. This visit sparked riots everywhere and led to the beginnings of a second Intifada. The invasion of Bethlehem and the siege of the Church of the Nativity by tanks, armored-personnel vehicles and infantry led to open warfare on the streets! The whole area was placed under curfew for more than 30 days!

My work then became visiting Muslim and Christian families to see if they required anything I might be able to obtain. During this time many of my Israeli friends called on a daily basis to see if they could help. I and the rest of the faculty at Bethlehem University tried to show Palestinian students that there are Israelis who are not hateful to students. I continue to invite as many kind Israelis as I can to meet my Palestinian students to foster respect on both sides.

At the time I am sharing this we find ourselves imprisoned inside a WALL that Israel built. It is at this time 403 miles long and 25 feet high. It encircles every Palestinian town and village and isolates the West Bank from Israel. This makes it impossible for Palestinians to leave their homes unless they have a permit which is very hard to obtain.

Throughout the years of suffering, problems, occupation, destruction and collective punishment the Palestinian people have never lost hope. The people pray and keep hoping that one day God will grant them peace with justice. One day there again will be a land that is truly their own. My duty today is to keep HOPE alive despite the terrible difficulties the Palestinians continue to face. So I pray with our people that the God of Peace will grant us and the whole world peace. I pray with Teresa of Avila, "God grant me the serenity to accept the things I cannot change, the courage to change the things I can and the wisdom to know the difference."

NOTES

[1]   A more extensive biography of Amneh Badran and the work of the Jerusalem Center for Women can be found on the Women Waging Peace website. www.womenwagingpeace.net/content/members/badran.html

[2]   An extensive and clear history of multiple organizations and people working for peace can be found in Janet M. Powers, *Blossoms on the Olive Tree: Israeli and Palestinian Women Working for Peace,* 1-13, 123-42, cited in ch. 2. Also see the website for Women Waging Peace, www.womenwagingpeace.net

[3]   These reflections were graciously sent by Patricia Crockford with permission to use them in this book.

5

Immaculee Ilibagiza, Rwanda

Immaculee Ilibagiza is a Tutsi survivor of the 1994 Rwandan genocide. Her story is woven through with beauty and peace, terror and suffering, hope and despair and finally with a deep sense that forgiveness can transform hearts even of oppressors.

Immaculee was born in the western Rawandan province of Kibuye in the village of Mataba. The beauty of lakes and mountains made her think she was close to paradise, at least as she imagined it to be. Childhood memories of climbing down the hill to the lake, swimming with her brothers and father and then returning up the hill for a good supper were happy ones. Her parents, Leonard and Marie Rose, were teachers and were also Catholic Christians who had a social sense of care for those poorer than themselves. Volunteer work was a way of life for the whole family.

Immaculee had two older brothers, Aimable Ntukanyagwe and Damascene Jean Muhinwa. Her younger brother was John Marie Vianney Kazeneza. Immaculee was only seven when the oldest brother Aimable went to boarding school. She remembers missing him so much that all she could write over and over in her letters to him was that she missed him. Her young brother Vianney was basically a pest who followed her everywhere.

It wasn't until Immaculee was ten years old that a teacher asked the children whether they were Hutu or Tutsi. A few children like Immaculee didn't know since there had not been any discussion about this. The teacher called them stupid and sent them out of class for the day. When she went home and asked her parents what she was they said that being a good person who cares for others had nothing to do with ethnic grouping. They did not tell her about the long history of Hutu and Tutsi hatreds.

At age fifteen Immaculee finished eighth grade as a top student. By now she was aware that her dreams of getting to a good high school and university were probably unattainable because she was a woman and a Tutsi. However, she underestimated her father's ingenuity. He took additional jobs and sold his two best cows to make enough money to get her into a good high school. She did well at school. However, she had one frightening experience that may have been a forecast of things to come.

One day some Hutu extremists came to the school and threatened the Tutsi girls. Later one of Immaculee's friends took her down to a room to show her how to end her life by touching a high voltage wire that was exposed. Stories were spreading of how the Hutu men abused young Tutsi women. Immaculee's friend believed taking one's life was a way to avoid the horrors.

When Immaculee went home for Christmas her junior year, she learned that her father was in jail. A Hutu neighbor had claimed her father was a political enemy so he was sent to prison. It was clear that even in their small village, ethnic tensions were increasing.

Immaculee finished high school near the top of the class and was awarded a coveted scholarship to the National University in Butawee. Her parents encouraged her to go to university even though they were well aware that a Tutsi woman would have a hard time at National University. Her scholarship included a monthly allowance that enabled her to have some spare money for social events. Some friends made her transition pleasant and exciting as two years flew by. However, an uneasy peace between Hutus and Tutsis was a concern.

Immaculee's brother Damascene warned her that she must avoid the growing number of Interahamwe, the brutal Hutu extremists who were gaining more power every day. In spite of peace accords in her third year at university Immaculee was awakened every morning by the hate filled messages and threats of the Hutus that came over the radio stations.

Immaculee and Damascene were both home after Easter. Damascene felt his family was unaware of the danger they faced. He witnessed many killings by the Interahamwe and pleaded with the whole family to leave the village. The names of all Tutsi families were on a Hutu list for killing. Immaculee's father insisted that in their village this would not happen. Hutus and Tutsis had always gotten along well in this village.

However, Immaculee believed her brothers Damascene and Vianney when they told their stories of Tutsis being murdered. She wanted to leave the village but her parents kept denying the problem. On April 7, 1994 after the assassination of the Hutu president the radio called for Hutus to pick up their machetes and start slaughtering their Tutsi neighbors.

The next day at dawn screaming began in the little village. The ten Belgian peacekeepers who were protecting the prime minister had been murdered. Immaculee's father who was a village leader woke up to about 10,000 Tutsis who had come up the hill to hear what he thought they should all do. He told them to pray to God and stand together against the Hutus. They managed to drive away the first stream of Interahamwe but the victory was short lived.

Immaculee's father insisted that she, Vianney and a friend, Augustine, should leave the house immediately and go to Pastor Murinzi's house. Even though the pastor was a Hutu, Immaculee's father was sure that the pastor would take in Immaculee, her brother Vianney and Augustine. On the five-mile walk to the pastor's house a gang of young Hutus surrounded them and threatened them with death until an adult Hutu friend stepped in front of the younger men with his spear and demanded they allow the children to pass in safety. The three children ran as fast as they could toward the pastor's house.[1]

Pastor Murinzi, a Protestant pastor, opened the door and welcomed them warmly. A good girl friend was there from school, but the young woman refused to acknowledge Immaculee's presence. It was painfully clear that now dividing lines between Hutu and Tutsi dissolved former friendship. Only the pastor's son Lechim remained friendly and welcomed the children and apologized for the extremist Hutus as he showed Immaculee her room.

It was not long before Immaculee's brother Damascene came to tell her that their village was burned to the ground but their parents had escaped on a motorcycle. He did not know if they were intercepted later. Damascene was afraid that none of them would survive the violence but he agreed to keep hopeful if Immaculee would. Their painful farewell was a final good-bye.

Immaculee went back to the bedroom knowing from the loud screams outside that the violence was now out of control. The bedroom door burst open as the pastor quickly admitted six more Tutsi women. There was pounding on his front door with men shouting they would kill any Tutsi woman. Immaculee noticed a hole in the ceiling and crawled up to look for hiding space. It was large enough for all of them to hide which they did for two hours in stifling heat.

The pastor came to the room and said he would take the girls to another hiding place after it got dark. He could not hide young men too so Vianney and Augustine went out into the night. The pastor took the women secretly into a hidden bathroom that measured about three by four feet. The women could hardly fit in the room, but they were glad for the protection. They were given instructions to never make a sound. They could flush the toilet only when they heard the adjoining toilet flush. Their life depended on them making no noise. The pastor promised the women that he would tell no one that the women were there, not even his children.

In the cramped space, when the women could no longer stand, the tallest four slid down to the floor with backs against the wall and the shorter women sat on top of them. They could not leave this space, so cramping and sleeplessness were part of the pain. When he could the pastor slipped some cold potatoes and beans into the small slit that served as a window. At intervals angry Hutus would burst into the pastor's house and demand to know where he was hiding Tutsis. The pastor kept proclaiming that he was a good Hutu and they could search the house if they wished. The searches were on the other side of the wall and did not turn up any Tutsi women. Yet the women were sure they would be killed. Immaculee recalls praying.

> Please God, blind the killers when they reach the pastor's bedroom.
> Don't let them find the bathroom door and don't let them see
> us . . . stop these killers from ripping us apart.[2]

After seven hours the pastor came to tell the women the men had left and they were safe for now. The women were too exhausted from fear to talk or to eat the food the pastor brought them. Immaculee noticed the large dresser in the room and asked the pastor to push it against the door to the bathroom so it would completely hide the door. The women returned to the small space and heard him slide the dresser against the door. It made them feel safer.

Every twelve hours the women would change positions. They worked out signals for dealing with menstrual periods, stretching, sitting together and standing, as well as for using the toilet and flushing at the correct moments. Killers gathered outside frequently singing "Kill the Tutsis." Any food brought to the women was dictated by the Hutu's presence outside the house so it could be hours or two days between meals.

The women could hear the conversations between the pastor and Sembeba, one of his sons who was a dedicated extremist Hutu. He informed his father that they had killed thousands of Tutsis and he was proud of it. The pastor got angry and informed his son that killing of any kind was against

God's will and the son should remember that his mother was a Tutsi. The son ignored this and the pastor told his son to leave and not come back until his hatred was gone.

Late that evening when the pastor let them out of the bathroom the women were informed that the government was assisting the genocide. Immaculee now had to admit that her father was wrong to trust the government and the world community. No one was coming to the aid of the Tutsis from inside Rwanda or from outside. Immaculee tried to pray for forgiveness for the Hutus but discovered she could not. So she prayed for the eventual ability to forgive.

> I desperately wanted God's protection, but I believed in my heart that they (Hutu killers) deserved to die. I couldn't pretend that they hadn't slaughtered and raped thousands of people.[3]

Slowly Immaculee felt pity for those who hate so much that they kill. Immaculee felt God had answered her request when she was inspired to pray that before each of these killers died they would be led to ask for forgiveness. The violence and cruelty of this part of their life made her feel pity for people who can hate that much. When a deep feeling of peace swept through her she knew it was God answering her prayer.

It seemed to Immaculee as she squinted out of the small space to the outside that every Hutu male in Rwanda had been given guns as well as machetes and spears. The UN had withdrawn its peacekeepers. Only one brave Canadian commander, Romeo Dallaire, had stayed on his own with about one hundred soldiers. He tried to get the world to send soldiers to help stop the continuing genocide, but no one seemed to hear. Major powers would not acknowledge that there was a genocide going on. Besides, they had their own concerns.

The only good news that was ever heard was that Paul Kagame still had a small group of Tutsi soldiers who were fighting in the north. Meanwhile the pastor was running low on food and told the women he would have to put them out if the fighting continued for another month; it did continue for another month.

The future was bleak and uncertain. Yet the constant hours of prayer seemed to transform Immaculee's vision of life's meaning.

> In the midst of the genocide I'd found my salvation. I knew that my bond with God would transcend the bathroom, the war, and

the holocaust . . . it was a bond that I knew would transcend life itself . . . I'd been born again in the bathroom and was now the loving daughter of God.[4]

When two more Tutsi women were added to the bathroom group the women heard more terrible stories from outside. The two women told them how they had been saved by the kindness of a Hutu man who gave them his identity paper. However, he was seen doing it, so a Hutu soldier chopped his head off in front of the two women. Their description of the numbers of stacked corpses all along the roads on both sides made the other women cry.

After seven weeks in the small bathroom there seemed to be more room due to the loss of weight of all the women. The heat and perspiring and minimal food made them all appear very gaunt. After twelve weeks in the cramped space of the bathroom the radio reported French soldiers were coming to Rwanda to set up some camps. Immaculee felt the Tutsi women would be safer with the French than with Rwandan Hutus. The pastor seemed relieved at the suggestion that it might be time to leave the bathroom.

That evening when the pastor let the women out he told them it was no longer safe for them to stay in that hidden bathroom. His houseboy was suspicious. A friend of the pastor's informed him that Hutus were coming back tomorrow to do a more thorough search. The pastor had information about how to get to a French-based camp. He told the women they would leave the house between two and three in the morning and the French soldiers would be waiting for them at the camp. When the time came the women stole glances at themselves in the mirror and were shocked at how much they now resembled the dead. Their bones were showing and their faces looked like starvation victims. Immaculee weighed 65 pounds.

For the first time the pastor's children saw the women. The pastor told the children that they could have been unfortunate like the women and he hoped it taught them that God wants all people to help each other. The only one who was angry was Sembeba who had killed many Tutsis. Immaculee prayed for him. "I prayed that one day he would find God's truth and forgiveness and wouldn't tell the killers about us before we had got away."[5]

The pastor and an older son walked with the women in the early morning darkness toward the French camp. When the French camp was in sight the pastor told the women to go ahead, and he and his son would keep watching to make sure they got in safely. Once inside the camp Immaculee spoke French explaining who they were. The French soldiers then lowered their guns and the women sobbed in relief. The French soldiers assured the women they were safe. No soldier would harm them. The men brought food for the women and told them to eat and then to lie down and sleep until the truck came to transfer them to a base camp ten miles away. Lying on the ground Immaculee stared at the beauty of the sky she had not really seen for months. Deep sadness descended as it dawned on her that things would never be the same again.

Immaculee decided to walk about the camp. In the shadows she recognized Jean Paul, a friend of her brother Damascene. Jean Paul recognized her immediately and they exchanged stories about the village and what they knew. Jean Paul told Immaculee that her parents were murdered a few days after his. Vianney and his friend Augustine had been killed in a stadium with a thousand other Tutsis. Damascene had escaped to Zaire but then was murdered.

Immaculee cried until she had no more tears. Then she heard the sound of the truck coming to take the women to a different camp. The women boarded the truck and were hidden by the coverings. There were a few roadblocks that the Hutus had set up. However, the driver kept telling the guards that he was bringing food to the Hutus in refugee camps. The capital city, Kigali, had fallen to Tutsi rebels and the Hutus were being driven to camps.

When Immaculee arrived at the next camp she walked around and was surprised to see her aunt and some cousins. Their bodies were filled with infected sores and their eyes swollen from insect bites. The odor from the bodies was strong but not enough to prevent her from hugging these poor gaunt relatives. "I said a silent prayer for all of them asking God to heal their hearts and promised myself that I'd do everything I could to heal their bodies."[6]

Stories were again exchanged. Here Immaculee found out that her brother Damascene had died of beatings he received because he would not reveal where she was hiding. Damascene had both arms chopped off and his head split open before he died. A school friend of his was part of the Hutu crowd of young men who saw the killing. This Hutu friend had cried for days after the brutal killing. He had played soccer and served as altar boy with Damascene for years. "I will never kill again," he said. "I will never get Damascene's face out of my head . . . It was a sin to kill such a boy—it was a sin."[7]

Immaculee befriended a captain who told her that he would kill any Hutu she named as well as any other soldiers or people she wanted killed. Immaculee was shocked at his anger and desire for revenge. If she had not received the grace to forgive perhaps she would have shared in his desire for revenge. She saw in a new way how the cycle of hatred was aroused by suffering and how difficult that cycle was to break. Then a new conviction grew. "I could see that whatever path God put me on helping others to forgive was a big part of my life's work."[8]

Because Immaculee spoke French she was quickly set apart as a translator for many others. One of the soldiers fell in love with her and wanted her to go back to France with him. She gently declined and assured him that God would find someone else for him. Immaculee was still too close to the suffering and death of all her family to be able to think about marriage.

War continued; more and more orphans began to show up at the camp. There was no other place for them. Immaculee tried to console them but they were so young that their loss had put many of them in a state of shock. The French soldiers were very kind to them.

When the camp got so large that another one had to be constructed the captain of the camp asked Immaculee if she would stay to help administrate the camp. About thirty refugees would stay at the camp; others would leave. A small group of friends around Immaculee agreed to stay and help with the ever new streams of refugees that would come into the camp.

One of the refugees who was in a wheelchair was a famous woman named Aloise who was a friend of Immaculee's parents. Immaculee did not remember Aloise but she knew that Aloise was a brilliant scholar. Aloise suggested that Immaculee and her friends come to live in Aloise's large house should they ever get back to Kigali.

In late August the French took the thirty refugees to a road that eventually led to the place where the Tutsi rebels had a camp. The refugees had no choice. Immaculee was hopeful that when the Tutsi soldiers saw them, the soldiers would be pleased to know there were some Tutsis who had not been murdered. However, the soldiers kept pointing guns at the group and demanding to see identity papers which none had. When Aloise charmed them a soldier pointed to a church and said there were some survivors inside. The groups were told to go into the church. The new group of refugees joined about one hundred others.

As suppertime drew near Immaculee walked behind the church to look for firewood. As she walked around she was surprised by a stench that nauseated her. She followed the scent and discovered hundreds of bodies stacked like firewood and covered by a blanket of flies. Walking further, she saw thousands of bodies that had been thrown into in a large pit behind the church.

> I'd have to leave the sorrow and suffering of this country behind, at least for awhile. In order to help heal others, as I knew God wanted me to, I needed the perspective that only space and time could provide. I had to first heal myself to be able to heal the others.[9]

An army truck finally took Aloise and her group to Aloise's house. It was still standing but needed work. Immaculee got a job with the United Nations in Kigali as a translator. When she had a chance to visit her former village she wept at the sight of her parents' graves and Damascene's. A friend of her father's took her to a prison to see the former neighbor who had murdered her family. As soon as the neighbor saw her, he recognized her and just wept and sobbed. Immaculee could not believe this was the person she once knew.

> I wept at the sight of his suffering . . . the evil had ruined his life like a cancer in the soul. He was now the victim of his victims, destined to live in torment and regret. I was overwhelmed with pity for the man . . . Felicien was sobbing. I could feel his shame . . . our eyes met. I reached out, touched his hands . . . and quietly said what I'd come to say, "I forgive you."[10].

In late 1995 Immaculee was at last reunited with her only living brother Aimable who was a successful doctor in Kigali. Immaculee continued to work for the UN, using evenings to pray and reflect and slowly heal as much as possible from the horror of the genocide.

In time she was ready to let relationships happen again. Bryan entered her life. He worked for an International Tribunal in Rwanda that was connected to the UN. Bryan and Immaculee shared much of their life stories; they married in 1998 and lived in the United States. After becoming a mother Immaculee went back to work at the UN in New York. As part of her job telling her story of the Rwandan genocide was built into a life given to reconciliation and healing.

> God's message extends beyond borders. Anyone in the world can learn to forgive those who have injured them . . . I know

that Rwanda can heal itself if each heart learns the lesson of forgiveness . . . If there was ever a time for forgiveness, it is now . . . The love of a single heart can make a difference. I believe that we can heal Rwanda—and our world—by healing one heart at a time.[11]

Immaculee continues to live in New York with her husband Bryan and close to their two children Nikeisha and Bryan, Jr. Immaculee has shared her life story with many because she hopes it will prevent new cycles of hatred in the world. Since all our lives are interconnected, "we're meant to learn from each other's experience. I wrote this book hoping that others may benefit from my story."[12]

NOTES

[1]   Immaculee Ilibagiza, *Left to Tell: Discovering God Amid the Rwandan Holocaust* (Carlsbad, CS: Hay House, Inc., 2006). The summary is from ch. 1-6, 1-56. Immaculee Ilibagiza has graciously allowed the selective use of her book for this chapter.

[2]   *Left to Tell*, 78. The summary is from 57-78.

[3]   *Left to Tell*, 92.

[4]   *Left to Tell*, 107.

[5]   *Left to Tell*, 114. The summary is from 79-114.

[6]   *Left to Tell*, 149.

[7]   *Left to Tell*, 155.

[8]   *Left to Tell*,.159.

[9]   *Left to Tell*, 179. The summary is from 149-79.

[10]   *Left to Tell*, 204.

[11]   *Left to Tell*, 210.

[12]   *Left to Tell*, xvi. The DVD *Hotel Rwanda* provides another version of this genocide.

6

South African Women Speak

The Union of South Africa was created from multiple territories on May 31, 1910. The official republic of South Africa independent from British control was formed on May 31, 1931 through the official statute of Westminster. In 1934 two former political parties merged to become the United Party which sought reconciliation between Afrikaners and English-speaking whites. In 1948 a party called the National Party was elected to power. This party began to implement a series of harsh segregation laws known collectively as apartheid. Apartheid became increasingly controversial in the latter half of the century as opposition forces rose up.

In 1990 the National Party took the first step toward negotiating itself out of power when it lifted the ban on the African National Congress (ANC) and other opposition forces. An opposition leader, Nelson Mandela, who had been in prison and hard labor camps for 27 years was released. His work and that of many others caused apartheid legislation to be removed from the statute books. The first multi-racial elections were held in 1994. The ANC won by an overwhelming majority and have been in power since then.[1]

An interim Constitution of South Africa set the stage for the foundation of a Truth and Reconciliation Commission. This vehicle was constructed to help the nation listen to the stories and experiences of both victims and perpetrators as each faced the others in a safe setting. Desmond Tutu was its first chairperson. The commission had three committees: the Human Rights Violations Committee, the Reparations and Rehabilitations Committee, and the Amnesty Committee. Public hearings were held around the country of South Africa so people could tell their stories of the gross human rights violations they had experienced. Until the truth of the suffering was laid out reconciliation among the races could not happen. The assumption was that there could be no future without forgiveness.[2]

The summarized stories that follow were recorded by a reporter for the Truth Commission named Antjie Krog. Like many other white South Afrikans Antjie had been unaware of the terrible forms of violence suffered by the black South Africans. Her reporting was a source of enlightenment and opened a door of understanding about the challenges that lay ahead for a continent trying to forge a future of peace out of terrible suffering. Her reports are found in her book, *The Country of My Skull.*[3]

Beth Savage

Beth was at a Christmas party when she heard something that sounded like exploding firecrackers. Then she saw a friend throw back her arms, fall over and die. She turned quickly to look at the direction the noises were coming from. A door opened and a man had an AK 47 pointed at her. When she woke up she was on a helicopter with someone telling her she had been in a terrorist attack. The next time she woke up she was in an ICU. A face kept appearing in the window looking at her while she was in the ICU. For some reason the face frightened her.

Who was that man? Much later her daughter showed her a photograph of one of the suspects from the attack. The photo was the same face looking at her through the ICU window when she was having hallucinations, the man who had been at the door with the AK 47.

Beth finally could come home but had to learn to walk all over again. Her children learned to bathe her, to dress her, to feed her and to do many things she could not do. The large hole in the aorta needed time to mend. Shrapnel still remained in various parts of her body. Yet she felt that she was lucky to be alive and was willing to forgive the violence she suffered. There could be no future without forgiveness.[4]

Anna Silinda

Anna recalled the day perfectly. It was only 6:30am when boys pounded on her door and said her son Frank had to come to a meeting. The boys made so much noise it woke Frank up from a sound sleep. Frank told Anna that he didn't know anything about any meeting. The young men claimed that it was a meeting of the comrades and Frank had to come. He hesitated so the young men forced their way in and then forcibly pushed Frank out the door. Once they had him outside one of the young men swung his axe and hit Frank in the head. Frank started running as fast as he could to find another house to hide in.

Anna saw what happened and was in shock. She saw Frank running and then he was lost in the distance. Not long after two boys from the house her son had run to came crying and shouting to Anna that Frank was being burned to death. In shock Anna started to run in the direction of the house the boys came from. They ran with her and said they didn't know what Frank did to make the others so angry.

Some women who saw Anna running pointed out the direction that her burned boy ran. By the time Anna caught up with Frank he was exhausted and collapsed in her arms. Anna asked who had done this to him. His whole body was burned with the exception of his face. His hair was now stuck in the blood that had dried from the blows to his head. Anna pleaded with Frank to tell her who had done this. He kept claiming he didn't know who the perpetrators were or why they did this. She pleaded that he had to tell her because she wanted to get justice. Frank looked up at her but before he could speak he died in her arms.

Anna Mtimkulu

Anna's story was about the death of her husband. She never knew why he was killed. One day her younger boy who was 12 came running home saying people were following him and calling his name and the name of his father. His father told him they were not going to the door. The son felt it must be friends so he insisted that he should open the door. Two men stood there waiting.

One of the men looked at Anna and asked if her husband was home. Her husband overheard the conversation and came to the door. The man told the husband he must come out. Once her husband went out curious people joined the group to see what the gathering was about. The men had whips with them that were the same kind issued to South African police. The boys had blades and slashers. As soon as Anna's husband stepped into the group the men and boys with the slashers and whips just started pushing and chasing him so he ran around the yard in an attempt to get away from the whips.

When he fell down they kept on beating him. One of the men came closer and said the husband would have to wear the tire. Quickly two tires were put around his neck. A 5 liter can of petrol was then poured into the tires and over him. Then the leader of the mob told Anna that she had to set her husband on fire. He gave her a lighted match. She blew it out. That happened two or three times. Finally someone in the crowd threw a battery at her which missed. Now the crowd was out of control and ready to be entertained by a burning.

Anna's husband was lit on fire before her eyes. The crowd laughed and then started to leave as he continued burning. Anna ran for a bucket of water but the water did not stop the burning. She started scraping soil from the earth and put it on the burning skin. Her younger son was so frightened that he ran off. Anna got a blanket but by the time she finally smothered the flames, her husband was almost dead. It took more time to get him to a hospital but he had been so badly burned that he had no will to live and died before the next day dawned. Anna never found out why he had been victimized or if there even was a reason other than just inflicting pain for the fun of it.[5]

Helena's Reflections

Helena's story is about her husband, a white South African, who was a policeman during the apartheid era. When she fell in love with him he was a very exceptional and loving person. He was liked by friends and was the type of man who made her feel safe in his presence. It was obvious that he cared about other people. He was the type of friend someone could always count on and she respected him for that.

One day he came home and said that he and his friends had been promoted to a special unit of South African police. It was a special forces unit and those chosen for it were the top policemen. He was clearly pleased by the promotion so she was too. She and he celebrated this promotion which made him and the friends promoted with him feel like they were now top policemen.

Helena was happy at first that the friends he worked with had good times together when they were not at work. Then things started to change. Sometimes the group would seem restless and then they would abruptly leave, saying they had to go on a trip and weren't sure just when they would be back. Her husband and the group would all drive off. Helena was like any other policeman's wife who has to be satisfied with not knowing what their husbands were doing or where they were doing it. Helena was just as glad not to know about the dangers that her husband faced as a special forces policeman. She trusted him even though she feared for his safety when he went on these special missions.

After her husband spent about three years with the special forces Helena became very conscious of changes that were taking place in her husband. He had become very quiet and withdrawn. There would be times when he would press his face into his hands and start to shake violently. She could hold him but the shaking wouldn't stop. He no longer could sleep through the night but would wander around the house from window to window. Whenever she woke up it seemed he was always moving in the house somewhere.

For some time she had noticed a great increase in his drinking. This was another behavior change in the man who had once been so disciplined and compassionate. At night she noticed other changes. On the most sweltering nights his body was ice cold and he started to have convulsions. His few times for sleeping were filled with nightmares that woke her up with bloodcurdling shrieks of fear and pain. She would try to wake him from the horrors he was experiencing. When he did wake up he would just stare.

Helena was afraid that her husband was slowly growing into madness. She tried to get him to go to the hospital or to see someone about all that was happening. He didn't want to let anyone else know of his private hell. Then Helena started to hear some of the stories the Truth and Reconciliation Commission was making public. She had been unaware of the degree of torture and brutality the police were inflicting on black South Africans. She now understood that her husband had been carrying out the orders of other higher up leaders of the country. The policemen who had any conscience left were probably reduced to the state of her husband.

Helena finally understood why the freedom fighters were so angry. She could forgive them for their violence against the white people. She might also have acted in violence if she had suffered the brutality others endured for years. She blamed not only the policemen for violence but all the top leadership for her husband's state. It was well known that the top leaders were not going to show up at the commission hearing and ask for amnesty because they did not really think they had done anything wrong. Helena had heard some of them claim very self righteously that they were good Christians after all including Mr. de Klerk. So let God judge them. What of her husband's punishment?

Helena knows his nightmares are a form of spiritual death he cannot escape. He is so close to despair that he cannot imagine any forgiveness for what he has done. She will continue to watch him closely and stand with him day by day. Spiritual death has entered into so many of the oppressors and it is a worse fate than physical death. At least with physical death, the victim is released from suffering and God can enter in. Those who suffer from spiritual death like her husband live in a wasteland and their suffering never stops.

Helena wishes there were some way to make the poor wasted people on both sides of apartheid whole again, but this healing will take generations. For now she prays to a compassionate God for her husband's sake and for the sake of all who were so victimized and dehumanized through apartheid. Helena's husband has told her that even if amnesty was formally granted to him a thousand times, even if God personally appeared to him and said he could be forgiven, he could never believe it. Helena's husband claims there is only one way that he can ever get out of his personal hell and that is to blow his brains out. So Helena watches him day and night as he simply sits and turns an unloaded gun over and over in his lap. There is suffering on all sides of apartheid.[6]

Mananki Seipei

Mananki lives in the Orange Free State of Tumahole. Her family was very poor, but she worked hard to provide for the children. Her oldest son Stompie had been in and out of various detention centers in South Africa for his participation in groups working to abolish apartheid. He was also a member of the Methodist youth group.

Mananki went to a detention hearing for Stompie in the middle of January, 1989, but he didn't show up. When she talked to the lawyer he claimed that her son was dead. She was puzzled by that announcement since none of Stompie's friends had been by to tell her that had happened. She knew they would have told her if her son was dead.

It wasn't until the end of January 1989 that two ministers from the Methodist Church came to see Mananki about her son. They said that Stompie had been taken from the Methodist Church meeting along with some others by Mrs. Mandela's football club. A few friends said Stompie and the others were probably at the house of Mrs. Winnie Mandela. The only people who really knew whether he was dead or alive would be the young men in the football club or the police who would have taken him to the mortuary.

In mid February the police came to Mananki's house and said she should go to Johannesburg with them to visit the mortuary. When they went to the mortuary Mananki was shown some remains of a young man who had been brutalized, killed and thrown into the river. Almost a month had passed so the decay and putrefaction made it difficult to identify him. She

Immediately looked for the signs that no one else would know. Though Stompie's eyes had been gouged out and the body had stretched from being in the water for so long a time Mananki recognized him. The birthmark on his nose, a small scar on his chest from a childhood fight, and another birthmark that still remained underneath the left leg convinced her this was her son. The tattered clothes were definitely Stompie's. Rumors were spreading that her son had been an informer which was why he was killed. Mananki insisted the accusation was not true. Finally when she got all the permissions for burial Stompie could be put to rest. However, some of the morticians who attended the burial still insisted this was not Stompie. Most people knew that the morticians were only claiming that because they wanted to protect Mrs. Mandela and her football team who had probably killed him.

The ministers from the Methodist Church assured Mananki that it was her son and finally she received a death certificate. Someone had betrayed Stompie. Mananki reflected that Jesus Christ was betrayed by one of his disciples, so her son could not expect more. Like Jesus she would pray to forgive those responsible. The commission thanked her for the painful retelling of her story.[7]

A Reporter's Reflections on the Post Apartheid Era

When the reporter Antjie Krog went home at Christmas time she knew many things were happening on the farm where she had grown up. She knew that the stealing of cattle from their farm and others as well was getting worse but was still shocked to see that her brothers were both armed and ready with their dogs to shoot at anyone who tried to steal their cattle.

Her mother explained that the cattle stealing was increasing and that farmers nearby had been killed by the night marauders. Even her brother's wife would be on the roof of the house with a night vision scope. That night Antjie heard guns go off and knew someone was shot because an ambulance siren was heard before her brothers returned to the family house.

This is still the way it is in some parts of South Africa as former victims are now taking back what they perceive to have been taken from them. At their last breakfast on the farm before Antjie left her two brothers laughed and talked like the old days. They claimed that the night before with the shooting was just like any other night. They informed her again that since the 1994 election more and more thieves had started to take back things from the whites. But most of the thieves are not armed so her brothers generally try to shoot into the ground near the thieves so they can scare them off instead of killing them.

Antjie wanted another side to the discussion. So in private she asked one of the black Africans who worked for the family why it is that the black people stand together even if it means lying about who stole from white people. The man said that blacks feel no one can destroy the whites because whites are too powerful. Black people will be wiped out by this power so they must stand together so they do not disappear. The same worker tried to explain why it is not wrong for black people to take white people's cattle. The white people have already stolen everything from black people. Taking cattle is a way of contesting power. Clearly much more true dialogue is needed if there is to be lasting peace in the land.[8]

Antjie returned to the Truth and Reconciliation Commission hearings for the next sessions. She had a little time when they ended so she returned for a quick visit to the farm. It was a shock to see a new sign on the farm that said anyone who trespasses can expect retaliation. Bushes had been cut down so that no one could hide close to the house. When the family gathered Antjie's brothers told everyone what they could and could not do. No one should walk before morning or after five in the afternoon when the gates were closed and three dogs circled the house. More than 19 farmers had been murdered in the past month.

There is much unrest and fear because Afrikaners who worked for land may have the land taken or at least the cattle on it stolen with no form of punishment. Antjie's brother said he would not die for the land although he would make sacrifices for the good of the country. A lot of conversation went on between them about the Truth Commission and amnesty and all the diverse opinions on the whole process. It was an occasion to talk about some of the challenges that lay ahead.

Each New Year comes and there are still divisions and many different proposals about the future and things that may work or may not work for building the future. There are still divisions among members of the Truth and Reconciliation Commission and the leaders of the Amnesty Committee. There are still differences of opinion about the unwillingness of De Klerk and Botha to make a firm confession of guilt about crimes against humanity.

Does that mean the process was a failure because some of those responsible for what went on in the country refused to come before the Truth Commission? No, perhaps everything did not work out as originally anticipated, but a lot of good happened that shouldn't be forgotten. Those who reported on the hearings of the Truth and Reconciliation Commission discovered that the process of joining in the stories of human suffering brought a new depth of community. Some degree of reconciliation resulted.

The Truth Commission was supposed to end mid-December of 1997 and submit its final report in July 1998. That wasn't possible because of the abundance of work that still needed to be done. Perhaps everything didn't turn out as well as one might have hoped. At the same time the process opened up the option for human beings to come together in common humanity. In spite of its failures the commission made space for all the voices who wished to speak to be heard. So there is a flame of hope that was kindled that still remains burning in spite of disappointments.

Discussion about victims and perpetrators as well as identifying the conditions for amnesty, justice and recompense will continue. Should the victims of violence receive compensation? Should the whole state ask for amnesty because the political system made injustice part of the law? These are not easy questions for a nation to answer with unanimity.

As an Afrikaner Antjie has joined her voice with many others desiring a future of true peace. With all voices she pleads for the oppressed and former oppressors to build a new South Africa together. There is always hope for a future when at least some of the people are willing to ask for forgiveness and when so many people are willing to try to forgive.

Reconciliation is far from complete. That is to be expected because people in a time of change have to form a new identity. There are many survival strategies that will be tested and tried before the power of reconciliation can happen. Hatred cannot be the end of the story. Hope through reconciliation and forgiveness are the end and beginning keys to a new South Africa. That is the future for this beloved country of grief and grace.[9]

NOTES

[1] www.wikipedia.org/wiki/South_Africa. This site has an abundance of further information about the multiple factors that continue to influence the evolution of South Africa as a nation. The overall history has been checked against other source material for accuracy.

[2] Antjie Krog, *Country of My Skull: Guilt, Sorrow, and the Limits of Forgiveness in the New South Africa* (New York: Three Rivers Press, 1998). The introduction by Charlayne Hunter-Gault reflects on the process of the TRC, v-viii.

[3] The work of Antjie Krog has been cited in no. 2 above.

[4]   Beth's story, 101-102.

[5]   Two women named Anna tell these stories, 185-186.

[6]   Helena's story, 193-5.

[7]   Mananki's story, 196-200.

[8]   Antjie Krog adds her story, 7-18.

[9]   These reflections are summaries of 363-79. The following DVDs/videos are a few of many available that can add to the understanding of South Africa's history and the period of apartheid. *Sarafina; The Power of One; Cry, the Beloved Country; The Country of My Skull; Mandela.*

7

Mercy Amba Ewudziwa Oduyoye, Ghana

At one time Ghana was inhabited by a number of ancient kingdoms that included the inland Ashanti kingdom and various Fante states along the coast. Trade with European states flourished after contact with the Portuguese in the 15th century. In 1874 the British established a crown colony here called the Gold Coast. In 1957 Ghana was the first black African country to obtain independence from colonial rule. A new constitution that restored multiparty politics was approved in 1992.[1]

Mercy Oduyoye is proud to be from Ghana. Her father Charles Kwaw Yamoah was a Methodist minister. Her mother Mercy Dakwan Yamoah was also involved with the ministry. Mercy recalls that she too was involved with the ministry of her father as a twelve-year-old. She was educated well and remembers the latter pieces of her education as transforming experiences that made a big influence on her life direction.

Methodist Girls Boarding School, Achimoto School, Kumasi College of Technology (now Kwane Nkrumah University of Science and Technology), The University of Ghana at Legon, Cambridge University in England and eventually Harvard University provided her with a sound foundation. She was a member of the Christian Students Movement at the University of Ghana. Some people there were influential in seeing that Mercy was invited to Geneva, Switzerland to work through the World Council of Churches (WCC) and the World Council of Christian Education (WCCE). When the WCCE eventually merged with the WCC's Department of Education Mercy became the Youth Education Secretary.

This work with the WCC enforced the ecumenical journey that would mark the remainder of her life, teachings and initiatives. Mercy has held positions with the Faith and Order Commission of the WCC, moderated many dialogues among people of various religious traditions, led multiple international assemblies of the WCC, initiated and helped produce the WCC Document on Men and Women in the Church, a decade long effort of the WCC to promote equality of women and men throughout the churches of the world.

Mercy consistently represented the Africa forum at multiple international meetings and was a major influence in initiating the Circle of Concerned African Women Theologians which began in 1989. Mercy was president of the Ecumenical Association of Third World Theologians from 1996-2001 and consistently encouraged African women theologians to join that group so women's voices and perspectives can affect African theology. At present Mercy directs the Institute of African Women in Religion and Culture, a place for African women to tell their stories, critically reflect on them, and come to new awareness of their humanity, their faith and their potential. She and others continue to give life to wisdom circles of African women which continue to grow in influence.

Her sensitivity about the need to universalize the interpretations of Jesus Christ for African peoples has resulted in volumes of writing. For Mercy, it is a struggle to look at the relationship between orthodoxy and creativity in the Spirit of Christ. How does one balance the eschatology of possibility with the reality of traditional faith perceptions? Mercy's works reflect her passion for justice and dignity not only for African women but for all people. Her global ecumenical work has deepened her conviction that peace among people will come only when "they" and "we" become "us" in the One Holy Mystery named God.[2]

Mercy's voice is best heard through her life spent to further justice and equality for African women. She has spent many years trying to change the forms of violence against women and the systems that foster it including some tribal religious systems. Whether in societies, cultures or religious groups, whenever women are not considered equal partners, injustice needs to be named and claimed if change is to happen. Mercy's voice in the selection of themes and perspectives that follow can provide a small glimpse of her horizons for the eventual transformation of religions and of the world.[3]

Exodus as a Symbol of the Journey Africa Travels

In the political struggles of Ghana, African liberation theologians like to use the symbol of the Exodus from Egypt as a meaningful paradigm.

Charismatic leaders like Nkrumah were often cast in the image of Moses who led the people out of oppression. The struggle for freedom was seen as marching away from colonialism which the people had known previously.

Yet all of Africa continues to struggle not just from its liberation from earlier forms of colonialism but also from the internal misgoverning of itself as those with power use it badly. The Exodus account can be used to judge leaders in Africa. As long as the leaders desired and furthered the well-being and dignity of the people they could be judged as leaders in the Spirit of God. However, once the authentic charisma of the Spirit departed, it was evident. Leaders chose their own power and wealth above the good of the people; forms of despotism set in. The people know when this happens. They reject such leaders because they feel God also rejects leaders who seek their own power above all.

The children of Israel were immigrants when they came to Egypt, and the native Egyptians remained dominant. That is not the case in Africa where the immigrant colonizers enslaved the native people and took away their human rights. This is different from the details of the Exodus story.

However, in both the biblical Exodus story and in African history there were those who refused to be part of this status quo of slavery and affliction. In the Exodus it was the midwives who refused to follow the law of the pharaoh to kill all male infants (Ex 2:23-25). The women were called God fearing. These midwives had enough compassion and wisdom to save Moses regardless of pharaoh's laws. Other people went along with the pharaoh's power without questioning the injustices. They would rather live in an unjust present than question power and move toward an unscripted future of equality.

There are people today who find it difficult to exchange a certain present for an uncertain future even if the present is oppressive. In the Exodus God didn't force people to act for their own good. People had to be involved in their own liberation and choose it, men and women alike. The situation of neocolonialism that now exists in many parts of Africa has made Africans strangers to their own potential. Many people cannot imagine any other way of organizing society! Yet true leaders are those who offer people new hope for a future they are making together. In Ghana it was Nkrumah who began leading the people like this so some considered him a new Moses.

The Exodus as a symbol can reassure oppressed and discouraged people that God is with them and still working here and now. Religious Africans believe that the river to the promised land has already been crossed. Leaders who try to reverse the process will eventually be eliminated because God's justice and peace are promised and God is true to the promise.[4]

Churches as Subtle Preservers of Discrimination

In Africa hardship has a ripple effect that is very visible as the wealthy become more powerful and the poor become even poorer. African tradition has a saying that means Africans should share with all people as the Creator wishes. This makes the World Trade Market an institution that needs critique from the African perspective. World trade market experts are brought in to lend money to Africans which only piles up debt for them. Rejecting local expertise means a loss of native Africans bringing a shared mentality to transactions. This lack of sharing is a danger to the neighborliness that the global community calls for in our time. It is not only political and economic lies that damage global neighborliness. Assumptions of some religions damage neighborliness as well.

There are many faiths beyond the biblical traditions of Judaism and Christianity. Can we say that we all really have the same God or at least a similar Holy One across religions? What is behind the mutual prejudices that have parents or neighbors say they will not accept as a true marriage one that occurs between persons who hold different religious faiths? While in theory the global neighborhood is a multi religious neighborhood how this reality plays out in local areas is a challenge for churches.

Are religions trying to foster global neighborliness by promoting awareness that the Holy Mystery is beyond any religion's human framing? Neighborliness across religions is possible since authentic religions foster the wisdom of loving the neighbor as oneself. Authentic religions then do not condone violence against other religions or peoples. The violence that has been caused to date between Muslims and Christians, Muslim and Hindu, or primal religions and both Christians and Muslims, or between Jews and many religions is a fierce cry against the neighborliness that all religions promote.

A lesser form of violence occurs when anyone insists that one religion is better than another. This insistence is religious chauvinism that often masquerades as fundamental faith. What religious chauvinism presupposes is that the Holy Mystery has given to one religious tradition a monopoly on insight and truth. This implies that all others must come to practice this religion, and that undercuts not only the roots of common humanity but the mystery of God who is beyond human imagining. Once humans learn to share spirituality across religious boundaries and national boundaries, we may all become truly the neighbors that a global world asks us to become.

This does not mean that we do not practice a specific religion. What it means is that violent or not so violent refusal to acknowledge others as equally religious and loved by God is an attitude that needs changing. One's neighbor is all people. Neighbor goes beyond gender, beyond particular faith expressions, beyond boundaries of race and geography. Any community in which gender or race or ethnic origin takes precedence over humanity as God's image will degenerate into marginalizing and even persecuting some people.

Neighborliness means speaking out and acting against the marginalization of people. Compassion is the heart of God and of faith who calls each to consider all as neighbor. What does it take to be a neighbor? It takes a self that truly sees a neighbor as oneself sharing common humanity in the Holy. Christians say to be perfect is to love one's neighbor as oneself. As we understand better the mystery of our common humanity we will understand better what God is trying to tell us about divinity.

The African church especially needs to empower women not only to speak for themselves but also to participate in the decision making that affects churches and all its members. The African church will not be a home for both men and women until both men and women are contributing fully to the theology that guides it into the future. Male blinders have turned African seminaries into male run theological factories where the particular church puts its stamp on seminarians who simply repeat the past. Christian theology must promote the interdependence of distinctive beings and incorporate inclusiveness and interdependence. The Spirit does not bring only one special group of humanity to perfection as God's image. Multiple gifts bring all humanity toward the fullness of holiness. In Africa the old order has not yet passed away in the churches. However, hint of hope for a globalized humanity moving together toward God is definitely on the horizon of some believers.[5]

Future Dreams

It is commonly acknowledged that two thirds of the work necessary for human survival is done by women. Yet few women have truly gained participation in current religious structure because the structures have been devised by men who sanctify their power in the name of God. So women are required to serve those religious systems without question. However, today there are women raising thoughtful questions because they have dreams about their involvement in the church and what it could be for all.

Women in Africa have survived because of their dreams and their empowering networks that have been built in community with each other. Many churches have organized women who bond as a support network. In Africa circles of women theologians have also supported and organized women to be supports and helpers of each other. As encouragement happens, dreams can come forth.

My call to my sisters around the world is about dreams. I sometimes call a church to put its house in order only because I have a dream of solidarity and freedom. I dream of a day when churches cease all forms of imposed subordination however subtly it may appear and however leaders may legitimate it by faith claims.

We remain free to tell our dreams today if we do not allow imagination to become captive to what is. The ability to dream, like the ability to feel pain, is a sign that we are alive. The ability to dream means we already have possession of what it takes to transform our lives. What transforms our lives as believers is faith, hope and courage. Dreams can affirm who we are and allow us to opt out of the power struggles that are destructive. Dreams call us to go to the desert of the unknown and make a promise that if we are willing to walk in the desert we just may find God and ourselves.

Dreams have always been part of the biblical tradition as people struggle against injustice and seek peace and true community. There is a prophetic heritage in Christianity that is about going toward the new, breaking the way into new life, going to a promised land where all are free. Today there are many culture bound images of God that have made God too small and an idol of human construction. Culture is not the final word or the final creator of paradigms for God or for human relationships.

Dreams for the future are about God's hope for humanity. So we humans try to ask the right questions. How can we work toward each of us and all of us becoming a global communion in God's image? Myths of human connectedness to date were too restrictive. Social structures created human beings into "races" and thus social structures can be changed to create human beings into one human race.

It doesn't matter that some human structures like "race" or in some cases false "religious groups" have become so dysfunctional that they have facilitated violence. What matters is that the power to dream of what can be can lead us to start shaping a future in which all participate in the future of equality and dignity. It is particularly women's full participation in these dreams that is the next battleground in coming decades. May the power to grow and to exhibit mercy and peace fill the hearts of all religions and all believing people so that there is at last a visible image of a God who remains life-giving and love sharing for all.[6]

Reflections on Redeeming the Church

In Africa homemaking is a part of women's experiences so it provides an image for theological reflection on the church. Women expect the household of any church to be a place where all are welcome and feel at home. Each is worthy to be there. Perhaps the word "hearth hold" is better for the church because that word for Africans means that here all are nourished from the same hearth space. In the context of church that nourishing hearth hold is Jesus Christ or God as Source of all being and the Spirit whose love and advocacy are for all. In Africa the hearth hold is a symbol for woman.

The church is a hearth hold with God as Mother, the whole earth as the hearth, and all human beings as the children. The community that claims a special relationship with Jesus Christ is the Christian Church within the hearth hold of the great mystery of the Sacred. A woman's true solidarity with the church is a solidarity with the church as it ought to be not as it is in practice. In practice women only remain in the church because they feel it is Christ who has called them to do so. It is not because the church fully represents the equality that Christ preached.

Most women stay in the church because they hope someday God will redeem the church from gender dualism and make all men and women truly participative in the mission according to the charisms they have been given. Women can find circles within the church that help sustain them in the midst of the pyramid that men run and interpret. In effect women have created for themselves a sort of church within a church. Unless churches radically change to allow women to use their gifts in mission and ministry there will be little transformation of the churches in our time. Justice and true peace will suffer.

It is clear that in New Testament times women and men could participate in evangelization according to their gifts. Many churches today have turned ordination into a mark that confers an official ministry only to men and not to qualified women. Partnership of men and women, ordained and not ordained, is a true partnership of the community called church. But it is not a full partnership until all men and women can share their charisma. When this does not happen that church is still in need of redemption.

Mission is the task of the whole church to the whole of humanity. To try to evangelize any people with the hierarchical pyramid that exists is not a becoming image of the household of God. To be a servant to all is an image that includes the diversity of servants as all the baptized in mission to the world. This means women and men, all races and all peoples. This would be a church that is a hearth hold and one that could be credible for African women.[7]

Who Will Roll the Stone Away?[8]

The stream of resurrection people that has flowed from the empty tomb of Jesus Christ has continued to broaden and deepen through the centuries. Women have stood in solidarity with Christ and with the church since the day Mary of Nazareth said yes to God (Lk 1:38). Through the centuries women as well as men have been supporters, promoters and community builders in their churches reaching out in mission. Today as society becomes more open to the full humanity of women it is essential that the churches also look at themselves and how women are treated in the churches. The World Council of Churches (WCC) wishes that each of its member churches look at whether it is acting justly toward women in an attempt to be faithful to God.

The church has claimed to be a voice for the voiceless. Women and children are among the voiceless. The churches throughout the world must look at the challenge to be in solidarity with women. They must deliberately and intentionally stand with women for what enhances the full humanity of all. The churches are being asked to continue the efforts of the United Nations who in 1979 officially tried to eliminate all forms of discrimination against women.

The WCC now takes up the same challenge. Solidarity requires this as part of faith. As a church the baptized are all one body. When any part of the body is not given fullness of humanity the whole body suffers. In the Body of Christ there are still subtle forms of sexism that prevent women from full partnership in church and community life. In the decade of solidarity with women it is hoped that women will be given equal place so that fresh approaches to the gifts of women and their ability to fully use their Spirit given gifts will come alive in a new way. Faithful women around the globe are asking, "Who will roll the stone away?" Will it be the World Council of Churches?[9]

Solidarity means walking hand in hand and developing strengths through unity. Solidarity means that together people accomplish common aims and their common interests are protected. If entire churches are to be in solidarity with women that means that the church must identify with hopes and fears that women live with both in society and in the churches. Looking at the Body of Christ as one church, to call for solidarity means that the church must show it cares by listening to women's descriptions as well as men's about how churches are and are not in solidarity with them.

Ideally in the church of Christ the common good means that women as well as men can use their gifts. While solidarity with women will mean different things to different churches in the Body of Christ discrimination against women means the church is not in solidarity with God. The call for solidarity with women is a call to life according to God's will. A church that acts in solidarity with women will be living out the Christian theology of creation that sees male and females as equally bearers of the image of God.

Jesus has handed over the care of humankind to the church. If the church does not act justly and does not extend solidarity to all as Jesus did it is not his body. Churches vary in their understanding of what it means to incorporate women fully into the body of Christ by baptism. Do not all the baptized have access to the Spirit who can give gifts as the Spirit wishes?

In some quarters of the WCC it is said that ordination should not be discussed because of the theological differences among churches. However, if ordination is the defining factor among churches that is no reason to ignore it or be afraid to discuss it. Can churches afford to maintain a posture of sacrificing women on the altar of visible unity because there is fear about discussing ordination?

Partnership and power among men and women in the churches remains unequal. Churches that claim equal partnership between men and women will be credible to the extent that the churches demonstrate willingness to share the exercise of power equally between competent women and men. The present state of the partnership of women and men in all cultures has not yet come to that obvious manifestation. For Christians, according to I Cor. 12 and Eph. 14, the Spirit of God, the Spirit of Wisdom, operates in women as in men for the common good of the community. The equal manifestation of gifts used by women as well as men is an essential element of the unity of the Body of Christ. As this dignified equality happens, there will be deeper renewal of the whole human community moving toward the eschaton.[10]

NOTES

[1] This information has been taken from *www.wikipedia.org/wiki/Ghana.*

[2] These particular reflections on Mercy's life are summarized from her introduction to her work *Beads and Strands: Reflections of an African Woman on Christianity in Africa* (Maryknoll, NY: Orbis, 2006) x-xiv.

[3] A list of Mercy's works can be found in Mercy Amba Oduyoye, *Beads and Strands,* 110-114.

[4] *Beads and Strands,* 3-10.

[5] *Beads and Strands,* 89-98.

[6] *Beads and Strands,* 104-8.

[7] Mercy Amba Oduyoye, *African Women's Theology* (Cleveland: Pilgrim Press, 2001) 80-89.

[8] Mercy Oduyoye, *Who Will Roll the Stone Away? The Ecumenical Decade of the Churches in Solidarity with Women* (Geneva: WCC Publications, 1990). The excerpts in this section are from this source. Section titles and pages will be indicated in the notes that follow.

[9] The Beginnings. The summary is from 1-10.

[10] Meaning and Signs of Solidarity, 40-55.

8

Jehan Sadat, Egypt

In 1882, ostensibly to protect its investments, the United Kingdom seized control of Egypt's government. A nominal allegiance to the Ottoman Empire lasted until 1914. Constant revolting by the Egyptian people led Great Britain to issue a unilateral declaration of the Independence of Egypt on February 22, 1922. The Egyptian government drafted and implemented a new constitution in 1923 based on a parliamentary representative system. Continued instability in the government led to a toppling of the monarchy and the dissolution of the parliament through a coup d'état in 1952. King Farouk I abdicated in support of his son King Ahmed Fouad II. On June 16, 1953 the Egyptian Republic was formed with General Mohammed Naguib as the first President of the Republic. Naguib was forced to resign in 1954 by Gamal Abdel Nasser who assumed power as president and declared the full independence of Egypt from the United Kingdom on June 18, 1956. His nationalization of the Suez Canal on July 26, 1956 prompted the 1956 Suez crisis. Three years after the 1967 Six Day War in which Egypt lost the Sinai to Israel, Nasser died. He was succeeded by Anwar Sadat whose story is woven through Jehan's story.[1]

Jehan Sadat, Woman of Peace[2]

Jehan was born in 1933 on Roda Island, a verdant island whose occupants saw the Nile flowing by and who heard the minarets of Cairo calling the people to prayer five times a day. Her father Safwat Raouf was an Egyptian surgeon who had met her mother Gladys Cortrell while he studied in England at Sheffield University. The two fell in love and married in spite of the protests of the Safwat's Muslim father. After three years the couple returned to Egypt. The children were raised Muslim as was the custom, but Gladys continued her Christian ways and in time Safwat's family learned to love her.

Jehan remembers asking her mother why the mother was Christian and the rest of the family was Muslim. Her mother gave her an answer she always remembered. "We are all what we are born to be. The important thing to remember is that all religions are expressions of one mystery . . . It does not matter how we worship . . . as long as we have faith."[3]

Although Jehan was raised as a Sunni Muslim she went to a secondary Christian school for girls in Cairo. Her family believed that women and men were equal in Allah's eyes. She was shocked when she discovered that other Sunnis did not practice this equality. Some women never ate until their husbands were entirely satisfied. The women disappeared when visitors came to see the husband. Jehan's father said that such practices were old-fashioned.

Jehan remembers loving Ramadan as a child because everything was made special. There would be no eating between sunrise and sunset. At sunset all the lights around the minarets would come on and people would share their table with others. It was a time for spiritual and social renewal that Jehan valued increasingly as she got older. Peace and justice were renewed. At the conclusion of Ramadan the three-day feast of Aid-el-Saghir was celebrated by giving extra alms to beggars and poor people. Children received new clothes and great feasting abounded.

Jehan was thirteen before she noticed terrible poverty. When she went to school outside her village she was told of an old woman who lived near a tree because that was the only home she could afford. Jehan began to take her own lunch and give it to the woman each day when she went to school. She was heartbroken one day when she went to visit the woman and was told that the woman had died.

By the time Jehan was fourteen she was praying at five points of the day. She also added short prayers at other times and fasted once or twice a week outside of Ramadan. In addition to her newly found adolescent religious fervor she became more emphatic about Egypt's liberation from British colonialists. Jehan's English mother encouraged Jehan's interest in politics and let Jehan go to Suez in summer to spend Ramadan with an aunt who shared similar interests.[4]

Jehan was visiting this aunt the summer she was fifteen when she met Anwar Sadat who was looked on as a hero in Egypt's liberation. Jehan's cousin

Hassan had been a colleague of Anwar's and had spent time with him in prison. Anwar came to the house shortly after being released from prison. Jehan loved Anwar at first sight. She quickly called her father to see if she could extend her stay with the cousin. Permission was given.

Anwar and Jehan spent a lot of time together. He was from a poor village, had been married as a very young man and separated, imprisoned twice, and now felt a strong dedication to better Egypt's future. He did not really expect his first wife or any future wife to understand the degree of his dedication. As they began to love each other Hassan agreed to be the ever present chaperone for good Muslims could not be romantically involved without a chaperone. Hassan accompanied them on their early morning walks.

It was clear that Jehan and Anwar should get permission from Jehan's parents to marry. Her father immediately said no as did her mother who felt Jehan was much too young for marriage. The blend of Jehan's persistent tears and pleadings and the sincerity and love of Anwar for Jehan moved the parents to agree to the marriage. Jehan's father knew that Anwar had little money, so he offered to buy a wedding ring and agreed that someday Anwar could pay him back. The place Jehan and Anwar chose to live was also a secret gift from the father who never told Jehan's mother how much he had assisted the young couple. The marriage was on May 29, 1949. The young couple felt their lives had been joined for a sacred purpose. They journeyed to the great Sphinx to see the sunrise in the desert and share a sacred moment.

> Often I have reflected at dawn in the desert. Surely it was God's will to draw us there to re implant in both of us our destiny and the destiny of our country . . . From that first dawn at the Pyramids my husband and I began the journey that had been charted . . . Love. Dignity. Honor. Peace.[5]

When Anwar had a hardship tour in the Sinai his wages doubled. They would not see each other very often but loved the times they spent together. Jehan went to stay with her parents and finish secondary school which Anwar encouraged her to do. "Anwar and I kept our own company, taking long walks in the desert in the evenings . . . We grew ever closer to each other with our separate strengths becoming the heart strings of the other."[6]

When Jehan visited Anwar in the Sinai she was shocked at the aftermath of the 1948 war that created Israel but left so many Palestinian' refugees. The once beautiful Gaza Strip that had been a tourist attraction was now lined with refugee camps. Jehan was moved by the terrible suffering she saw. Her eyes were opened to a new depth of social consciousness she had not known before.

Like other native Egyptians she began to resent the growing wealth of King Farouk and those around him as poor people became poorer. On January 26, 1951, Black Saturday, the unrest boiled over. Finally King Farouk was expelled and at last Egypt was ruled by Egyptians. Anwar Sadat had been one of the major players in this restoration so he and Jehan became important and well-loved persons. Poor people now trusted Jehan to listen to their stories of the hardships they were suffering. She did all that she could to assist them.

Jehan began to get migraine headaches as she feared the opposition to Anwar's work. By the time a new constitution was approved in 1956 the Sadats had two daughters. Egyptians were delighted at their newfound freedom to govern themselves. President Nasser nationalized the Suez Canal so Egypt would receive benefits. The Suez War followed as Israel invaded the Sinai and the Canal Zone with the assistance of the US and Britain. The UN called for a cease-fire, but only Egypt accepted the call to cease fire. In this turmoil in November a son Gamal was born. A fourth child, Jehan, was born in 1961. The UN ordered a peacekeeping force to stay in the Sinai until 1967.

Meanwhile, anti-Jewish sentiment among the Egyptians was growing. Soon thousands of Jews who had lived peacefully with Egyptians for centuries were expelled or else fled from Egypt. At one time Muslim neighbors had gone into Jewish homes on the Sabbath to turn on lights or do other chores for them that the Jews could not do on their Sabbath. Now that former harmony seemed forever destroyed.

On Fridays Anwar took Gamal to the mosque. Jehan prayed with the girls since they did not go to the mosque.

> Acting as the imam it was I who would lead them in the ritual. Both Anwar and I wanted the children to gain peace and understanding we ourselves had gained from a religion. Very early I taught the children to know the holy book, to pray and fast.[7]

Anwar had now become a speaker in the Parliament so Jehan felt she too had to act for the people. Jehan also began a small cooperative among the women of the villages to make and sell products. This helped the women help themselves and their children move out of poverty. This also meant that some men would not be happy to have their wives making money.[8]

In spite of the many positive things that were happening both Jehan and Anwar knew that there was unrest manifesting itself again in Egypt. President Nasser's reforms included the Committee for the Liquidation of Feudalism seizing assets from the wealthier Egyptians and humiliating them in the process. People were being put out of their homes and abused as they were stripped of wealth. Jehan's family members were among those being stripped of their wealth. Many middle-class people turned against Nasser.

In spring of 1967 Israel's invasion shocked the Egyptians. Egyptian planes were destroyed before they even got off the ground. More than 15,000 Egyptian soldiers were killed and thousands of Palestinians were exiled from Israel. Like other Egyptians Jehan volunteered in an Army hospital assisting soldiers or comforting them as they lay dying. "Who can see the things that I have seen and not believe in peace? In the summer of 1967 I was learning firsthand that war should never be an answer to any conflict."[9]

Anwar thought Jehan was spending too much time away from home. Jehan's work for the hospitals, for peace and for the betterment of village women was taking more and more of her time. Jehan saw that the Israelis were killing not only soldiers but also women and children in the Canal Zone. She was more and more distressed at this cruelty. The Israelis won the war and occupied the land. Egypt was further shocked when Abdul Nasser died at age 52. Anwar Sadat was quickly sworn in as President.

Anwar Sadat knew the people were disillusioned. The Muslim brothers were getting stronger and their conservative ways were a source of concern to many people. Anwar's moves toward democracy and away from repressive actions like the secret bugging of phones angered these fundamentalists. The Islamic fundamentalists also disapproved of Anwar's peace initiatives. Anwar announced to Parliament that if Israel would be willing to withdraw forces from the Sinai, Egypt would be willing to reopen the Suez Canal. He also said he would extend a three-month cease-fire and sign a peace agreement with Israel mediated through the United Nations.

Jehan legitimated her roles outside the home by making a claim to Egyptian history. The Egyptian Queen Hanshepsut launched successful military expositions and had the image of herself carved on her massive tomb in Luxor with a beard since that was the sign that Egyptian women also had power. Jehan made it clear that it was only recently that women had been assigned inferior roles by men and she would use her powers for good.

I felt that God had given me the power to help the people and
the ability to understand their problems and to work with them.

> As the wife of the new President . . . I knew that some would
> criticize me for my work . . . How I made use of this gift from
> God would be up to me.[10]

Jehan and Anwar knew that the most conservative Muslims and even some of the fanatic Muslim fringe groups lived in Assiut in northern Egypt. Jehan hoped she could win them over and lessen opposition to Anwar. She went to ask these people what they thought of her willingness and desire to be of service. It would mean she would be working away from home and not clad in traditional veil and clothing. Should she stay at home as other wives of presidents have done? Or should she assist her husband?

> Am I going to share the burdens of Egypt working with women
> and children, the disabled and poor, or am I going to leave my
> husband to do everything alone? . . . I want to help my husband
> to do whatever I can for my country . . . I believe that God has
> sent me this mission . . . What is your answer?[11]

After a few moments of silence the applause swelled with strong affirmation. Jehan thanked them and then continued her journey. The times continued to get worse. Some former supporters of Nasser were in prison and the Minister of Defense had given orders to arrest Anwar Sadat. A police officer loyal to Anwar brought a tape to him that revealed particular plans for his assassination. Anwar remained calm while Jehan urged him to do something.

On May 11 when the ministers jointly resigned as a sign of a coup, Anwar had them placed under house arrest. That night tanks were heard moving toward the Sadat house. Jehan wanted to send the children to their aunt's house in case this was going to be some form of assassination. The children had already decided if the parents were killed they wanted to die with them. Jehan was moved by their bravery and prayed fervently that the family would somehow come through this. The phone rang with General Nassif assuring the family that he had ordered the tanks to the Sadat house to be a form of protection.

In the morning Anwar Sadat addressed the nation. He said any repressive moves that had been made by his enemies in their power positions were now rescinded. Many political prisoners were then released. Jehan had made a promise to Allah that she would go on pilgrimage if such a positive resolution happened. In 1971 she prepared for the pilgrimage to Mecca.[12]

Preparations included prayer, removal of makeup and jewelry and wearing a white scarf over her hair. Once in Mecca she joined with many other pilgrims on the journey through the Gate of Peace and into the courtyard of the Holy Mosque. This courtyard space was large enough for half a million people to assemble. It was a moving experience.

> Praying with the others, I was at once humbled and uplifted. Before God there was no discrimination between races, classes or even sexes . . . To actually see the Kaaba with my own eyes, to be close to the one object that binds Muslims all over the world, was a profound sensation. Draped over the entire building was the famous *kiswa*, an immense black velvet cloth embroidered in gold with verses from the Quran.[13]

The Kaaba is circled several times, beginning each circle with praising Allah as great. Jehan prayed in all four corners of the Kaaba as was the custom. She prayed for her husband, for their family, for friends and for peace. After leaving the Kaaba she journeyed to other holy sites as part of the ritual of conversion of heart. After the prayers and rituals of cleansing the celebration of the Feast of the Sacrifice recalls God's compassion to Abraham who was willing to sacrifice his son. The celebration lasts for four days and all other business affairs cease. The completion gave Jehan a sense of deep inner peace as she returned to Cairo.

Jehan continued her work. She was as moved by the Israeli soldiers who were suffering in Egyptian hospitals as she was by the Egyptian soldiers who were wounded. She received a letter from an Israeli soldier's mother that reflected on the need for peace so that all mothers could once again keep their children from early death. Jehan answered the letter. She was surprised to find out later that the letter had been reprinted in the Israeli press. In the letter she clearly stated that the young have dreams of the future they deserve to know rather than the fears of war that destroyed them and their dreams. "We have to know that love and friendship are better than enmity . . . I wish that all women would devote their time to hard and constructive work to realize peace."[14]

After the war ended Jehan became very involved in a number of social organizations that dealt with women's rights, rehabilitation centers for crippled war veterans, fund raising for new limbs and other needs of the veterans. They deserved better than selling pencils on the street to make money for food! Whenever Jehan accompanied Anwar on official state visits she asked to see what that particular country had in terms of disabled assistance. She also worked to set up special villages for orphaned children in which either Muslim or Christian women served as mother figures for the orphans. Jehan and her own children were sponsors. By 1980 there were over 1600 day care centers in Egypt to assist with this form of child care

At 41 Jehan decided to go back to school in an attempt to emphasize the importance of education for women in Egypt. During this period she ran for political office and won the 1974 election for a seat on the People's Council. She was reelected until she had served the maximum term which ended in 1981. Meanwhile, she had graduated in 1978 with a first degree and in 1980 earned an MA degree from Cairo University. As she started work toward a PhD, she also initiated international conferences to discuss the issues of justice for the poorest people.

Queen Alia of Jordan and Jehan became close friends. Queen Alia became very involved in the social affairs of her own country of Jordan. Queen Alia was tragically killed in a helicopter crash on her way to visit a hospital. The sudden death of this young and vital woman was a blow to Jehan and to all who knew and loved her.[15]

Once in a joking manner Anwar asked Jehan what she wanted for her birthday. She responded she wanted more equality for women. Although it was asked in humor on June 29, 1979 Anwar Sadat wrote two official decrees about women. The first decree set aside 30 seats for women to be members of the Egyptian Parliament. The decree also set aside 20% of seats on the People's Councils for women representatives. The second decree called for reforms of the so-called *status laws*. These reforms called for men to let go of some of the former controls they exercised over the life of their wife and daughters. In the end parliament approved.

Anwar Sadat decided to go to Israel in a gesture of peace making. Upon landing in Israel he was greeted by heads of state including Golda Meir. Jehan had often held up Golda Meir to Anwar as a woman representing the leadership that women were capable of exerting. As the motorcade wound its way to the meeting place in Jerusalem many mothers were waving signs along the route welcoming Anwar Sadat a man of peace. That same night Jehan went to the hospital for the birth of their second grandchild, a beautiful baby girl. When Jehan called Anwar to tell him about this new life Anwar was on the way to morning prayer at El Aqsa Mosque, the third most holy shrine of Islam.

Later that afternoon as Anwar entered the Knesset he was greeted by a standing ovation. A global audience watched the history making address.

Anwar began his address with a prayer. "Peace and the mercy of God Almighty be upon you and may peace be with us all, God willing."[16] Anwar proceeded to set forth principles for peace. He concluded his address by citing the holy books of Muslim, Jewish, and Christian tradition to show their similarity in the call to love, justice, and peace. He concluded by praying for God's peace on all.

When Anwar Sadat returned to Egypt people lined the streets to applaud and cheer his bold efforts for the peaceful future of their land and its people. As 1978 dawned he was hailed as *Time* magazine's "Man of the Year" in recognition of his daring and bold moves for peace. The peace he negotiated was not popular with many Arab leaders who refused Anwar's invitation to come to a peace summit. Various negotiations for peace continued in spite of the opposition. In 1978 during Ramadan, Anwar agreed to go to a summit meeting called by President Jimmy Carter of the United States. As Anwar arrived back in Egypt the people were delighted to hear of the peace accord between Israel and Egypt. In October 1978 the Nobel Peace Prize was shared by Anwar Sadat and Menachem Begin for their joint efforts at peace.

By 1980 the embassies of the Arab countries in Cairo were shut down to protest Sadat's peace agreements with Israel. Threats against Anwar's life began to increase. Jehan lived in fear but Anwar responded in his typically calm way. "What more could any man want? I have fulfilled my mission set out by God . . . I do feel that my life, by God's grace, has made its contribution to destiny."[17]

On October 6, 1981, Jehan and the family were seated in the stands for the review of the troops. It was always a day of national pride. Anwar in full dress uniform was with others in the reviewing stand. As the jets roared overhead and Anwar stood and looked up loud explosions were heard. Grenades, gunfire and screams came from the stand. A barrage of bullets started flying. The carnage was a nightmare. The bodyguards of the Sadat family quickly ushered them into a helicopter. The helicopter took them to the hospital. Jehan sensed that her husband was already dead. The family went into the operating room to recite the traditional Muslim prayer for the dead. Vice president Mubarak was sworn in. Anwar's coffin would be laid in the tomb so it would face Mecca. His body was wrapped in the Egyptian flag as a symbol of his life that had always been given for his country.[18]

Anwar Sadat's funeral was attended by many world leaders. However, only two Arab leaders came. Thousands of letters of sympathy came from around the world and thousands of others paid their respects during the three-day mourning period. On the day of the funeral three former United

States presidents came. So did the Prince of Wales and Menachem Begin. While these tributes were being paid people in Baghdad were dancing in the streets at Anwar Sadat's death. This type of reaction to the life of a man of peace caused additional suffering to the family.

In time both America and Britain awarded peace medals to Jehan Sadat who accepted them in Anwar Sadat's name. Looking back on their life together Jehan has some regrets that they did not spend their later years together as much as they might have. Yet he fulfilled his mission in his own way. Jehan continues to live her life inspired by his spirit which encourages her efforts for peace and equality.

> I work for peace to raise the standard of the poor, to train the disabled to care for themselves . . . I try as much as possible to be the best person I can while I am on the earth. And after death I know I will meet my husband again.[19]

Jehan Sadat earned a Ph.D. from Cairo University. She has been a senior fellow at the University of Maryland in the United States where the Anwar Sadat Chair for Peace and Development has been endowed. She has written poetry, is the recipient of multiple national and international awards for public service and for multiple humanitarian efforts benefitting women and children around the world. At the time of this writing Jehan has received more than 20 honorable doctorate degrees from colleges and universities around the world. She continues to spend part of the year in Egypt and another part in the United States as a visiting scholar at American University in Washington, D.C., the University of South Carolina, Radford University and many others. She continues to spend her life working for peace.

NOTES

1. The rich history of Egypt's culture can be found at www.wikipedia.org/wiki/Egypt.
2. Jehan Sadat, *A Woman of Egypt* (NY: Simon and Schuster, 1987).
3. *Woman,* 40.
4. *Woman.* The summary is from 34-70.
5. *Woman,* 107.
6. *Woman,* 115.

[7]   *Woman,*. 169.

[8]   *Woman.* The varieties of ways Jehan assisted the women to make money and be enterprising are detailed in 181-209.

[9]   *Woman,* 237.

[10] *Woman,* 257.

[11] *Woman, 260-62.* The context can be found between 256-61.

[12] *Woman,* 261-71.

[13] *Woman,* 275. Tradition holds that Abraham built the first house of worship here where Kaaba marks the spot. This is the spot to which Muslims turn five times daily.

[14] *Woman,* 298. The entire correspondence can be found on 297-98.

[15] *Woman,* 298-363 describes the friendship of the two women.

[16] *Woman,* 389. The entire address can be found on 380-83.

[17] *Woman,* p.441. Anwar Sadat's popularity and peace efforts can be found between 380-443.

[18] *Woman,* 13-31.

[19] *Woman,* 459-60.

9

Latifa, Afghanistan

Afghanistan declared independence in 1919. In 1921 the Treaty of Kabul marked the end of British presence and overseeing. From 1933 to 1973, Mohammed Zahir Shah, an Afghan king, ruled the country. The influence of his wife and the west as well as his own education and history caused many changes that helped the social status of women. By 1959, women were no longer required to wear the veil, but they could if they chose to do so. In 1964, women obtained the right to vote. The first elections in which everyone voted were held in 1965. In 1973, Mohamed Zahir Shah was overthrown by Mohammed Daoud. Daoud established the first Republic of Afghanistan and served as its president.

A coup in 1978 resulted in a communist party victory. The second Republic of Afghanistan with a communist regime brought restrictions and cruelty that caused a visible rise of various Islamic movements for change. In 1979, the Soviet military intervened to preserve the communist regime. The mujahadeen (literally means resistors) began guerrilla warfare against the Soviet Army and the Afghan army who fought with them. This went on for a decade before other nations acted to broker peace.

In April 1988, an UN sponsored agreement was signed by major parties of the US, the USSR, Pakistan, and the Kabul government representatives. This agreement saw to it that the last of the Soviet troops left Afghanistan in 1989. A short time after their departure, civil war began between multiple ethnic groups of the mujahadeen forces.

A ruthless mujahadeen warlord named Hekmatyar was known especially to women because he had been stirring up militant Islamic student groups since the 1960's. His uncritical students of Koran were called "talibs."

This group of fundamentalist students became the Taliban. Their biased interpretations of Islamic law (Sharia) bolstered their own importance and power over women. Many young men from Pakistan rallied to the cause in Afghanistan as well to get part of the power and importance they had not felt before.

The only opposition to Hekmatyar and his growing number of Islamic fundamentalists was General Tajik Ahmed Shah Massoud. Massoud united and then led the groups called the Northern Alliance to control the northern provinces, including the city of Kabul. The Taliban who were financially and militarily supported by Pakistan, were successful in the south, capturing Kandahar in 1994. Kandahar became the stronghold center for the Taliban and Osama bin Laden.

The Taliban continued to grow stronger and take over more and more of the land. After General Massoud was assassinated on September 9, 2001, the Taliban dominated the land.

It was that same September in 2001 that the two towers of the World Trade Center in New York were destroyed. Soon after, American forces intervened in Afghanistan. By November 2001, the Taliban had abandoned Kabul and the Northern Alliance forces declared victory. In December 2001, Hamid Karzai was sworn in as leader of an interim government. Karzai's interim government had thirty representatives including several Afghan factions who formerly were fighting each other. In March 2002, a series of earthquakes struck Afghanistan with the loss of thousands of lives. In addition to the challenges of rebuilding and ongoing skirmishes, bands of bandits continued to roam and to steal from Afghanistan's rural people. The Taliban continue to resist and fighting continues in Kabul and other areas in Afghanistan in spite of the presence of international peacekeepers. Latifa's story unfolds in this period and can be found in the fine Hyperion Books publication, *My Forbidden Face:Growing Up Under the Taliban, A Young Woman's Story.*[1] Latifa has written her story under a fictitious name to prevent punishment from the Taliban should they happen to discover her work.[2]

Latifa remembers well the morning of September 22, 1996. Rocket fire around the city had gone on for most of the night so she was still asleep in mid morning. Her young cousin Farad woke up her family by his loud knocking. Latifa's father opened the door and the upset Farad said the white flag of the Taliban was now flying over Kabul. The family turned on the battery powered radio to see what was happening as Farad continued to talk. He told the family that he had seen one of their Pushtan government leaders and his brother who was wearing a western suit were hanging in the public square. The Taliban were forcing people to look at the bodies. Latifa wondered why the Taliban would hang a Pushtan since many Taliban were Pushtans.

Had the Taliban really taken Kabul over? In Kabul, women were not imprisoned in their own homes as they were in Taliban ruled places. In Kabul. Latifa and her friends were still going to school. Other women were still going to work outside the home. Rumors abounded that the Taliban in other places forbade these things, took teen age daughters from houses and raped them, burned the villagers' houses and forced the men to join the Taliban Army.

The people of Kabul knew that the Taliban were not all from Afghanistan. There were many who were from Pakistan and other Muslim countries. These extremists often did not speak Afghan. The young men demonstrated their manliness through brutality, even cutting off limbs as punishment for breaking laws which they themselves did not observe. This was done in the name of Allah, but Latifa and others knew the claim was really a facade for self importance

Latifa's family was a very affectionate and religious family. All observed the essence of Islam to be compassionate to all. Latifa's father was liberal with respect to women, a perspective that he felt Islamic law affirmed. His wife was a professional woman who worked outside the home. Latifa had just passed the first part of university entrance examinations prior to her study of journalism. Her father and mother and everyone else in the family wanted her to finish her studies at University and fulfill her lifelong dream of being a journalist. Latifa now wondered if the white Taliban flag flying on the mosque marked the end of making her dreams come true.

An adventurous teenage friend of Latifa's called to say they should go see what was happening. Latifa's father drove them toward the town. Latifa could see the shock and the tears in people's eyes as they saw what had happened in the square. The hanging bodies had obviously been physically abused by the Taliban. Latifa was horrified and afraid.

The group went home and again turned on the radio. The radio had already been taken over by the Taliban. There was religious chanting and then a man's voice reciting verses of the Koran. A decree of the Taliban was read in a harsh, singsong voice.

The prophet told his disciples that their work was to forbid evil and promote virtue. We have come to restore order. Laws will be established by religious authorities . . . For reasons of security, we ask that women stay in their homes during this first period of transition.[3]

Latifa's father told the family he had better turn in his weapons so that the family would not be at risk should the Taliban raid the house. He was sad to turn in the swords that were family heirlooms. Latifa had a lot of rock music and posters of Brooke Shields and Elvis Presley. The Taliban forbade all those kinds of things and everything else that was western. Latifa and her sister Soraya were grim. Soraya was an airline stewardess who came home in between her airline flights. She had her flight attendant uniform hanging in the closet ready for the next flight but knew she could never wear that uniform again if the Taliban remained in Kabul.

Then the sisters looked in their closet for their chadors. They still had them although they did not wear them. The chador was a prayer garment worn for prayers made in the privacy of one's room. It was Latifa's brother who insisted that his sisters must now wear the chadors when they prayed. Latifa's father did not approve of his son telling the girls what they should wear when they prayed. At the time, the family did not realize that the son and brother was already beginning to be influenced by the severity of Taliban interpretations of the Koran. The brother insisted that Soraya and Latifa should lengthen their skirts and to make all their necklines higher. He told the girls he worried about them because it was clear the times were changing.

On Saturday, September 28, 1996, Latifa woke up and realized that life had changed and would not be getting back to normal. Her house would be her long-term prison. She decided she would get up and continue beginning each day as she always did. She would say her prayers on the lovely prayer rug her father had brought her from Mecca. Then she would live one day at a time. That she had passed the examination for university didn't matter anymore. As a woman, she could not go as long as the Taliban were in charge of Kabul.

The radio station carried only religious chants and the multiple daily decrees that kept imposing more and more restrictive laws of the Taliban. Daily the mullahs would announce more restrictions. Reading of verses from the Koran was all that the radio station now carried other than the decrees of the Taliban. Only men could walk freely on the streets to see what was happening. So Latifa's father was the one who could bring news. He would return with news about streets full of gloomy people who saw that most of the stores had been closed, TV sets had been pulled out of homes and all TV's and video and cassette tapes were destroyed.

An Islamic system as interpreted by the Taliban would be imposed on the country. All foreign ambassadors would be sent out. Women and girls would not be permitted outside the home. If women were obligated to leave their homes, they had to be accompanied by a man. Buses would now be segregated for men and for women. Men had to let their beards grow to hand's length, wear a white cap or turban and no longer wear any Western dress. All forms of neck ties were forbidden. Women and girls could not wear bright colored clothes beneath the chadors or wear nail polish, lipstick or any other form of make up. All prayers were to be said at exactly the right time. No more conversations could happen between young men and young women who were not married. If an unmarried young man and woman were seen talking, they would have to be immediately married.

Latifa and her friends had always chuckled at the unstylish chadors. In Afghanistan, some country women had always worn the chadors but younger women in the cities did not. When Latifa and her friends tried them on, they found it difficult to breathe and to see.

> The small embroidered openwork peephole covering the eyes and nose frightens me . . . The cloth sticks to my nose. It's hard to keep the embroidered peephole in front of my eyes, and I can't breathe . . . This isn't clothing. It's a jail cell.[4]

There could be no listening to music and no more photographing of anything. All names of children had to be Muslim. Non-Muslims had to wear yellow clothing or a piece of yellow cloth and mark their homes with a yellow flag. Hindus, Jews and Christians all had to be marked. Female undergarments and alcoholic beverages could no longer be sold. Anyone who broke any of the laws would be punished in the public square.

All Latifa wanted to do was go to her room and cry. Each day the radio brought additional laws and practices to be imposed on all the people. Everyone had to stop whistling and they couldn't own whistling tea kettles. No more dogs or birds could be kept as pets. Latifa's dog was smuggled to an uncle's house in the country. The pet canary was let out of the window. Maybe someday the people would be as free as the canary outside the cage. Latifa's father grew a beard as instructed. However, he insisted that his beard might belong to the Taliban but nothing else did!

Many friends of Latifa's father were disgusted by the way the Taliban distorted Islamic religion. The friends saw nothing familiar in the brand of Islam that the Taliban were forcing on them. One man told Latifa's father he had been stopped five times by the Taliban and forced to pray each time he was stopped. Another man admitted to Latifa's father that when it was time to ask God for one's deepest wishes, he asked God to get rid of the Taliban. The men were careful about when and how they shared their true feelings.

Latifa's mother could no longer go to work so women came to her in secret. One day three young women came in secretly and began crying. The crying teens told Latifa's mother that they were raped multiple times by the Taliban and abused in many other ways. The young women had done nothing wrong. They were just walking on the street accompanied by a male as dictated by the Taliban. But as the Taliban approached, the young male was frightened and ran away. The Taliban raped and abused the teens for being unaccompanied. Latifa's mother had no access to painkillers, but she helped cleanse the young women and did what she could to comfort them.

Everyone soon began to hear more such stories about women being beaten on the streets for no reason. One day Latifa saw a Taliban police unit screech to a halt and four young men jumped out with whips and started beating four women until blood was flowing on to their shoes. The women were screaming but no man on the street would dare come to their rescue. Latifa and a friend were close enough to witness this but were afraid for themselves so they did not attempt helping the young women. They raced for home. Later they found out that the Taliban beat the women because the women were wearing white shoes. Since white is the color of the Taliban flag, women cannot wear white because that disrespects the flag. These and many other rules are not in the Koran but the Taliban insist Allah wanted it this way.[5]

Latifa's brother, Wahid, who had been in the army, was imprisoned about nine miles north of Kabul. When the family visited him, his stories about the tortures and killings made Latifa ill. Money could be used to bribe head guards or less important officials. So Latifa's father bribed some of the guards in order to keep her brother safe. Some prisoners were scalded to death; others were stabbed or beaten to death. The cruelty was difficult to hear about. Latifa and her sisters prayed daily for their brother!

On a visit to see the brother, the family stopped at the mosque in Mazir-I-Sharif, with its blue dome. The festival of the New Year was in progress. Latifa and her family observed the cure of a blind man who had been praying daily for a year at the mosque in hope of a miracle. The mosque contained the tomb of Ali, a holy Muslim, whose tomb had been the site of miracles. Latifa was told that she could pray for something to God and the wish would come true. "I prayed for mama to be healthy and for God to protect my whole family."[6]

On August 12, 1998, the Taliban took control of Mazir-I-Sharif and massacred many of the people who had been so welcoming to the family when they visited the holy mosque. The people had done nothing to upset the invading Taliban. Latifa recalls saying to herself that if she could visit the tomb of Ali again, her prayer would now be to work a miracle for the Afghan people.

> I would pray that those Taliban-who in their ignorance of the Koran dare invent laws that are inhuman and contrary to sacred scripture-learn to respect the holy book, humbly, as we Afghans do and have always done.[7]

One morning Latifa's friend Farida came to visit. Farida opened a window overlooking a courtyard of the mosque. She and Latifa saw the mullah (Islamic cleric) holding a stick which he used to strike the hands of a little boy who either made a mistake in his recitation of Koran or else wasn't fervent enough in his swaying movement and recitations. As the two young women observed this mode of education, they knew that their own education had been so much better. The girls had been taught to be critical of things they were learning. What a contrast!

These little boys wearing their white hats at age eight or nine were learning nothing of the outside world except its sinfulness. The boys would be learning only the kind of brainwashing the mullah was putting into them. There was no independent thinking or reasoning. The girls had an idea! They would discuss education with the mothers in their building and see if the mothers wanted their girls to be educated more broadly. The schools under Taliban rule meant the education was a very restrictive and biased one. Only the little boys could go to school and they were not being taught about science, mathematics, the world's history, Afghan history and other subjects. Farida and Latifa decided their "school" would be an alternative.

They would model it on the school one of their former teachers was now running. Like that school in Kabul, this school would expand the knowledge and global awareness of the children. The women knew their former teacher was caught running her school by the Taliban who threw the woman down the stairs. Latifa and Farida admired their former teacher for taking the chances she did. They decided to go visit her with their idea after they met with selected parents in their unit. These women in the unit could be trusted. They would not report Latifa and Farida to the Taliban.

The plan for education required the unit pupils to meet at different hours in the daytime. The young teachers would use the plans of their former teacher and figure out how to get basic supplies. The people in the unit as well as Latifa's family and Farida's family agreed to the plan. Each of the young women would take seven or eight girls and boys into the home and begin their education program. Latifa and Farida, would meet regularly to go over lesson plans, to correct papers, to discuss how the children were doing and to evaluate the whole process. The students lived in the same unit as the teachers so no one had to go on the street.

Latifa's brother, Daoud, said he could get basic materials like pencils and old books and each family could pay him when they were able. It was hard to get books, including those to teach English language, but among the three of them, they managed to obtain materials. Each child would be getting a much better education than if the Taliban were the instructors. The little girls were especially lucky since the Taliban frowned on the education of girls. The Taliban had never been educated themselves to have any critical sense of what they were taught. They had all been brainwashed so they did the same thing to the little boys they taught.

The school of these two women was a delight for the parents and the children. It was small but very successful. Whenever the Taliban were seen circling the apartment while the children were at the alternative school, the young teachers would keep the children outside. If the Taliban forced their way to the steps connecting the apartments, they never broke into the home areas that were the school. Latifa and the parents remained delighted with this school.

One day Farida and Latifa received word that their former teacher, whose materials they were using, had been called back by the Taliban for questioning. Her husband was being forced to divorce her, which he refused to do. The punishment was that his wife's head would be shaved and the children, all younger, would be thrown in the river to drown. So the woman had her head shaved because her husband would not divorce her. Then the woman and her husband were forced to go down to the river. The Taliban threw the little children into it. The woman was hysterical and jumped into the river to try to save all of the children, but she could only save one of her sons. In shock, her husband divorced her and she fled to Pakistan with her son.[8]

In July 1998, Latifa's brother Daoud decided to get married. The bride's family suggested having the wedding in the garden behind their house which was hidden from street view. The policing Taliban couldn't really see what was happening. Because the family was on such good terms with neighbors, they felt it was safe. Guests were carefully chosen to protect all concerned. The young couple looked lovely although Daoud could not wear a suit and tie because these were forbidden. As the couple exchanged their vows, one of Daoud's friends played a forbidden cassette and a video cam was also on. A neighbor shouted that the Taliban was coming. The dancing stopped and all tried to act normal as the Taliban broke in, found the video cam and cassette and began beating some young people while others ran away. The garden was devastated. Fortunately, the new bride and groom were happily in love with each other and that lessened their sadness over all that accompanied their wedding event.[9]

Latifa and her friends continued their subversive and secretive efforts to make a difference. In addition to the secret school, Latifa and her friends decided to put out a small newsletter that they would then distribute to certain people to inform them about happenings in the world and in Afghanistan. This might give people some hope!

In spring, 2001, the French were looking for a woman who would come to Paris to talk about the plight of women in Afghanistan. A woman's magazine wanted to launch an information campaign about this. The invitation went to a woman doctor, Dr. Sima. She was one of Latifa's friends and also a good friend of Latifa's mother. Dr. Sima was afraid that if she went, and the Taliban found out that she had an underground clinic and training facility for women, all would be in danger. Latifa and her mother agreed to go in place of Dr. Sima.

Her father said he should go with them since they needed to be accompanied by a man. They went to Pakistan first since they had visas for Pakistan. Officially the family was going to Pakistan to take their mother to the hospital. Once in Pakistan, they would telephone the Afghan embassy in Paris. The ambassador had already agreed to prepare plane tickets for them so that the Taliban would have no way of finding out that the family actually went on to Paris.

Once the family arrived in Paris, a representative from the embassy was waiting. The next morning the family was accompanied to Brussels and the European Parliament. Now the whole family was looked upon as ambassadors for the women of Afghanistan. Once there, Latifa and her father addressed the Parliament. She spoke about how women had been robbed of their voices. She talked about women her age who had been robbed of their careers by Taliban rules. She detailed the many forms of injustice that the Taliban were falsely claiming to be Islamic teaching. She detailed the systematic purge of much of the Afghani culture by the Taliban. She spoke movingly about the women who could no longer work or go to school or even walk down the street without a man. The women couldn't show themselves except through the peep space of the chador and that was dangerous for crossing streets. It had been more than 20 years of war and the Taliban had taken away not only the guns and other means of defense but the spirit of many people. Her message was heard!

When the event was over, Latifa asked her father what difference any of this would make. He was always an optimist and assured her that in time it would make a difference. People of the world would now understand what the Taliban were doing to young women like herself and to all women. Then he assured Latifa that if a Taliban tells a woman that she is nothing and he is everything, he is an ignorant man who does not know the Koran. All men are born of a woman and all saints have mothers. So women are something far more important than nothing.

On the last day of May, the family received a fax from the French Embassy sent by Daoud who was now in Pakistan. He said the Taliban had issued a decree against all women who denounced their regime and that some of Latifa's activities were now known to the Taliban. Daoud learned from friends that the family's apartment had been gutted by the Taliban who had moved into the family apartment. Where would the three of them wind up? The Afghan Embassy in Paris said they would help the family find a new place to live as refugees. In October of 2001, the Americans went to war against the Taliban. The Taliban were temporarily defeated in December but war continues to wage in many portions of the country.

Latifa dreams of a day in the future when she will be able to return to Afghanistan. For now, that remains a dream to be accomplished in some future time.

> I pray God that whoever will lead our country may be, in his heart, as much Pashtun as Tajik, as much Uzbek as Hazara; that his wife may counsel and assist him; that he may choose advisers of great character and wisdom . . . I will do more than pray, because when the last Taliban has put away his black turban and I can be

a free woman in a free Afghanistan, I will take up my life there
once more and do my duty as a citizen, as a woman, and I hope,
as a mother.[10]

Latifa continues to hope that one day the Taliban will either retreat or be
permanently defeated. Then her life can return to some degree of "normal"
and her dreams can be pursued. For now, these dreams remain on hold.

NOTES

[1]   This summary was taken from the history that winds through Latifa's *My
      Forbidden Face: Growing Up Under the Taliban: A Young Woman's Story*, in
      collaboration with Shekeba Hachemi and trans.by Linda Coverdale (NY:
      Hyperion, 2001).

[2]   All Summaries and occasional quotations are from *My Forbidden Face*, cited
      as *Face*.

[3]   *Face*, 17-18. Summary material is from 1-18.

[4]   *Face*, 46-47. Summary material is from 18-47.

[5]   *Face, 48-72.*

[6]   *Face*, 116. Summary material is from 73-116.

[7]   *Face*, 118.

[8]   *Face*, 119-56.

[9]   *Face*, 140-62.

[10] *Face*, 201-2. Two videos, *Daughters of Afghanistan* and *Osama* provide a similar
      picture of the repression of the women of Afghanistan and the misuse of the
      Koran to justify violence.

10

Shirin Ebadi, Iran

Shirin was born on June 21, 1947, in Hamedan, a city in northern Iran. Her parents were practicing Muslims. As a child, Shirin worried that her mother might die. Shirin remembers the experience of praying to God in the attic. "An indescribable feeling overtook me . . . In that stirring, I felt as though God was answering me . . . Since that moment, my faith in God has been unshakable."[1]

In Shirin's household, she and her brothers were treated equally, to the surprise of their servants. Rewards, affection, discipline and attention were given equally to all the children. Shirin entered law school at Tehran University in 1965. At the time she entered law school, the Shah was enduring protests of various kinds. Demonstrations to her were simply "an afternoon shot of adrenaline before we walked over to the coffee house near the university where we sipped café glace, vanilla ice cream drowned in coffee after class."[2]

Shirin became a judge in March 1970, when she was 23 years old. She was one of two highest ranking students in the class. In the swearing in ceremony, she and the other student carried in the Koran, were sworn in, and began what they considered a lifetime of serving justice to all who sought the court's assistance. In 1975, she and Javad Tavassolian were married after a period of testing whether they were meant for each other. "After my father, he was the second central man in my life who tried to strengthen, rather than inhibit, my independence . . . That Javad championed my career was itself tremendous; if the balance of household work swung entirely in my direction that was a compromise I was willing to make."[3]

On the bitterly cold day of January 16, 1979, the shah left Iran. This ended two millennia of rule by Persian kings. On February 1, 1979, the Ayatollah Khomeini came back to Iran as the espoused leader of the revolution against the shah. The Ayatollah said nothing about Iran becoming an Islamic state on that day he arrived. However, he did call on God to cut off the hands of Iran's enemies. Members of the military forces who were faithful to the shah imposed a curfew which the Ayatollah told people to ignore. On February 11, the Ayatollah was deemed victorious over the shah's loyal army and many of the army just merged into the streets with the people and changed sides. It took about a month for Shirin to realize that by participating in the revolution, "I had willingly and enthusiastically participated in my own demise. I was a woman, and this revolution's victory demanded my defeat."[4]

Shirin and Javad were concerned about starting a family. Shirin had two miscarriages so the couple then made arrangements to go to New York to visit a fertility clinic. Their time in New York was productive and hopeful. They returned to Iran and went back to work. Now motorcycles instead of cars were parked outside the ministry where she worked. The men inside could no longer wear ties or suits, symbols of the west. No cologne could be used since that was a symbol of wealth. Clothes were worn dirty to identify with the poor. In time, Shirin was encouraged to take a lesser job than judge. When she said no, she was told that a purging committee could demote her to court assistant. Shirin had published many articles by this time and been involved in important cases. As a public figure, she felt bad things would not happen to her. When she became pregnant, her joy made the country's situation less important.

In November of 1979, Ayatollah Houmeini congratulated the young men who had taken the staff of the U.S. Embassy as hostages. "When I think back to these times, my own naivete astounds me. Hostage taking contravenes international law . . . we were too overwhelmed by the sight of our own Tehran collapsing around us to realize that rules and justice would be lost in the chaos, as is the case with all revolutions."[5] Iranians opposed to this kind of behavior were afraid to speak out. That hostage situation lasted 444 days. Many of Iran's future politicians came from that student group who had taken the Embassy.

In the final days of 1980, Shirin was stripped of her judgship and given an inferior position. As a sign of protest, she went to work but refused to do any work as symbol of her anger at the unjust demotion. One morning, the newspaper announced that the penal code had been rewritten. In spite of the importance of writing a new penal code, there had been no consultation of the people and no consultation of lawyers or of anyone else who knew Iranian history and law. These new laws turned back the clock 1400 years.

Women's rights were turned upside down. Now the value of a woman's life was half that of a man if she were killed. A woman's testimony in court was worth half as much as a man's testimony. If a woman wanted to file for divorce, she needed her husband's permission. Law professors from Tehran University wrote a letter of protest. They lost their jobs but in time got them back because no one was found to replace them and the university had to go on.

On April 21, 1980, Shirin gave birth to a daughter, Negar. "I had not been very fond of children until I had my own . . . I was captivated . . . (Negar) was such a respite from the ugliness outside, the executions and purges that would not abate."[6]

A new chapter in the life of Iran occurred with Saddam Hussein's invasion. His cruelty to others in the Muslim world shocked the population. Saddam finally offered a truce but Iran was in the midst of its own civil and political factions vying for power. A militant version of Islam kept the war going but when it ended, civil strife continued. The Ayatollah's followers hunted down enemies and executed or arrested those of more liberal persuasion.

In 1983, Shirin and Javad had a second daughter, Nargess. The childhood antics of her two girls, age three and an infant, were a source of joy in Shirin's life at a time when work was depressing. By 1988, Iraqi air strikes were a daily occurrence in Tehran. Many Iranians left the country if they could. Shirin, Javad and the girls moved north, but returned to Tehran when the war ended. Morality police now combed the area and reported on women or others who were not strictly observing the laws. "After I was arrested myself once or twice for bad hejabi, or improper Islamic dress, I concluded that there was little one could do for protection against a state that simply wished to impose a climate of fear."[7]

Throughout the nineties, the number of women with college degrees rose and women began to outnumber men in universities. In neighboring Afghanistan, the Taliban forbade women to read. In Saudi Arabia, women could not drive. Nervous clerics in Iran tried to impose a quota system on how many women could go to university. They did not really need to worry since a woman's opportunity contracted once she left the university. Gender discrimination prevailed in the job market as well as in most other parts of life.

In 1992, when the judiciary permitted women to practice law again, the Iranian Bar Association granted Shirin a license. She was quickly disappointed at the lack of justice she witnessed in the courts, especially around human rights issues. She decided to set up her own office apart from the ministry. She gave up taking cases that paid her and decided to take on cases *pro bono* so that she could "showcase the injustice of the Islamic Republic's laws . . . Iranian culture, for all its preoccupation with shame and honor, with all its resulting patriarchal codes, retains an acute sensitivity to injustice."[8] She had many stories of injustice from her own experience. It did move the listeners even if the tactic did not necessarily get courts to act justly. Raising people's awareness of their rights was often the best that some of her cases could do within a system that was inherently unjust. The court of public opinion is a strong court even when things do not change as well as one would hope.[9]

Shirin recalled one article that she wrote which excited so many literate people in Tehran that the magazine sold out and the article was reprinted. This kind of public power did not go without notice. She was publicly threatened for her views. "I realized for the first time that the system might actually fear me and the growing public resonance with my work."[10]

After one of her trials received not only national but international attention, Shirin realized that she was a more powerful personality than she assumed. That was less important to her than the issue of human rights in Iran and the international view that Iran was known now as a theocracy unwilling to reform its unjust and repressive laws. In the early 1990's, human rights' groups started documenting the waves of executions and the abuses of human rights in Iran. Death squads varied their techniques. They began to use things like car accidents or shootings during bank robberies, or street stabbing or injecting potassium to cause heart attacks. These could hide the actual number of assassinations in an attempt to preserve the ruling regime.[11]

On May 23, 1997, Mohammed Khatami was elected. He was a refined leader, bookish, and an alternative to the power driven clerics of the past twenty years. His landslide victory made it clear that Iranians wanted change from the oppressive regime. For a brief time, the freedom given to the press and the optimism of the people was a justified reason for hope. However, senior officials still held power from the last regime. Unrest continued. Though President Khatami was the elected official, the doctrine of divine clerical right to rule was invested in Supreme Leader Ayatollah Ali Khameini. By summer, 1999, things were back to the oppressive atmosphere of fear.

On June 28, 2000, Shirin was taken to a prison without a real trial and without an accusation that would stand up in a court. "Hours turned to days and days turned to weeks in the suffocating sameness of my cell. I prayed five times a day. I stretched and attempted calisthenics."[12] The cells were simply an endurance contest for anyone forced into them.

After her release from prison, Shirin returned home a changed person. In 2003, her daughter Negar announced that she wished to be an engineer and wanted to go to Canada to school. Shirin wondered if such a western experience would keep her in Montreal. Would Negar wish to return after her graduation? The night before Negar left, Shirin "pulled out the Koran and held it high in the door frame, so that she could pass beneath it three times on her way out, a ritual of departure we have performed too many times for our loved ones since the revolution."[13]

Shirin's reputation as a human rights lawyer was growing to international fame. In September 2003, Shirin was invited to attend a seminar in Paris. The Iranian embassy in France protested this invitation saying that Shirin held views that were counter to the official position of the government of Iran. The organizer of the seminar stuck to the position and invitation. Shirin decided to bring her younger daughter Nargess to Paris. The seminar went well and Shirin took Nargess to see and admire the sights of Paris. On the morning Shirin and Nargess were going to leave Paris, they said good by to their friend, Dr. Lahiji. Just as Shirin and Nargess were getting their suitcases ready, the phone rang. The voice on the phone told Shirin she had won the Nobel Peace Prize. Shirin called her friend Dr. Lahiji, who said she should put off her return to Tehran by a day because she should hold a press conference. He set it up.

At the press conference, Shirin was typically measured and civil about her response regarding why she was the recipient of this prize. She did no direct attacking of the government of Iran. Once she and Nargess had boarded the plane, they got moved up to first class. Other passengers kept sending notes of congratulations during the flight. The captain called the flight a flight of peace and invited Nargess and Shirin into the cockpit. Once Shirin had quiet time to reflect on the meaning of the prize, she realized that she received the prize because she often repeated the same refrain. An interpretation of Islam that is in harmony with equality and democracy is an authentic expression of faith. It is not religion that binds women, but the selective dictates of those who wish them cloistered. That belief, along with the conviction that change in Iran must come peacefully and from within, has underpinned my work.[14]

Upon her arrival in Tehran, Shirin was humbled by the numbers of people who had come to greet her at Tehran airport. Many had walked miles just to be part of the moment when the first Iranian and the first Muslim woman to receive the Nobel Peace Prize returned home as a world citizen of renown. Now her work would be overshadowed temporarily by the preparations that had to be made for the trip to Geneva to receive the prize.

Receiving the Nobel Peace Prize

On December 10, 2003, Mr. Ole Danbolt Mjos, the chairman of the Norwegian Nobel Committee introduced Shirin Ebadi with high praise for her efforts to further democracy and human rights, especially those of women and children. Shirin had suffered for her beliefs and her actions to defend the defenseless victimized by an authoritarian regime. She had been imprisoned and demoted from her position once a fundamentalist regime came into power. She never lost hope or quit her efforts to secure rights, especially for women and children who had few rights under Islamic sharia law.

Mr. Mjos praised Shirin's courage to act at multiple times in his introduction. In a way the prize awarded to Shirin was not just for her but for "all those who are campaigning for human rights and democracy in your country, in the Muslim world and in all countries of the East and West . . . She (Shirin) has been very clear in her opposition to patriarchal cultures that deny equal rights to women."[15]

Citing her professional expertise, courage and willingness to defy danger to herself and her own safety, Shirin was congratulated for being truly a woman of and for her people. "At a time of violence, she has staunchly upheld the principle of nonviolence . . . she has emphasized that information and dialogue constitute the best avenue toward a change of attitudes and a settling of conflicts."[16]

Although Shirin is a conscious and devout Muslim, she sees no conflict between Islam and fundamental human rights. She knows that for Muslims today, justice and equality are crucial issues with a diversity of interpretations. However, she is confident that women have a role to play in the interpretations. Why should it be only elderly men who interpret the tradition? She knows there are no fundamental conflicts between the values of Christianity and the values of Islam. It pleased her that the Roman Catholic Pope was among the first to congratulate her upon hearing of her selection.

Shirin stepped to the podium and began her acceptance speech "In the name of the God of Creation and Wisdom . . . Today coincides with the 55th Anniversary of the adoption of the Universal Declaration of Human Rights, a declaration which begins with the recognition of the inherent dignity and the equal and inalienable rights of all members of the human family . . . Unfortunately, however, this year's report by the United Nations Development Programme . . . spells out the rise of a disaster which distances mankind from the idealistic world of the authors of the Universal Declaration of Human Rights."[17]

Shirin went on to cite some 2002 statistics. Approximately 1.2 billion humans earned less than $1 a day, more than 50 countries were at war or recovering from natural disasters, 22 million people were dying of AIDS and more than 13 million children were turned into orphans. Her passion for justice and the law came through strongly as she identified the violations of human rights and international laws that were happening under a pretext of fighting terrorism.

> Hundreds of individuals who were arrested in the course of military conflicts have been imprisoned in Guantanamo, without the benefit of rights stipulated under the international Geneva conventions, the Universal Declaration of Human Rights and the (United Nations) International Covenant on Civil and Political Rights . . . why is it that some decisions and resolutions of the United Nations Security Council are binding while some other resolutions of the council have no binding force?[18]

With pride, she stated that her country and she were descendants of Cyrus the Great, the Persian emperor who promised he would never rule over his people if they did not wish it. The Charter of Cyrus the Great, an important 2500 year old document, guaranteed freedom of religion and faith to all the people. It was an outstanding statement of human rights.

> I am a Muslim. In the Koran, the Prophet of Islam has been cited as saying: 'Thou shalt believe in thine faith and I in my religion.' This same divine book sees the mission of all prophets as that of inviting all human beings to uphold justice . . . Iran's civilization and culture has been imbued and infused with humanitarianism, respect for the life, belief and faith of others . . . avoidance of violence, bloodshed, and war.[19]

She went on to clearly distinguish between what the religion of Islam sets forth and the counter view of those who misinterpret the religion.

> The discriminatory plight of women in Islamic states . . . has its roots in the patriarchal and male-dominated culture prevailing in these societies and not in Islam. This culture does not tolerate freedom and democracy, just as it does not believe in the equal rights of men and women, and the liberation of women from male domination because it would threaten the historical and traditional position of the rulers and guardians of that culture.[20]

She believed that awarding her the Nobel Peace Prize would inspire many others like herself who are working in Islamic states to continue working for the realization of equality, justice for all and democracy. If human rights fail to be manifested in codified laws or put into effect by states. Human beings will be left with no choice other than staging a rebellion against tyranny and oppression.

Reactions to Shirin Ebadi's reception of the prize were diverse and most positive. Sheila Sahar writing in *Sister Namibia* said among other things, Shirin demonstrated an intelligent and enlightened interpretation of the Quran. Adapting the laws to fit more modern understandings was especially needed in laws pertaining to women. Abolition of judicial penalties such as stoning and amputation of limbs was on the list of priorities.

> Upon hearing the news that she had won the Nobel Peace Prize, the elated and surprised Ebadi called for the release of all political prisoners in Iran . . . she emphasized that while people in the Middle East need international support to create democracies, 'no country is allowed to invade another in the name of democracy, since human rights cannot be promoted through tanks and weapons but through the people of a country.' The next day, a woman member of the parliament announced a delay in the planned execution of Afsaneh Noroozi.[21]

The article concludes by naming other Iranian women who were in the forefront for social transformation in the years between 1906-1911. During the Constitutional Revolution of that period, women formed the first committees for women's rights in the Middle East. The movement wanted a reduction in the power of the clergy. In 1979, when Ayatollah Khomeini decreed compulsory veiling, forced expulsion of women judges from the courts, and a host of other restrictive measures against women, thousands of women marched to protest the counterrevolutionary direction the new rulers were taking.

The International Journal of Humanities and Peace agreed with Shirin Ebadi's statement that awarding her the prize would send rays of hope to all who work for human rights around the world. "It could hand Iranian reformers what they've been craving-a leader with the clout to rattle the entrenched theocracy."[22]

In one of many interviews after she had received the Nobel Peace Prize, Shirin was very clear about her perspective on her religion. She is a devout Muslim who insists as a lawyer that human rights are compatible with Islam. Human rights should not depend on who holds power at any particular time in Iran. At a speech at Syracuse University in May 2004, Shirin's view was very clear. "One urgent task is to learn about the dynamic spirit of Islam and its nature of inclusiveness, to realize we can accept modernity without the risk of losing our faith. We should realize that Islamic governments do not have the key to paradise."[23]

In the interview, Shirin repeated much of what she has said many times about the ways to secure equal rights for all. First, separate Islam from interpreters who are despots and separate Islamic law from patriarchy. Shirin insists that good Muslims faithful to Islam's beliefs can strive for commitment to human rights and better laws. A mind set that makes women second class citizens is not equated with Islam. Misogynist interpretations are the issue. Second, all children and adults need to be educated about their rights and educated to respect the rights of others. As more women attend university, there should be a greater sense of this. Progress in women's rights is progress in human rights and the degree of social justice any society wishes to practice. Protecting the rights of all is a responsibility of society. Fourth, political and social changes as well as economic ones will be needed to safeguard rights and instill laws for protection.

Shirin continues to work for the reformation of her own country's laws in many ways. Her writings are a powerful weapon for change if they can get into the hands that wish to read them. Several years before she won the Nobel peace prize she was in a round table discussion about the issue of women's rights. The penal code of the Islamic regime discriminates against women which is obvious in laws that state a woman's life is worth half that of a man, financially. Under the present regime, a thirteen-year-old girl is considered to be a mature adult who can be married. But she cannot vote until she is sixteen. If she gets a scholarship, she cannot use it without her father's permission. If a husband dies and she is not yet fifteen, she cannot get a job. The new penal code of 1991 dismisses the wisdom of earlier codes.

At the end of this particular interview, Shirin responded to the question of whether feminism would continue to cause ripples of social discontent and disturbance in Iran. Her response was consistent with the deeply held beliefs she has stated in many ways to many different groups around the world.

> Does it create disturbance to say that God created men and women as equals? To spread and sponsor the attitude that God has said that the foundation rests on piety, does this create disturbance? We must all, together, declare that human equality is good and discrimination against people based on their gender, social status, language, race or religion is unacceptable . . . What I say is not based on feminism; it is based on demanding social justice . . . I emphasize once again that the problem is not with Islam; the problem is the sexist, patriarchal attitudes of the legislatures. Some people behind closed doors sit around a table and write their opinions as if God dictates them . . . The roots of the problems are here.[24]

Final Reflections

Shirin's daughters are now grown and successful women. So should Shirin slow down or retire? Perhaps she might slow down but as she reflects on retirement, she muses that she can't retire just yet "That would mean Iran has changed, and that people like me are no longer needed to protect Iranians from their government. If that day comes in my lifetime, I will sit back and applaud the efforts of the next generation from the seclusion of my garden," but for now she "will continue as I have done, in hopes that more of my fellow Iranians will stand at my side."[25]

NOTES

[1]   Shirin Ebadi, with Azadeh Moaveni, *Iran Awakening: A Memoir of Revolution and Hope* (New York: Random House, 2006), 10. Similar perspectives of

Iranian women and their attempt to stay free through the efforts of their literature teacher can be found in Azar Nafisi's *Reading Lolita in Tehran: A Memoir in Books* (New York: Random House, 2003). Two videos that can provide background are *Mystic Iran: the Unseen World*, which focuses on the religious spirit of Iran and *Iran: Days of Crises*, which details the hostages taken at the American Embassy that Shirin will allude to in her memoirs.

2 The citations from *Iran Awakening* will be indicated as *Iran. Iran,* 17.

3 *Iran,* 29.

4 *Iran.* 38.

5 *Iran,* 44.

6 *Iran,* 54.

7 *Iran, 103.*

8 *Iran, 111.*

9 A list of the many writings of Shirin Ebadi can be found in her official autobiography that was written as a recipient of the Nobel Peace Prize. The official biography can be accessed at the web address: nobelprize.org/peace/laureates/2003/ebadi-bio.html

10 *Iran,* 119.

11 Some of Shirin's cases during this time are noted in *Iran,* 132-41.

12 *Iran,* 178. The ordeal of various prisons and interrogations are described on 164-78.

13 *Iran,* 183.

14 *Iran,* 204.

15 presentation, 2

16 presentation, 3.

17 nobelprize.org/peace/laureates/2003/ebadi-lecture-e.html 2.

18 ebadi, 3.

19 ebadi, 3.

20 ebadi, 4.

21 Sheila Safur, "Iranian feminist wins Nobel peace prize," in *Sister Namibia.* Vol.15:5-6 (Nov. 1, 2003), 36.

22 "Nobel Peace 2003 Winner, Shirin Ebadi," an abstract in *International Journal of Humanities and Peace*, Vol. 19:1 (January 1, 2003). 6.

23 Cited by Fereshteh Nouraie-Simone, "Shirin Ebadi: A Perspective on Women's Rights in the Context of Human Rights," in *On Shifting Ground: Muslim Women in the Global Era,* ed. Fereshteh Nouraie-Simon (NY: Feminist Press at the City Univ.of New York, 2005) 267.

24 Fereshteh Nourai-Simone, 281.

25 Feresheth Nourai-Simone, 280, 281.

11

Mairead Corrigan Maguire, Northern Ireland

Periods of Civil War between Irish Catholics and English and Protestant peoples have occurred since 1649. In that year, Irish Catholics revolted against the English and the Protestants who denied the Catholics equality. After a brutal war, Oliver Cromwell's efforts on behalf of the English Commonwealth were successful. One third of Ireland's population was either dead or in exile. As punishment for the Irish Catholic rebellion, land owned by Irish Catholics was confiscated and given to British settlers. Catholics revolted again unsuccessfully in 1689. This resulted in great brutality against Catholics as British Penal Laws were enacted. The Great Famine of 1740-41 killed about 400,000 people. Almost sixty years later, another unsuccessful rebellion in 1798 resulted in Irish self-government being abolished by the 1801 Act of Union.

In 1823, Daniel O'Connell began a successful campaign to achieve Irish emancipation, conceded by Britain in 1829. The potato famine of 1845-49 led to a massive emigration of many Irish people. Some four million people who stayed endured starvation. In the 1850's, a national school system required that English be the language taught and used in the schools. Children would no longer learn the Irish language or about ancient Irish culture through the school system.

In the 1870's, Charles Parnell and the Home Rule League initiated debate on Irish self government. Tensions between Irish nationalists and Irish unionists increased. A 1914 Home Rule Act passed by Britain led to continual disagreement between nationalists and unionists. A 1916 Easter Uprising to attain total independence for Ireland was not successful.

In 1919, an Irish Republic Parliament met in Dublin. The group decided to form a thirty-two-county Parliament for all of Ireland which would maintain ties with Britain. Again disagreements led to bloodshed. The Irish Republican Army waged another War of Independence for two years. Finally, a Republic of Ireland formed out of 26 united counties in 1949. The Republic of Ireland officially left the British Commonwealth while the remaining 6 Northern Ireland counties remained members of the British Commonwealth.

The founding Prime Minister of Northern Ireland declared that these six counties would be a Protestant state for Protestant people. Discrimination against the Catholic population led to civil rights marches in the 1960's. The events of Bloody Sunday and Bloody Friday in the early 1970's started another period of violence and tensions known as "The Troubles." By the 1990's, peace hopes continued to grow. The Belfast Agreement of 1998 gave both Unionists and Nationalists control over limited areas of government. In July 2005, the provisional IRA agreed to end its armed campaign.[1]

Efforts to foster peace agreements were initiated through women like Mairead Corrigan Maguire. The historic Spring, 2007 Agreement between Ian Paisley and Martin McGuiness was well covered by international media. The media did not name the decades of peacemaking that preceded this through marches and movements by women like Mairead Corrigan Maguire and her coworkers in the Peace People Movement. However Mairead's efforts were not lost by the Nobel peace prize committee, which the following pages will eventually detail.

Mairead Corrigan Maguire's Experience of Violence

Mairead was born in Belfast, Northern Ireland into a Roman Catholic family. She personally experienced violence in Northern Ireland through multiple incidents. Once she and others were tear gassed while attending a funeral for a friend. The friend was murdered for being a Nationalist. Mairead's brother was arrested and held without any trial for his opposition to oppression of Catholics. A turning point for Mairead's life came in 1977. In that year, a Protestant extremist shot a young IRA member, Danny Lennon. Danny was driving a car that then careened into Mairead's sister and children who happened to be on the street at the time. Anne, the mother, survived but the children, 8-year-old Joanne, three-year-old John and 6-week-old Andrew died. Betty Williams, a passerby, assisted as best she could before the victims were taken to a hospital. Anne was too critically injured to attend the children's funerals. Eventually, she did recover physically but not mentally.

These tragic deaths and many other senseless killings were the sparks that caused Mairead, Betty Williams and Ciaran McKeown to initiate peace marches. The peace marches were supported by many Catholics and Protestants in Belfast were repulsed by the tragedy of the children's deaths and the deaths of so many other innocent people. The marches for peace grew in number and were supported by thousands of people from all religions, all ages, all ethnic communities and all kinds of workers and students. In time, these marches gave birth to the Peace People Movement. That movement was officially born in 1976 with its agenda for peace.

> We want to live and love and build a just and peaceful society. We want for our children, as we want for ourselves . . . lives of joy and Peace. We recognize that to build such a society demands dedication, hard work, and courage . . . every bullet fired and every exploding bomb makes that work more difficult . . . We dedicate ourselves to working with our neighbors, near and far, day in and day out, to build that peaceful society in which the tragedies we have known are a bad memory and a continual warning. [2]

Today the work of The Peace People is a global movement. Its work is to heal divisions, to assist and empower all people who wish to work for peace, to engage in dialogue and to protest against violence across the globe. While the movement was growing in 1981, Mairead married Jackie Maguire. They continued to live in the Belfast area although Mairead spends much time speaking to groups around the globe about peace. She is the recipient of numerous honorary doctorates as well as many peace and leadership awards from many nations.[3]

Mairead's message for peace takes as many shapes as her audiences and their context of violence. Themes of compassion and freedom reflect her own deep seated nonviolent and compassionate spirituality. Hints of that spirituality of non violence filter through the following reflections.

An Open Letter to the IRA, 1993 (written in a Belfast church)

I was born a short distance away and went to a school around the corner . . . I love this place. More than that, I love the people of this community . . . Here, the desire for peace is passionate, tangible. You feel you could reach out and touch it. Without their having to explain it to you, you know that the people here have a deep sense of what peace is, and what peace is not.; something born in them out of a long history of never knowing real peace . . . I sense in this community an excited anticipation that the time is now and that the opportunity for a genuine peace has never been greater. The people want this creative peace.

In 1976, during the Peace People rallies, more than half a million people walked for peace. This movement began when my sister Anne and her husband Jackie's three children, Joanne (8), John (3), and Andrew (6 weeks old) were killed in a clash between the army and the IRA . . . I hoped and prayed at the time that the deaths would be the end of all violent deaths in our country. They were not. In the past 25 years, more than 3,000 people have died leaving unimaginable pain and suffering to their families. You and your comrades in the IRA take responsibility for your part in causing this . . . In the republican movement, you are now faced with the need to change radically-to move away from the armed struggle and into a nonviolent alternative . . . The way of active nonviolence is in tune with your Christian roots and heritage . . . Jesus with a machine gun does not come off as an authentic figure.

Wisdom means the tough decision to walk the path of nonviolence. That risk of faith will take all your courage . . . A new vision and a fresh wisdom are not only necessary for the republican movement. They are necessary for the future of humanity . . . I have come to know that our first identity is not nationalist or unionist, but our humanity. I have come to know for certain that love and compassion are the greatest and strongest forces operating in our world today. I believe and work for a nonviolent, demilitarized, northern Irish society, and I hope our friends in the south of Ireland will also begin to work for a demilitarized nonviolent Ireland. Then we will truly be light in a highly militarized world.[4]

Address to Women's Ordination Worldwide Conference, Dublin, 2001.

My dear brothers and sisters in Christ,

"MY SOUL DOTH MAGNIFY THE LORD AND MY SPIRIT HATH REJOICED IN GOD MY SAVIOR." I love these words of the Magnificat. They are the words of a woman who has found inner freedom. This woman feels fulfilled and her 'spirit' dances with joy and gratitude to God. Mary says 'yes' to becoming the mother of Jesus, and through the working of the Holy Spirit, the impossible becomes possible . . . .

Just as Mary said 'yes' and gave birth to Jesus, so too each one of us is called to give birth to love and truth . . . And that is why I am so happy to be with you all at this Conference. We come together in celebration of women's call to a renewed priesthood in the Catholic Church. I want to acknowledge my joy at being here in the company of some of these women to whom God has given a priestly vocation. And while I myself do not feel called to Ordained Ministry, I fully support these women, and this movement . . . .

For a long time I have believed that woman's ordination in the Catholic Church will happen; it is only a matter of time. However, before now, I did not feel the need to seek out and listen to women who had such a calling. Now, I have listened . . . .

I never much thought about how difficult it must be for women who receive this call from God. We (Catholics) are so culturally conditioned to think of priests as men only. We grow up in a sexist church, which excludes women from ordination. Catholic theology teaches that priestly ordination is for men only. The Vatican's reasoning for this is that Christ chose his Apostles only from among men. They seem to think that maleness is more important than any other attribute which Jesus possessed. Yet, in the Gospels, Jesus' divinity and humanity were more important than his maleness. But, I believe, once we ourselves break through the cultural conditioning of thinking only of male priesthood, there is no reason why women should not be ordained and very many reasons why they should . . . Women's ways of nurturing, mediating, meditation, counseling, would help 'feed the human spirit' and would enrich both priesthood and people.

However, the most important reason is that our Baptism confirms us as sons and daughters of God and we are all equal in God's sight. In Gen. I: 27 we are told that male and female God made them, and that 'in God's own image, they are made'. As the spirit of the Holy Trinity lives in all our hearts so we too share in the divinity of God and are loved equally. Why then does the Vatican not realize how deeply offensive it is to women to be told that because of their 'biological' make-up they cannot be ordained? Many Catholics are coming to see that this kind of theological argument based on 'biology' is nonsense. Moreover, people are coming to realize the spiritual violence being done to men and women's consciences by the Institutional Catholic Church . . . the spiritual violence is experienced not only by women, but also by theologians, priests, religious and laity.

We are all aware of the Vatican's practice of 'silencing' those whose opinions differ. In a time when 'Dialogue' is being called for by both secular, state, and church bodies, Irish society is permeated with fear among clergy and religious, fear of speaking out on issues such as women's ordination. Indeed they have tragically been forbidden from doing so . . . This is a form of spiritual abuse. It is an assault on the sanctity of a person's conscience, and the removal of the right to freedom of thought and speech. This kind of spiritual abuse is causing very grave damage to many priests and religious who love their faith, but feel torn between conscience and church rules and regulations. I have met such good people, whose spirit, like a wilted flower, calls out in the words of Gerard Manley Hopkins "Give my Roots Rain."

I myself give thanks to God for the gift of faith and conscience. Born into a catholic family, from childhood I have been surrounded with nuns and priests who have blessed me with their friendship. They accompanied me down into the valleys and up onto the mountaintops. I want to publicly thank them today. I have great hope for the Church in the new millennium, and it is because I have met many good shepherds—Bishops, nuns, and priests. I see so many wonderful new forms of discipleship being developed by the laity of all churches, and faiths, but above all, I believe Jesus and take his divine promises very seriously. From time to time also, we see the prophetic church shine through, and the spirit of Jesus comes alive. Such was a time during Vatican II when we heard such sweet words of freedom as 'grace lives in the hearts of all men and women.'

We also took great hope from the Council which taught us that we should follow our formed conscience and that our conscience is our most secret core and our sanctuary. I loved this. I undertook a vigorous process of discernment and began to try to inform my conscience, by reading relevant church doctrine, pondering tradition, praying, seeking spiritual guidance . . . sometimes my decision did not coincide with the Church's teaching . . . I always asked myself 'what would Jesus do'? and after making my decision, refused to allow man-made traditions to destroy the joy and beauty of my faith in God's presence with me on my journey.

Today the institutional catholic church is in the eye of the storm. When the apostles were in the boat and the storm blew-up, they were fearful. There is fear and anxiety in the boat today. But there is also hope and joy, because Jesus is present with us on the journey . . . Many people are rejecting religious authority, but they are passionately looking for religious truth and experience. They can tell the difference between religiosity and spirituality.

Can we change the 'power-thinking' that is a throwback to older darker days when the Church vied for wealth, and worldly power? Can we rediscover the beautiful nonviolent tradition of Jesus and the early Christians who lived unarmed, loving each other and their enemies? I believe so! I also believe when the Church rediscovers and lives out of its nonviolent roots, it will warm people's hearts and rekindle their spirits.

Perhaps the time is coming soon for a new Vatican Council, a new Pentecost in the Church, a time to assemble as the people of God, in the spirit of humility and simplicity, and receive the gifts of the Holy Spirit, of happiness, creativity, fulfilment, and freedom. This then is my vision of a renewed priesthood and church. With Mary, I say 'yes' to this vision, and ask the Holy Spirit 'but how can this be'? Only a deep profound silence comes back to me, the silence of the spirit of truth and love at work in the hearts of all men and women in our world. God's deep peace to you. Deo Gratias![5]

Address at Marquette University, USA, 2003.[6]

Northern Ireland is a deeply complex situation . . . It has social, economic, historical and religious roots going back centuries. But that mixture of all of these different problems needs a multidimensional approach to solve it. It will not be solved quickly and it will not be solved easily, but it is solvable . . . If we can do it in Northern Ireland, it can be done anywhere.

In the first six months of the Peace People, we were privileged to see a 75% decrease in violence. It was shown that the people of nor5thern Ireland came together and said, "Let's do something and change this." But we were also not naive about it because we realized the root cause of our violence had to be tackled. Violence is only the flower of the root of injustice. You have got to deal with the injustice . . . .

The conflict in northern Ireland is not about theological differences. It's not over religion . . . It was essentially over a lack of basic human rights that brought the civil rights movements into existence, which was started in the universities by students . . . .

Two traditions, cultures, religions have grown up alongside each other, but never learned to become friends. And they put so much into their identity that they could become murderous, and they have murdered over this identity. That's very important to understand . . . if people put so much into their flag and their country, and their religion becomes the way in which they define themselves with passion, then if that is challenged in any way, it becomes fearful . . . it can very easily be manipulated by government to go to war against those who happens to think differently

If we are going to make a difference, no matter where we live, we only do it by winning our own inner freedom. Once you receive that inner freedom, you see beyond color and creed and religion . . . 'You have that right to life and when you realize your life is sacred and precious and wonderful and beautiful, you don't want anybody to kill you and you don't want anybody to hurt you because your first human right is your right to your life. Then you recognize a natural justice that you must give the right to life to every single person you meet.

We have got to learn to work together . . . It' s not enough when you live with diversity. It's not enough to say we will tolerate each other. That's a very negative attitude. It's not enough to say we will respect each other. We must be proactive and proclaim people's right to think differently and to act differently . . . So we can no longer have a superior attitude to each other . . . We want to create a culture of nonviolence that's built on an absolute respect for human life and for the environment . . .

In the old days, we had "fight or flight," but now we know the third way of nonviolence. It is wrong to stand by when there is evil in your society and not do something . . . Is there such a thing as a just war? I studied the just war theory . . . it never has worked.

The message to me from the cross is love your enemy. Do not kill. And for me the cross is the greatest symbol of nonviolent love and action . . . we can find that message again in our personal lives . . . And in Ireland today, if we could get the Catholic churches to proclaim and dedicate themselves to Jesus' nonviolence, then we could build a wonderful society . . . We have learned in Northern Ireland that Militarism doesn't work; paramilitarism doesn't work. The only thing that works is love.[6]

A Letter to My Son, Luke[7]

Always know, Luke, that you are deeply loved . . . But as you grow up and begin to ask questions for yourself, you will know that men and women have a need in their hearts for something more, something deeper than that found even in the very best of human love . . . .

As you grow up in the Christian tradition, pray to be more loving, compassionate, courageous, gentle and peaceful. Try to see Christ in everyone, especially the suffering Christ . . . and try to remove the causes of that suffering when you can . . . as you would ask natural justice of your

fellow travelers in respecting your right to life, then you too must give justice
and respect every person's right to life. This means, my little son, that you
must never kill another human being.

It will not be easy for you to refuse to kill . . . it will take all of your
courage to walk unarmed and refuse to hate and kill, in a world which insists
that you must have enemies and be prepared to kill them before they kill
you . . . only love can bring down the barriers of hate and enmity . . .

Pray also for the gift of wisdom. It is a wise man who soon comes to know
that the human family's real enemies are those of injustice, war, starvation,
poverty . . . when human life is held as so sacred that no one can kill, then
justice will reign in people's hearts and in all lands. Wars will be no more.
Justice will mean that no one has too much while some have nothing. Greed
and selfishness will turn into feeding the hungry and removing all poverty . . .
You just have to refuse the old ways of thinking and doing things and begin
to think and act in a way more in tune with magnificent goodness . . . .

Be happy, be joyous, live every minute of this beautiful gift of life.

World Summit of Nobel Peace Laureates, 2004.[8]

We need urgently to move on to a new road. We can choose to do this
individually, by seeking truth and living our lives with as much integrity
as possible. But in order to bring about the enormous changes necessary,
we have to demand our Governments change their current national and
foreign policies which are destroying the lives of millions of our brothers
and sisters on the planet and damaging the earth itself. We have to challenge
our governments . . . as a united human family.

I suspect when Mr. Gorbachev initiated Perestroika, it was because he
recognized that the Soviet Union and the world were on the wrong road . . .
He gave hope to humanity . . . We too shared his vision of stopping the
nuclear arms race. We believed that everyone could share in the Peace
Dividend. We too wanted to stop the madness of such huge military
spending, and opened it instead to tackle the real enemies of the human
family, poverty, disease and so on . . . .

There will be no quick fixes . . . but at least if we change on to a new
road now and insist our government do likewise, then we can travel together
united as the human family, celebrating the gift of life, the gift of each other,
and the joy of simply being alive. For the journey, we gain inner strength
by following our own spiritual paths, but also from the example of others
whose courage and self-sacrifice uphold and uplift us.

Meeting with Pope Benedict XVI, November 23, 2005.[9]

On Wednesday 23rd November, 2005, I had the privilege of meeting in St. Peter's Square, Rome, with Pope Benedict XVI. After his public address, he greeted a delegation of Nobel Peace Laureates present in Rome to attend the Sixth Nobel Peace Summit.

In his address, to the St. Peter's Square audience, the Pope spoke of unconditional love. I could not help asking myself: "Why if the Catholic Church, speaks so much about unconditional love do so many Christians facilitate and participate in violence, armed struggles and war?" . . . .

When I met the Pope, I took the chance to ask him to 'abolish the Just war theory, and proclaim the nonviolent gospel of Jesus'. He smiled. (Four years ago Pope Benedict, then Cardinal Ratzinger, made a statement saying the time is coming when we will have to get rid of the just war theory). I told him I was from Northern Ireland, and invited him to visit us. The moment's encounter was brief and intense and I was moved by his quiet, peaceful, and listening *persona*. Understanding, that I would not get to speak much to him, I had written him a letter. In this letter I asked the Pope, as this was the year of the Eucharist, the sacrament of nonviolence, to consider calling a Council to declare 'No Just war and proclaim the Nonviolence of Jesus' . . . .

The Catholic Church officials will argue that they are for peace, and always have been. But tragically the practical gospel message of "no killing, and love your enemy" is often, for the Church, a step too far, and hence since the third century and the time of Constantine, Christians have been amongst the most warlike and violent people on earth. Even today, in the recent war and invasion of Iraq, carried out mostly by USA and UK Christians, the justification of invasion, torture, and use of phosphorus chemical weapons on people is described by some as 'just war', or justifiable to 'stop terrorism'. They seem blind to the fact that war is terrorism!

To all our shame only a handful of Bishops in the USA actually opposed the war against Afghanistan, and very many American people from Christian background supported war and the invasion of Iraq. And in Ireland, how many continued to support paramilitaries and the 'armed struggle'? How many put aside the message of love of enemy and non-killing? How many regarded it as a nonissue, a non-thought?

I believe, if there is to be any future for humanity then we must transform our violent cultures into nonviolent ones and begin to build non-killing societies where we live. In developing such a new culture, all faith traditions have a role to play, by bringing peace and nonviolence to the center of their theology. The human family faces violence on many fronts, war, nuclear weapons, poverty, environmental, human rights, women's rights. We await with hope, what His Holiness Pope Benedict XVI and our world's Spiritual Leaders have to say to us on such issues of our time.[9]

NOTES

[1]   www.wikipedia.org/wiki/History_of_Ireland The summary of the 24 pages has been checked against other sources. There are many Videos/ DVD's that present particular periods of Irish history. *Michael Collins; My Left Foot; Enemy Mine: Northern Ireland; Bloody Sunday* and *Angela's Ashes* are but a few of these.

[2]   A full text and information can be found at www.peacepeople.com/PPDeclaration.htm

[3]   Many of these are listed on the Peace People website. Mairead Corrigan Maguire has graciously given permission to use the cited texts in this chapter. Visit the Peace People Website for additional resources about peace and non violence. www.peacepeople.com/MaireadCMaguire.htm

[4]   www.peacepeople.com/LettertoIRA.htm

[5]   www.womenpriests.org/wow/maguire.esp

[6]   *www.marquette.edu/cgi-bin/advprint/print.cgi?doc=http*

[7]   Excerpts are from a reprint of the monthly paper of Peace People.

[8]   www.wagingpeace.org/articles/2004/11/10_maguire_united-world-divided-world.htm

[9]   www.peacepeople.com/ 30.11.2005

12

Mary Robinson, Republic of Ireland

Mary Robinson was born in Ballina, County Mayo on May 21, 1944. Her full name was Mary Therese Winifred Bourke. Mary's parents were medical doctors. Mary had two older brothers, Oliver and Aubrey, and two younger brothers, Henry and Adrian. Henry recalls that whenever Mary got into trouble as a child, she would make her case. Mary was fond of saying, "Look, it's not the way you see it . . . you're blowing it up."[1]

When she was ten, Mary was admitted to the Mount Anville Boarding School in Dundrum. Mary was impressed by the strong sense of social justice that the nuns of the Sacred Heart demonstrated. It had a lifelong effect upon her own integrity and idealism. Mary's grandfather who was a lawyer also affected her sense of justice. He thought it was right that wealthy landowners should have some of their property redistributed to poor people.

After finishing school at Dundrum, Mary went to Paris for a year to attend the Foyer du Sacre Coeur. In Paris, her spiritual inspiration grounded in justice deepened. Here her eyes were opened in new ways to the use and the abuse of power not only in politics but in the church as well. "I was very angry at a lot of what the church stood for at that time, at how religion could become a power play and oppressive, undermining the true sense of spirituality."[2]

Mary returned to Ballina after her year in Paris. She began to study for a scholarship to Trinity College in Dublin. She won the scholarship but Catholics who wanted to attend Trinity College in Dublin were required to get a bishop's permission. Her father secured permission by informing the local bishop that attending Trinity College was a family tradition.

While a first year student at Trinity College, Mary and her future husband Nick took first class honors in their first year. In the second year, Mary won a special undergraduate scholarship honoring young scholars. This scholarship paid all fees, paid a small quarterly salary and paid for part of her food bill since women could not attend meals in the Commons at Trinity College. Between 1965 and 1967, Mary became editor of the student law review, *Justice.* She also was an auditor for the Law Society. She received her LLB degree in 1967, the Degree of Barrister of Law from King's Inns, Dublin in 1967 and won a fellowship to Harvard Law School in Boston. She left for Boston within a day of her last exam at Trinity.[3]

At Harvard, her perspectives about justice were enhanced and reinforced. By the time she returned to Ireland with her LLM degree in 1968, she had a new self confidence and a strong sense that a lawyer could practice law and still have an ethical conscience! She accepted the position of junior counsel on the Judiciary's Western Circuit. She quickly recognized the difference in a woman barrister's position in Ireland and the experiences she had in the United States. She was relieved and honored to be appointed Reid Professor of Constitutional and Criminal Law at Trinity College in Dublin in 1969. At age 25, she was the youngest person to hold the prestigious Reid Professorship Chair that had been established in 1888. The same year Mary became the first Catholic senator for the upper house to be selected by Dublin University. She ran as an independent candidate. In spite of opposition to some of her ideas of justice, she was elected as an independent senator.[4]

In 1970, she married former classmate Nicholas Robinson. They had three children, Tessa, William and Aubrey. The Robinson household functioned with a sense of equality and responsibility. Responsibility and family sharing of it was necessary as Mary became a member of the English Bar in 1973 while holding the position of Reid Professor at Trinity College. She was a lecturer in European Community Law at Trinity College in Dublin from 1975-90. During this time, she remained a member of the Irish Parliament, serving in the upper house for 20 years until 1989.

She decided not to seek another election to the Senate. However, the Labor Party asked her to become their nominee for president. She finally agreed and became the first Labor Party candidate for president. She was also the first woman candidate for president. She eventually won the support of the full Labor Party, the Workers Party, independent senators and a majority of the people. She was inaugurated at a joyful celebration at Dublin Castle on December 3, 1990.

From the time she took office, Mary made it very clear that she was a president for all the people. The invitation list for the inaugural celebration demonstrated her intent. Representatives from women's organizations, homeless coalitions, disability groups, politicians from both sides of Northern Ireland's troubles, people working for peace, members of government who shared her ideals for a better future and church representatives all gathered to hear Mary's inaugural address.

"The Ireland I will be representing is a new Ireland, open, tolerant, inclusive." After reminding the people that there were four provinces in Ireland, Mary said she wanted to address *the fifth province*. Where is that fifth province? "It is a place within each of us—the place that is open to the other, that swinging door that allows us to venture out and others to venture in . . . If I am a symbol of anything, I would like to be a symbol of this reconciling and healing Fifth Province."

She offered her official dwelling, Aras an Uachtarain, as a place "where emigrant communities could send representatives for a get-together of the extended Irish family abroad." She identified the face of modern Ireland as local, participatory communities and promised to represent the local as well as the global. "Ours is a truly beautiful country and the Irish people are wonderful race." She continued to assure the people that she would contribute to international protection and promotion of human rights in their name. "We have a long history of providing spiritual, cultural and social assistance to other countries in need . . . May God direct me so that my Presidency is one of justice, peace and love. May I have the fortune to preside over an Ireland at a time of exciting transformation when we enter a new Europe where old wounds can be healed."[5]

A Presidency of Justice, Peace and Love for All People

As a constitutional lawyer and a human rights lawyer, Mary was uniquely prepared for the challenges that would come. She had questioned the constitutional foundation for the practice that prevented Irish presidents from speaking out on relevant and controversial issues of the day without first seeking the approval of government. She knew this had to change!

She decided to do what she saw fit. Her priorities were made clear when she attended AIDS benefits, ate with cross-border groups from Northern Ireland, visited women's prisons, attended events at a rape crisis center, participated in Third World development projects and gave many interviews to varieties of media representatives. Attempts were made by some government officials to stop these actions because the actions were giving this president a new and different profile. A showdown between the keeper of the old, Charles Haughey, and the profile of the new, Mary Robinson, came over the future visit of the Dalai Lama.

The Dalai Lama had personally written Mary to thank her for forcing a debate in the Irish Senate in 1989 that condemned Chinese violation of human rights in Tibet. She responded in 1991 by inviting the Dalai Lama to visit her at her official residence. Government officials notified Mary that they disapproved of this meeting. It carried political overtones. Mary responded by saying she was meeting the Dalai Lama at her residence. This made it a personal visit by a friend. Technically, it was not an official head of state meeting. "I met the Dalai Lama, and he clearly knew more; he knew what a struggle it had been . . . it was a price I knew I had to pay."[6]

Mary's sense of justice affected her budgeting. The majority of her budget would not be spent on grand state dinners for very important heads of state, although some of it would be assigned to this. The majority of her entertainment budget would be used to entertain the powerless rather than the powerful. People in groups from all over Ireland who wanted the president to hear their concerns would be invited to come to talk to her over tea.

One group from Mercy Center in Dublin's inner city came to tea. One of the women recounts that she had borrowed shoes for the meeting but the shoes were too small. Mary noticed this and told the woman to take off her shoes so she could be more comfortable. The woman then challenged Mary by saying that Mary had more room in this one area of Aras than these women had in their flats. Besides that, their children had only a minimal space in which to play. A few years later, Mary met this woman again as she formally opened a playground at their Mercy Center. Mary recognized the woman and went to sit with her and other women of the center instead of eating with the more publicly prominent people present.[7]

Mary's graciousness extended to many. She learned that years ago during the Irish famine, the Choctaw tribe had raised $173 for the relief of Irish famine victims. It was a lot of money to donate at the time. Mary journeyed to personally visit the tribe in Oklahoma and to thank the Chief and people for being so generous to a suffering Irish people. Mary thanked the Choctaw Nation for using their own suffering as an empathetic strength to help others. The response to Mary's visit was a return visit. The Choctaw Chief made her an honorary Chief of the Choctaw nation in May 1992 at her residence. She was honored by the thoughtfulness.[8]

In 1993, Mary became the first Irish president to visit Queen Elizabeth II at Buckingham Palace. Mary had been invited to tea with Queen Elizabeth II. Both Mary and the Queen received government opposition to this unofficial tea. Past and present tensions between the English and Irish made governments uneasy! Both women realized this but the tea went forward graciously as the two leaders enjoyed each other's company. This experience led them to set an official visit of the heads of state to be held in Buckingham Palace in June 1996.

The formal welcome to Buckingham Palace in 1996 followed the protocol for all heads of state. Prince Edward walked Mary as a head of state to inspect the Irish Guard of honor. The Irish national anthem was played. The flying of the flag of the Republic of Ireland and the official guard all saluting the Irish president symbolized clearly that this was an official State Visit of the Republic of Ireland to England. Those who considered Ireland and England as past enemies realized that this was a new age for a new England and a new Ireland.

While Mary was in London, Prince Charles expressed his wish to visit Ireland and visit the place Lord Mountbatton had been murdered. Mary knew that Charles was as interested as she was to send a signal that it was time for reconciliation for this event as a symbol of deeper reconciliations in the future. Charles ignored the advice of his advisors and a trip was arranged for 1995. The official visit began as Charles had dinner with Mary Robinson at Aras. Then Charles proceeded to western Ireland, met with the people and a healing took place. Mary became aware that both shared deep hopes for peace and would do whatever it took to obtain it.[9]

Mary made plans to deal with getting the more than seventy million Irish emigrants back home. Whenever she traveled, she always addressed the emigrants with the hopes that a changing Ireland might welcome them to return. In accord with Irish custom to guide the stranger, Mary kept a burning candle in her kitchen window in Aras an Uachtarain that became a public symbol for all who saw it, It also helped remind the people that they must hope and work for a day when the emigrants could find their way back home.

Mary became a global traveler when affairs of state or when human rights issues were involved. Her visit to regions of Africa and the days she spent with suffering people left a lasting impression on her. She was ashamed that neither she nor probably many others knew the extent of the terrible suffering she had witnessed first hand. It was not known or being responded to by her nation or by many other nations. The experience prompted her to stop in New York on her way home and plead with the Secretary General of the United Nations, Kofi Anan, to encourage UN action.

Mary's growing awareness of the need for human rights and justice now gave her presidency a more international agenda. She made trips to other parts of the world that were in need of humanitarian aid. The Irish government provided emergency relief to victims. She continued making visits to effect some change in the great suffering and violence in Africa. She was very outspoken about the need for a more efficient and less bureaucratic United Nations organization that could act more quickly in response to humanitarian crises.[10]

In 1994, Mary journeyed to Africa for the inauguration of Nelson Mandela as President of South Africa. She took time to visit many sites that she was expected to visit as an official Head of State. Her outspoken passion for human rights brought her to the attention of Kofi Anan as her knowledge of an international agenda became very clear.

Meanwhile, Mary's popularity in presidential rating polls was 93%, one of the best ratings for any Irish president. As Ireland's President, she was able to sign into law some of the reforms that she had furthered for years with considerable opposition. Her sense of compassion and justice moved her to make visits to Northern Ireland where she would meet with any representatives who requested it. This meant meeting men and women and groups who represented many positions on the troubles in Northern Ireland. Her willingness to listen first and then speak may have eventually assisted the Easter accord that cleared the way for a temporary cessation of violence.[11]

At a 1996 International Women's Forum, Mrs. Kennedy Smith, US ambassador to Ireland, pointed out that Mary Robinson had reshaped the Irish famine to become a source of strength, concern and responsibility for all the world's hungry people. "The belief that all of us are members of the human family, that we all share common origins and a common destiny, is embraced and articulated by President Robinson wherever she goes."[12]

Mary had audiences with Pope John Paul II, Mother Teresa of Calcutta and many heads of state. She also met with numerous other groups with whom she could discuss the AIDS-HIV issues in Africa as well as other humanitarian issues. Her human rights interest and her lawyer's training to deal with them helped her decide not to seek a second term as president. The people were disappointed since the people trusted her to be a voice of conscience. She was a president for all people as she had promised. She had revitalized the identity of the Irish people through fostering the Irish language and arts as the bulwarks of Irish identity.

On March 12, 1997, Mary announced her decision not to run for a second term because she knew her name was being considered for the Office of High Commissioner for Human Rights in the United Nations. However, she would need her own government's support before she could allow her name to remain as one in consideration. In time, Mary received that official support from the government with a mix of pride, gratitude and some sadness. Mary officially resigned as president of Ireland in September 1997, a few months before her first term ended so she could become the High Commissioner for Human Rights[13]

Some Reflections of the High Commissioner for Human Rights

Human Rights, Hope and History. Oslo, Norway, August 13, 1998

In an address to religious leaders of the world, Mary emphasized the link of common understandings among religions about the essential questions of existence, and of the source and destiny of human freedom. "This is the gift of fundamental belief—liberation in truth . . . The fundamentalist believer or unbeliever becomes a substitute God." Mary continued by saying that fundamentalists try to force their beliefs on others. In contrast, major religions "see themselves in particular as defenders of the deprived, the poor, the discriminated against . . . They must ensure that their own internal practices are not discriminatory grounds of gender or race or class. They have to learn from the good practice of wider society as well as teach it."[14]

Acceptance of the Erasmus prize, Amsterdam, November 9, 1999.

"Human rights are all about collective responsibility. Their underlying message is that we belong to one global community and that we are responsible for what happens in that community." Mary assured the gathered audience that as Human Rights Commissioner, she would act with quiet diplomacy when it seemed like the best way to get results. However, she never shied away from making public comments to leaders when that seemed to be a better way to get results. "I have assumed the burden of listening; listening to the pain and anguish of victims of violence; listening to the anxieties and fears of human rights' defenders . . . and will continue to speak out for those who have no voice or whose voice is ignored."[15]

Women, human rights and sustainable development in the 21ˢᵗ century. Pretoria, South Africa, August 31, 2002.

"I have seen the effects of violence against women in victims of trafficking in Cambodia, in victims of rape and forced marriage in Afghanistan, and in many other women in too many countries . . . Many practices that violate the rights of women have avoided human rights scrutiny because they are seen as cultural practices that can deserve tolerance and respect . . . Domestic violence can be difficult to condemn if traditions and culture allow men to abuse women or insist that family privacy is more important than the rights of women or children who are abused."[16]

Farewell Speech to Staff at the Office of the High Commissioner for Human Rights, Geneva, September 10, 2002.

Mary named the ongoing threats to human rights that still exist. She included governments that pay lip service but do not act for human rights, international organizations that refused to mainstream human rights and gender rights and also those civil societies that have relaxed vigilance about human rights. She continued with her reflections on terrorism. "Responding to terrorism will remain a major focus of international affairs over the coming years. But we must all continue to insist on respect for basic rights and fundamental freedoms in countering terrorist threats." What was needed now, above all, "is the building up of national protection systems to ensure implementation of agreed human rights law." Building a culture of human rights throughout the world still remains a great challenge. However, the human rights mandate will not be lost because the opening word of the Charter of the United Nations is a statement of human rights. "We the peoples . . ."[17]

Kofi-Anan's Praise of Mary Robinson

> She brought to the task a leader's vision, a lawyer's precision and a believer's conviction . . . She never shied away from controversial issues. Here was a clear voice for human rights when a clear voice was needed . . . When Mary left the United Nations in 2002, she left the world a better place than she found it. And her work for the cause of human rights continues.[18]

Human Rights as a Private Citizen

Kofi Anan knew Mary Robinson would always be an advocate for human rights and peace. After leaving her position at the United Nations, she initiated *The Ethical Globalization Initiative: Realizing Rights*. She was its president and remained active with the team and the Board in executing varieties of actions around global issues like equitable trade, HIV/AIDS response in Africa, human migration policies and numerous other issues

Mary Robinson has received multiple honors and awards. These include being the 24th Chancellor of Trinity College in Dublin, its first woman chancellor, recipient of the 2002 Sydney peace prize, being honorary president of Oxfam International, chairperson of the International Institute for Environment and Development, a founding member and Chairperson of the Council of Women World Leaders, director of the Ethical Globalization Initiative, Professor of Practice in International Affairs at Columbia University and multiple other honors. Mary remains a popular national and international speaker on the issue of human rights.

Mary has also been articulate about the role of religion in a world that is being globalized. When addressing a meeting of Catholic Major Superiors of Women and Men Religious in 2004, Mary again linked spiritual voice with a human rights' voice. She urged the group to make their governments accountable "for implementing rights to food, safe water, to health and education, and for doing so without discrimination." How could religions more actively support the empowerment of women? The culture of patriarchy is the chief obstacle and so are the forms of fundamentalism that continue to deny women's rights. "I believe it's necessary for faith adherents to place the empowerment of women at the center of their own strategic thinking. Women must be able to participate fully and equally in decision-making within the faiths themselves, and their concerns need to be embraced as priorities in prayer, advocacy, and activism." She concluded by encouraging interfaith activism in the areas of violence against women, especially sexual trafficking, gender dimensions of HIV/AIDS, and women's health, as well as exploitation of women in the workforce. The pattern of power relationships needs to be addressed. It is here that religious bodies may be able to have some influence if they have the courage to be changed themselves.[19]

Mary Robinson's life is an active proclamation of how one woman is living out a sacred journey grounded in a spirituality of nonviolent transformation. While not explicitly discussing personal spirituality, Mary's life witnesses to it. She remains grounded in global compassion and works toward the day when all people will experience and act as one human family

NOTES

[1] Olivia O'Leary and Helen Burke, *Mary Robinson: the Authorised Biography* (London: Hodder and Stoughton, 1998) 11. Hereafter this will be cited as *Biography.*

[2] *Biography,* 19.

[3] *Biography,* 23-39.

[4] Lorna Siggins, *The Woman Who Took Power in the Park: Mary Robinson,* (Dublin: Mainstream Publishers, 1997) 51-58.

[5] Fergus Finlay, *Mary Robinson: A President with a Purpose* (Dublin: O'Brien Press, 1990) These excerpts are from the full address that can be found between pp. 155-60.

[6] *Biography,* 156.

[7] *Biography, 159.*

[8] *Power in the Park,* 194-95.

[9] *Biography,* 184-87.

[10] *Biography,* 249-62.

[11] *Power in the Park,* 165-75.

[12] *Power in the Park,* 210.

[13] The final chapters of Fergus Finlay's *Mary Robinson: A President With a Purpose,* describes the many accomplishments of Mary's presidency. The accomplishments are too many to be included here. A list can be found between pp. 148-60.

[14] Kevin Boyle, ed. *A Voice for Human Rights: Mary Robinson* (Philadelphia: Univ. of Pennsylvania Press, 2006) 312-13. Further citations will be noted as *Human Rights.*

[15] *Human Rights,* 19-20.

[16] *Human Rights,* 60-61.

[17] *Human Rights,* 355.

[18] Kofi Anan's *Forward* in *Human Rights,* vii-viii. It is clear in the remarks of Kofi Anan that he had great expectations of Mary Robinson and that these expectations were met.

[19] Visit realizingrights.org for further information. This website also contains useful information about present issues of justice and human dignity.

13

Ama Adhe Tapontsang, Tibet

Ama Adhe's story emerges out of a long history of Tibet that went from self rule to rule by multiple other powers. The roles played by China, Britain and India in the history of Tibet are long and complicated. Only the unfolding of history in the last one hundred years will be summarized in this chapter since it is this history that has impacted the life story of Ama Adhe and Tibetans of this time.

In 1912 when a new Republic of China was formed Chinese troops stationed in Tibet eventually returned home to China. This retreat made it safe for the Dalai Lama to return from his exile in India to Tibet in July 1912. In 1914 the Simla Convention brokered a treaty in India about territorial rights which were being negotiated by representatives of India, China, Tibet and Britain. The actual negotiations broke down over territorial rights for each of the four countries. Resulting tensions paved the way for the eventual Sino-Indian War of 1962 that continued the fighting about boundaries and who had power over whom.

That war caused a new interest in Tibet by Western powers who had basically lost interest in Tibet after World War I. A civil war in China led to loss of interest in Tibet by both the Chinese and Indians who were fighting in the civil war. The general loss of interest by the former boundary players enabled the 13th Dalai Lama to rule Tibet in peace. The government of Tibet controlled all the territory that today coincides with the borders of the Tibet Autonomous Region. Once the civil war ended China claimed Tibet as its territory which gave rise to the Tibetan rebellions of the 1950s. The CIA supported the Tibetan rebellions until late 1969 when support was withdrawn for political reasons. This loss of support led to the 14th Dalai

Lama and other government principals fleeing to India. The Chinese set up their representative, the Panchem Lama, as a figurehead in Lhasa. The Chinese claimed that the Panchem Lama headed the legitimate government of Tibet because the 14th Dalai Lama had fled from Tibet. The Panchem Lama ruled until his mysterious death in 1989 which was shortly after he criticized the Chinese. The Chinese had destroyed thousands of Buddhist monasteries, massacred countless Buddhist monks and nuns, destroyed centuries old Buddha statues and priceless works of art in Tibet. They also imposed brutal suffering on the people. In the late 1990s major economic changes occurred in Tibet. The repression of the people of Tibet continued into the new millennium. However, most religious freedoms have been officially restored, provided the lamas do not challenge the rule or practices of the People's Republic of China. Some official government and human rights watchers still occasionally protest the situation in Tibet, but generally governments recognize both the sovereignty of the People's Republic of China over Tibet and the legitimacy of the exiled Dalai Lama's Tibetan Government in Exile.

The exiled Dalai Lama is the person who encouraged Ama Adhe to tell her story and the story of the Tibetan people so that it will not be forgotten. Ama has pledged her life to make the plight of her people known. She still hopes that in her lifetime her people of Tibet will again take charge of their country, although that seems improbable. Ama's story follows, a story about a life of action, prayer and hope that someday Tibetans may become again a free people.[1]

Life as a Tibetan[2]

Ama Adhe was born in 1932 in the Kham region of Tibet which was peopled by nomads and farming families. Like the Adhe family many Tibetans were semi nomads. In the summer months the family moved their herds to the mountains for grazing and the children played in the wild flowers in the sun filled days. They had horses, cattle and female yaks; the family lived in tents during the time they moved the herds for grazing in the mountains. At the end of October each year the family moved back to their permanent home for the winter months.

Before eating Adhe's family always prayed to Dolma, also known as Tara, a female Buddha who was a protector. In the evening the children would listen to stories of the elders about the great religious tradition of Tibet and of the holy city of Lhasa where the Dalai Lama reigned. This city held famous monasteries and the Jokhang shrine which held the famous sacred image of the ancient Buddha Shakyamuni. This was a site for many miracles and a center to which thousands of pilgrims came. The elders would tell stories and talk about the Chinese and the centuries of disputes over Tibetan lands. Sometimes the elders used the stories about Chinese brutality to keep the Tibetan children well behaved!

Adhe's family moved to the peaceful vicinity of Karze when Adhe was still young. There were thirty-one Buddhist monasteries and nunneries here. The monastery of Kharnant had more than 450 monks and lamas (religious teachers) who prayed and resided there. Each family had a religious teacher who would come to the house chapel and assist the family. The chapel was a special place in the home. In the center was an altar with the statues of the Buddha and the many manifestations in the form of Tibetan deities. Below the statues were flowers and seven prayer bowls filled with water. Only when the lama came did the whole family gather in this space. Otherwise individuals would go into the quiet space alone. Adhe did this often. She was taught the teachings of the Buddha by her father who stressed the harmony that comes from being good to all others. "Leading a life in which there is compassion and the practice of virtue brings charity and peace."[3]

The Buddha stressed the Eightfold Path and Adhe was moved by the stories of the Buddha and his life of compassion. Her father also taught her the long prayer of the female deity Dolma whose compassion was as wide as the wind. Dolma is a *Bodhisattva,* an enlightened one who returns to earth to aid the people in the form of a compassionate mother. Adhe also learned about the great leader of Tibet, His Holiness the Dalai Lama, the human manifestation of unconditional compassion. Chenrezig had his first incarnation in 1391 but continues to reincarnate as the Dalai Lama to guide the Tibetan people. The thirteenth Dalai Lama died in 1933. The fourteenth Dalai Lama was born in 1939 and all the people celebrated his return.

Adhe's family took her on pilgrimages to Kharnang monastery countless times to receive blessings. Both her father and brother Jughumo each had a monk guru from Kharnang monastery. The monk guru would occasionally visit the family, pray special prayers for the family and remember all the family members who died. Life in Karze was peaceful for Adhe, her brother Jughamu and her older sister Blumo. In Karze the Tibetans revered deities of the sky and mountains. Here Tibetans looked upon the earth as a manifestation of living essence. The heritage of balance of people and nature made it hard to imagine that all would change.[4]

Traditionally an arranged marriage was set for Adhe when she turned sixteen. She did not know her future husband Sangdhu Pachen. However, her girlfriends told her she was lucky because he was handsome and kind. The couple married in 1948. The family religious leader conducted the brief ceremony. After the wedding ceremony and a celebration for three days and three nights the bride traditionally lived with her family for another six months to a year before being considered "officially married." In spring 1949 Adhe was considered formally married so she left her family home to reside in Sangdhu Pachen's house. Her mother-in-law greeted her so warmly that Adhe knew everything would be fine. There were the usual adjustments but all went well and both families grew close.

In spring 1950 the Chinese army entered Karze. They held a public meeting in a large field and claimed that they were there to help the people although the army was well armed. For a time the Chinese army projected an attitude of respect for the people and were reverent toward the many religious practices. Smiling Chinese soldiers even helped with the harvest. The Tibetans felt this was a temporary occupation and nothing to be concerned about.

Adhe's father was a respected leader of the people. In 1953 he was among the 30 influential people the Chinese chose to visit China and to see and appreciate the culture of China. The delegations were given a supervised tour but they did not see the poorest people. It was not until the delegation was at a marketplace that Adhe's father was enlightened. An older man pulled Adhe's father aside and said that the Communists were plundering every family for riches. Moments later when a truck of women prisoners arrived the man said these women would be lined up and shot like other Chinese prisoners. Adhe's father was horrified. When he got home he threw the pictures of Mao and Stalin into the fireplace and warned the people about the Chinese intent, but it was too little too late.

Soon Chinese paper currency began to be used instead of Tibetan money. The Chinese took Tibetan coins and melted them down for their own use. The Chinese claimed that people would be better off now that everyone would be using Chinese money. The people were forced to share whatever wealth they still had. Tibetan elders could see what was really happening and they urged Adhe's husband to take her to Lahsa where the family could be safe.

In spring 1954 Adhe's father died. His last words to her were that no one should trust the Chinese. More and more Chinese troops kept coming into Tibet. Later in 1954 his Holiness the Dalai Lama was invited to visit China and asked to participate in the drafting of a Constitution by the Chinese National Assembly. At first his Holiness thought this was an invitation that would help his people. However, some members of the Dalai Lama's party were suspicious and insisted that the Dalai Lama travel by an old route because they feared a trap. Other advisors insisted it was not a trap and insisted that they would go as the Chinese had directed them to go. These men were all killed on the way.

The Dalai Lama arrived in China by the old route. He was kept in China for nearly a year and was constantly told that China was the greatest power in the world. Even in his partial isolation the Dalai Lama observed that the Chinese people had lost all sense of individuality. Everything was regulated including all the clothing the people wore. The Dalai Lama returned to Tibet in April 1955 to the joy of the people. However, then the first persecutions of the monasteries began. In an about face the Chinese declared that all religious life and religion was useless. The Chinese tried to force monks and nuns to marry and break their vows. Suicides within the monastic community occurred on a large scale as a public protest against the Chinese propaganda and demands.

The only happy part of the year was the period of time in which Adhe gave birth to a son Chimu. Like so many Tibetans Adhe secretly resisted the teachings of the Chinese. Stories were told of the punishments of those who were caught resisting the Chinese propaganda. These people who resisted publicly had bamboo sticks put under their fingernails until they would name others who were also refusing to follow the Chinese ways.

By spring of 1956 opposition forces against the Chinese sprang up in many places. Adhe's husband was one of the men who joined and fought with opposition forces resisting the Chinese. The day before he was going to take Adhe to a safer place Pachen's food was poisoned and he died quickly. Oppression increased and brutal persecution of the monks and nuns continued. Treasures from the monasteries were stolen and claimed by the Chinese. The former respect for the land was lost as the Chinese began cultivating all available land to feed their thousands of troops. There was no attempt at crop rotation or preservation of resources which the Tibetans knew was essential. Tibetans considered this ravage of the earth as a direct affront against the deities of the soil, of the mountains, of water and of the sky. Perfect balance with the surroundings of earth, air and water was part of the religious heritage of Tibet, but this was totally ignored by Chinese practices.

The Chinese leaders began a direct campaign to force some Tibetans to denounce other Tibetans who did not comply with Chinese propaganda.

Children began denouncing their parents, servants their employers and even some young monks denounced their abbots and lamas. The religious teacher of Adhe's house who had become a good friend to her brother was publicly humiliated in the village when a communist woman soldier tied a rope around the monk's tongue, led him like an animal in the street, poured urine on his face and forced him to drink it. It was now very clear that the Tibetans were facing a long period of suffering.[5]

Between 1956-57 thousands of Tibetan people were massacred for taking part in the resistance movements against Chinese oppression. To Adhe and others it seemed that there were decaying bodies everywhere. The only joy Adhe remembers at this time was the birth of her daughter Tashi. However, Adhe never got to know Tashi because Adhe was accused of being a resistor to Chinese rule. One October morning Chinese soldiers stormed into Adhe's house. They dragged her forcibly away and cared little about leaving a crying son and baby daughter alone in the house. Neighbors who witnessed this eventually came to take the children for they knew Adhe was going to prison. She felt she would never see her children again.

In prison Adhe was beaten. Her hands were cuffed, and she was made to sleep on a damp stone floor. She had splinters inserted under her nails, was forced to kneel on sharpened points of sticks and was kicked so vehemently that in later years she retained a permanent lump from all the beatings. After months of torture she asked the guards to kill her. They laughed and continued the abuse.

For eleven years Adhe could not wash her body because the prison had no forms of sanitation. Many people committed suicide if they could find a way. Adhe's sister Bhuma was in the same prison, but they rarely met. When the eleven-year sentence was finally over Adhe hoped for release. But since she had been a strong resistor she was sentenced to an additional sixteen years in prison with no recourse.

In July 1959 Adhe was taken to Dartsedo prison to be part of a work force that carried stones from a quarry. The abuse that was part of this experience was dehumanizing. Adhe was especially sorry for the monks and lamas in the work force. They suffered more than others due to their religious beliefs. There were interrogation sessions after the day's hard labor that were often conducted after injections of serums which were supposed to lessen resistance. For the work force there was so little to eat that stealing food from the pig sty and eating it became a treat. One autumn day in 1960 Adhe was called with other prisoners to march to a new place. They walked for four days. Adhe thought about how she might jump off a bridge to kill herself because she feared that the new prison might be worse than the one she was leaving.[6]

The next prison camp in the valley of Gothang Gyalgo was another labor camp. The 10,000 prisoners there looked like skeletons to Adhe. Raw lead was being extracted from the tunnels by day, and more propaganda lessons were forced on them by night. In spite of the suffering Adhe always tried to pray to Dolma the protector and compassionate one.

Starvation was always a possibility at this camp. However, some brave local Tibetans came in secret at night and left food close to the fences at times when the prisoners would find it before the guards did. It was decided that Adhe and other prisoners who were still healthy enough would go to another labor camp to grow vegetables. Once there the prisoners working in the vegetable garden would secretly eat some of the vegetables and bring additional vegetables hidden in their clothing for the bedridden prisoners or those in solitary confinement in the camp.

In 1966 Adhe was transferred to another labor camp in Na Fan Dui. Here as before, there was typical mistreatment and propaganda lessons. Prisoners were forced to cover the holes of the inner walls of their camp place with plaster made from precious Tibetan religious scriptures. For Buddhist prisoners like Adhe, this use of scriptures was humiliating, but they had no choice. In 1967 doctors came into the camp and extracted great amounts of blood from the healthier prisoners. No one ever knew why this was done, but the blood loss weakened the prisoners for months after. There was no lessening of the work expected.

In 1974 when Adhe's sentence was officially over for a second time she was not released but kept under detention and eventually transferred to another prison at Mian Fen Chang. This prison had a "Thought Correction Center." In addition to the thought correction propaganda at night the days were spent making tiles which required squatting for most of the work day. Prisoners were not allowed to stand up. After a 12 to 14 hour work day it was difficult to move. When Adhe was sent to a logging operations camp she was very happy!

Getting to the logging operations camp required walking four hours to and from every day. The logging labor required quotas that were difficult to meet. Each person had to drag their logs on mats to the proper station up the mountain. The loads were too heavy for women Adhe's size. In Adhe's case a man named Rinchen secretly tried to help her meet her quota. Rinchen had been a model prisoner so he got away with helping. He was also allowed to go outside the camp. Each time he returned, he would bring back sad news of Tibet's increasing downfall. A once happy and harmonious culture was being devastated.

In January 1976 Chou Enlai, Prime Minister of the People's Republic of China, died. The concentration of power was now broken after his 40-year rule so the period of the Cultural Revolution was over. By mid-July of 1977 it looked like there would be changing policies toward Tibet which caused great hope among the Tibetan people.[7]

In March of 1979 some Tibetan prisoners were released, but Adhe was not among them. Meanwhile, the Chinese government agreed to a request by the Dalai Lama to allow an official fact-finding delegation from his exiled government to enter Tibet. The Chinese told the people to wash themselves, put on the new clothes the government gave them, smile and to carry the prayer wheels so the delegation team could see how happy they were.

Adhe had spent 21 years in detention camps. The Chinese allowed her and other people to line the streets when the first delegation appeared even though freedom of assembly had been banned for more than 20 years. The official delegation saw a staged Tibetan scene. No political or other prisoner could speak to any member of the delegation. After the delegation left the new clothes had to be returned and life went back to oppression.

However, now the Chinese authorities claimed a new age of goodwill and a change in policy. The authorities allowed Adhe to make a 15 day visit to her native Karze. They told her to present her official papers to the authorities in Karze. She left with some hope of seeing her city again. As she walked into her devastated city she was recognized by a few older neighbors. They told her that her mother died of starvation. Her son Chimi had been despondent after her arrest and drowned himself. Her sister had gone mad but was still alive. Her daughter Tashi was alive and well. A friend quickly agreed to arrange a brief meeting. When the time arrived for the meeting Tashi appeared and kept a shy distance. She was an attractive young woman now. As Adhe approached Tashi met her with an embrace, and their tears said all that had to be said.

Adhe took her official release papers from prison to the authorities to verify that she was in Karze with permission. After she left the authorities other women who had been part of the resistance came secretly to thank her for not giving their names to the Chinese. The women had secretly helped raise her children while Adhe was in prison. There were other nephews who found her and said they would like to go with her to the graveyard to give thank offerings to the spirit of the departed family members. This was a forbidden act, so they all agreed to go at night. In the graveyard Adhe told the deceased family spirits everything and hoped that they could still feel her love as she could feel theirs.

Adhe returned to prison and was finally released permanently the day after the Tibetan New Year in 1985. She was warned that she must never tell what really happened in the prison camps. If she told anything negative about the Chinese treatment she would be back in detention for the rest of her life. Adhe had already spent 27 years in Chinese prisons and intended to spend no more time there. Her daughter Tashi came to get her and take her home. Adhe still carried the home sewn mattress pad she slept on for so many years in prison. It was made from scraps of clothing from the many prisoners she had met, so she wanted to keep it.

The new Chinese administration gave the Tibetans a small degree of freedom as long as they did not speak badly about the Chinese authorities. Adhe felt that she must tell the Dalai Lama about the suffering of their people. He had been in India for years with the Tibetan Government in Exile. In spite of some small reforms the Chinese authorities still forbade people having a portrait of the Dalai Lama displayed in their homes or carried on their person.

Due to her brother's influence Adhe was able to make a pilgrimage to the holy city of Lhasa where the two oldest statues of the Buddha were located at the shrines of Jokhang and Ramoche. The life size statues represented the Buddha at ages eight and twelve, respectively. The statues were 1300 years old and among the most sacred objects of Tibet's religious heritage. Adhe's friend Rinchen traveled with her to be of assistance on the pilgrimage.

At Jokhang, Adhe was moved at the sight of so many pilgrims whose strong faith was still obvious in their eyes and on their faces. With them she turned the great Eight Pointed Wheel of Dharma and prayed for the protection of the Tibetan faith and its people. Then she entered the magnificent shrine and walked past the stone statues of the deities that guarded the four directions of the earth. The shrine, in spite of its beauty and sacred atmosphere, showed the ravages of the Cultural Revolution. Many of its former statues had been destroyed and the beautiful frescoes on its walls defaced. Many monks had been killed, beaten publicly or abused. Other monks remained in prison. The once breathtakingly beautiful courtyard had been turned into a pig sty. Many chapels were closed. Some of the most revered and beautiful statues had been cut in half, stripped of all gems and gold leaf and then thrown into a heap in an old storehouse outside Beijing.

Rinchen could not help but pray loudly for his Holiness to return and for Tibetans to regain freedom and independence. Others quickly joined the prayer. The sentiments made the caretakers nervous so they forced the people to move along quickly and not cause a disturbance. Adhe was joyful that so many Tibetans were still praying together for the return of the Dalai Lama and for the country to once again be free and its people happy.[8]

Rinchen and Adhe decided to go to India to visit the Dalai Lama. When they were at the western border of Tibet and ready to enter Nepal customs authorities searched them carefully and looked through their bags. Adhe told them she and Rinchen were going to Nepal to get her brother and bring him home to Tibet which pleased the authorities.

All the while Adhe was praying to the deities to protect them and give them safe passage all the way to India. She wondered if she and Rinchen and other pilgrims were leaving Tibet for the last time. Her brother Jughuma now lived in Nepal. He had been one of the official guards protecting the Dalai Lama when he escaped from Tibet in 1959.

At the time of Adhe's visit the Dalai Lama was 82 years old and living in a monastery in Dharamsala. He spent most of his time turning the large prayer wheel and praying for his own people and also for the world's people. He invoked the deities to help people stop the greed that was responsible for so much suffering in the world. Adhe and Rinchen finally got to Jughuma's house in Nepal. Jughuma gave them directions to get to a place where the Dalai Lama would soon be making an appearance among the people.

Adhe and Rinchen traveled to Varanasi to hear the Dalai Lama. He drew immense crowds from great distances. While it was moving to hear him speak she and Rinchen decided they had to visit him at his monastery and talk to him directly. Adhe continued to pray to the deities of Tibet to guide them. After hours of riding on buses and getting a variety of directions they finally found the road that led to the monastery of his Holiness the Dalai Lama. It took a few days before they could get a personal audience. Adhe had waited her entire life to see this holy man up close. When he appeared she was in awe and couldn't move. He smiled with great love and gestured her to come forward. She still couldn't move. He looked at her and smiled and said she should come closer.

She did, and when the greetings were over she proceeded to tell him about the fate of so many teachers in the monasteries of Tibet. She told him of the suffering of his people and of her own years in prison. When he took her hand and looked in her eyes he could see how much she was still suffering. Gently he told her that she should record her experiences so that the world would not forget. As she left his presence she felt that he was right and a new peace came over her. If she was meant to tell the world about Tibet, a way for her to do so would appear.

In 1989 the way appeared. She was invited to attend an international hearing concerning Tibet which was to be held in Bonn, Germany. Rinchen accompanied her. It was the initiative of a German couple that ultimately got Adhe to come and tell her people's story. The couple met her and Rinchen at the airport, provided hospitality and took her to the hearing. Adhe's testimony moved so many people that a group formed to encourage Germany to be a venue for justice and peace for Tibet. This could be a means for Germany making up for some of the destruction and horror of the Second World War. The German couple generously offered to provide permanent residence in the country for Adhe and Rinchen. However, the two decided they had to return to Nepal to take care of Jughuma. In spite of leaving Adhe and Rinchen felt such a bond of communion with the German couple that gave hope for a better future.

Adhe and Rinchen returned to Nepal where Adhe cared for Jughuma. She had time each day to spend long periods in prayer. As she climbed the hill to the temples with their medicinal trees and lovely settings her heart was overjoyed. She always had prayed to the deities for direction, and they seemed to give it to her. Now she waited to see what else would come.

In November of 1989 Adhe was invited to go to Copenhagen to address another support group for the Tibetans. She hoped the hearing would have the outcome of acknowledging His Holiness the Dalai Lama as the official representative of the government of Tibet in exile. Such a move might anger the Chinese, but the nation of Denmark did not mind. They made that choice and agreed to try to get other governments to join them in that diplomatic move. The Danish parliament and the people of Denmark could not have been more hospitable or more supportive of the cause. This made Adhe feel like the Dalai Lama's words to her were a direction for her life.

In 1989 Adhe moved permanently to Dharamsala. Her brother had a last request to be taken to the place where the Dalai Lama was going to make a visit. She took him to the grounds where there were more than 150,000 pilgrims. To see that many people together burning lamps and candles and saying prayers with such devotion to the Lord Buddha, the deities and his Holiness the Dalai Lama, was a moving event. To hear prayers for all humanity brought peace. Jughuma died soon after in peace.

Now in her later years, Adhe is a free citizen in India. She has written her story and told it to many audiences as part of a life's mission to help an oppressed people. In spite of all the suffering she experienced she still believes that there is nothing on earth more powerful than the truth and love of people. Her life story is not told to get sympathy for herself but rather to show that conflicts cannot be reconciled by force. The only way to resolve conflict is to work toward a day when hearts can join together in justice and peace.[9]

Adhe has learned through a long life that the world is a far bigger place than she had ever dreamed, and yet its inhabitants are somehow connected to each other. Sooner or later actions of love or destruction have an effect on others near and far. Adhe will spend the rest of her life trying to help Tibet know once again the peace and freedom derived from the Buddhist way. With many other Tibetans Adhe awaits a day when Tibet can be truly "home," and they can claim to be at home. Meanwhile, they remain sojourners in their own land.

NOTES

[1]   The website *www.en.wikipedia.org/wiki/Burma* has a very detailed history of Tibet with additional information about the geographic, political, economic and religious history.

[2]   Joy Blakeslee and Adhe Tapontsang, *The Voice that Remembers: One Woman's Historic Flight to Free Tibet* (Boston: Wisdom Publications, 1997). The summaries and quotations in this section are all from this work. It has been used with permission from Wisdom Publications, 199 Elm Street, Somerville, MA 02144, USA. Wisdompubs.org

[3]   18.

[4]   The summary is from 5-28.

[5]   The summary is from 35-73.

[6]   The summary is from 74-115.

[7]   The summary is from 117-85.

[8]   The summary is from 186-215.

[9]   The summary is from 216-42.

14

Sadako Ogata, Japan

Japanese civilization goes back to at least 10,000 bce. Clay vessels from this period are some of the oldest surviving examples of pottery in the world. The influences of China and Korea in the early centuries of the common era influenced Japanese culture until a strong central Japanese state emerged in the 8th century that was centered around an imperial court and Emperor. Japan's feudal era was characterized by the emergence the Samurai, a ruling class of warriors along with the shogun rulers who were appointed by the emperor.

During the 16th century traders and missionaries from Portugal reached Japan for the first time which initiated a period of active commercial and cultural exchange between Japan and the West. In 1854 Commodore Matthew Perry and the "Black Ships" of the United States Navy forced the opening of Japan to the outside world with the Convention of Kanagawa. The Boshin War of 1867-1868 led to the resignation of the shogunate which was followed by the Meiji Restoration which adopted some western political practices but still remained centered around the emperor. The early 20th century saw a brief period of "Taisho democracy" overshadowed by the rise of Japanese expansionism and militarization.

On December 7, 1941, Japan attacked the United States naval base in Pearl Harbor and declared war on the United States, the United Kingdom and the Netherlands which brought the United States into World War II. In 1945 the US dropped atomic bombs on Hiroshima and Nagasaki that destroyed millions of lives and resulted in devastating radiation effects on successive generations. Japan agreed to an unconditional surrender on August 15, 1945. The war left its destructive effects on Japan's industry and infrastructures.

In 1947 Japan adopted a new pacifist constitution emphasizing democratic practices and in 1956 was granted membership in the UN. Japan has become the second largest economy in the world. The power of the emperor is limited and defined by the constitution as "the symbol of the state and of the unity of the people." Power is held chiefly by the prime minister and other elected members of the diet. Sovereignty is vested in the Japanese people. Japan is the world's second-largest donor of official development assistance with 19% of its GNP in 2004. About 84% of Japanese people profess to be believers of both Shinto, the indigenous religion of Japan, and Buddhism. About 7% of the people profess Christianity. Healthcare services are provided by national and local governments. Payment for personal medical services is offered through a universal health care insurance system that provides relative equality of access. Patients are free to select physicians or facilities of their choice.[1]

The care and generosity of the Japanese people to others in need is embodied in the life of Sadako Ogata who was born in Tokyo in 1927. She graduated from the University of the Sacred Heart in Tokyo. She studied at Georgetown University and its Edmund A. Walsh School of Foreign Service in the US and earned a PhD from the University of California at Berkeley in 1963. She returned to Japan to teach international politics at Sophia University.

Sadako became well known as a scholar of diplomatic history and political science and a fine administrator. She was invited to be a member of the Japanese delegation to the United Nations General Assembly in 1968 which was her first direct participation had in the UN. Because her two children were still small she needed encouragement from her husband and parents to go to New York for the meeting. This marked the beginning of an involvement with the UN that would continue for over a decade.[2]

Within a year, Sadako was asked to be minister plenipotentiary at the Permanent Mission of Japan to the UN in New York. In 1979 she led the Japanese government's mission to plan and provide assistance to Cambodian refugees. Sadako had gained some experience of refugee issues while serving on the UNICEF executive board for several years, made field trips to Asia and had participated with some peacekeeping operations of the General Assembly. With her experience and dedication to suffering people Sadako was a ready choice to represent Japan on the UN Commission on Human Rights from 1982 to 1985. In this position, she saw firsthand some of the many horrors related to the violation of basic human rights.

The sudden resignation of Thorvald Stoltenberg, the High Commissioner for Refugees of the UN, left this post in need of a successor. The Japanese government asked Sadako if they might put her name in nomination for the job. Near Christmas 1990 the Secretary General of the UN phoned to say that he wanted to present her to the general assembly for election. She was elected and left for Geneva in late February 1991 in the midst of the Gulf War. She had to be briefed and then immediately start planning some action. Sadako spent a few weeks going through a host of internal briefings and learning about the multiple agencies and groups that would combine to respond to this crisis and future crises. The implications of her new job came on her quite suddenly when three major crises confronted her in the first four weeks she was in Geneva!

First, Kurdish refugees were fleeing by the thousands to seek safety in Turkey. Second, Ethiopia was experiencing the return movement of about 200,000 Ethiopians who had taken refuge in Somalia. In addition there were at least 450,000 Somalis who were also seeking refuge in Ethiopia to escape from the lack of security in their country. Third, thousands of Albanians were crossing the sea to get to Italy because they knew their own country would soon erupt in unrest again. Italy had more opportunity for a better future than their country could offer. In this same year after Chechnya declared its independence from Russia, an additional 250,000 refugees were on the move to neighboring Russian republics for safety. The High Commissioner for Refugees and her workers were the main responders to the multiple crises. Sadako urged the UN to exert pressure on nations to take part in humanitarian assistance to refugees. It was often discouraging to see the results or lack of results of direct aid as the genocide and ethnic cleansings continued. How were the people going to cope with the aftermath of mass atrocities? Sadako's commission tried to rebuild communities and initiated programs to assist former enemies to coexist once the period of atrocity and war was over. It was no easy task for there were two major obstacles.

First political concerns blocked the humanitarian response that could be made by compassionate nations. Everyone was aware that strategic interests held by major states affect what the response will be to a crisis. Political concerns can become an excuse for non-action.

Second providing ongoing assistance for peace making among former enemies was not part of the usual plan. A safe haven may be provided temporarily but how to give returning refugees some kind of security as they repatriated was not a priority. Training the former military combatants to be peacemakers needed much more attention! The genocide in Rwanda and the spread of fighting in the Great Lakes region of Africa were two obvious examples. In countries like Rwanda and Afghanistan governments may insist that they are in charge of the overall reconstruction of the nation. The UNHCR must then work with the government within its structure to provide services. Even though the government in Afghanistan assumed multiple responsibilities for shelter, water supply, education for all and fostered both health and sanitation programs, there remained a problem. The continuing power feud between the warlords and the violence among diverse ethnic groups was difficult to stop. Planning for the next generations to know peace requires multiple partnerships with the right range of organizations all cooperating. Sadako tried to get interfacing among political, military, humanitarian and developmental groups in strategic partnerships which was essential for a long term future of peace and reconciliation.[3]

Sadako Ogata's Farewell and a Briefing[4]

On December 20, 2000, Sadako looked back at what had been accomplished during her time as the High Commissioner and also at what still had to be done. After thanking her staff she identified present and future needs. Globalization would continue changing the way people moved across borders and why they moved. Some refugees were looking for safety. Others were looking for work and a better life. Others were being trafficked and were dying or being abused in the process. This human trafficking is not under the auspices of the UNHCR but cannot be ignored because of its human rights violations. Sadako wanted it to be someone's concern!

She felt the issues of asylum and migration needed to be kept separate by governments and met with different forms of assistance. Clarity is still needed on these two issues. There also remains a gap between emergency assistance and long-term developments for peaceful futures. These difficult challenges will be adequately addressed only by perseverance and creativity.

Staff and workers of the UNHCR need to remain free in their thinking and not constrained by bureaucracy. Academic life had taught Sadako that humans are always free to think beyond the bureaucratic. Her training and experience taught her that in a globalized world overly bureaucratic organizations will soon become irrelevant. Why?

Contact with real people and real situations opens up possibilities that can only be addressed by going beyond bureaucratic plans or solutions. Commission members cannot give up on a project just because it won't fit traditional schemes or bureaucracy. Her program for ethnic enemies,

"Imagine coexistence," did not emerge out of a bureaucratic solution but came from needs of real people for a long term peace. It was a new approach to help the UNHCR fulfill its core mission.

A challenge for many of the commission workers was the burden of so much suffering and death that many workers experienced while working with the refugees around the world. Nothing can compensate for the deaths of thousands of refugees who perish but also friends who die assisting refugees, in spite of the commission's best efforts to save all life. Many workers for the UNHCR leave the job because of this burden of suffering. Sadako urged her workers to look at the good they accomplished and work to change the systemic weaknesses.

In a final address to the UN Security Council Sadako noted two major areas that required immediate attention: peace operations and peace building.

Peace operations in changing environments of the world require more than simple humanitarian assistance. The Security Council needs to be vigilant in overseeing more than humanitarian assistance for refugees. They also need to oversee and plan for training security forces so that the humanitarian agencies and their workers, like the UNHCR, are not left alone to confront violent situations. Staff security, the security of refugees and the security of the host groups who are housing refugees remain of utmost importance. This means that a ready response unit of trained local or international security forces, trained police and trained military personnel need to be put into place quickly for the security of all concerned.

Clearly this has not been part of the planning in many troubled areas of the world. Supporting the regional police and military units with logistics and communication people and with liaison officers to work with the community is essential. Securing areas in and around refugee sites is another necessity for effective peacekeeping. A humanitarian department today must include members who know how to work effectively with agencies that have trained peace operations people. Humanitarian action and peace operation action need to work side by side. For the UN there is a challenge to keep refining the operational nature of these relationships and how each group can support the other.

This may mean expanding peacekeeping beyond a country's borders in spite of the political hurdles this would cause. Today the insecurity spilling across borders from countries in conflict affects not only the refugees but the countries that host them. There are many nations who could benefit from this expansion of peacekeeping beyond borders.

A second and related point is that peace building needs much more attention and action than is presently the case. During the decade that Sadako was High Commissioner she and the UNHCR were criticized for going beyond their actual humanitarian mission as defined by the bureaucratic UN. The bureaucracy was not pleased with creative peace building projects like the "Imagine Coexistence" project which trained local people to look to a future together in peace. This meant they had to start building relationships in spite of the past sufferings they had both inflicted and endured. This mode of reconciliation has to be addressed if there is to be a lasting peace, and such peace building involves more UN agencies than the UNHCR.

In this context there is a special need for the former military personnel to be assisted in the process of reintegration into the community after they put down weapons of war. UNHCR has witnessed that disarmed soldiers will go back to their lucrative military activities if they are not given real opportunities for a future. Peace is fragile when former fighters or soldiers are not consciously brought into the peace process. Security and peace partnerships must be built as part of a better future. The Security Council needs to assume this leadership in working with and supporting the High Commissioner of UNHCR. Uprooted people in the world continue to work bravely for a future of peace in dangerous areas. The Security Council must assist that hope and work to build strong cooperative processes.

A Spirituality of Compassion and Corporate Hopes for Peace[5]

Now that Sadako Ogata has completed her term as UNHCR she is President of Japan International Cooperative Agency which oversees plans and actions for Japanese assistance to developing countries. The company has offices in 54 countries. In spite of being in her early eighties Mrs. Ogata remains an active president who visits the programs and people involved in many developing countries. At the time of this writing she is in some country overseeing projects on the average of one week of every month.

In spite of her busy itinerary on June 3, 2007 she was willing to take time out of a harrowing schedule to share tea and some thoughts about her life and work. My questions were basic but her responses were typically clear and reflective.

First I asked how she developed such a universal sense of authentic compassion and care for people around the world especially refugee victims of war. She was quick to name her father's influence. He always wanted to discuss world situations and needs. "Like many young people growing up I pretended I was not really interested in reading all the material he had about people around the world. Looking back now I can tell that his influence on my outlook was very strong. He set strong foundations and interests that did in time influence my own educational choices. I chose international politics as my field and became a scholar of diplomatic history and political science. In time that led to my being Dean of the Department of Foreign Studies at Sophia University."

Having read some brief biographies of Mrs. Ogata, I then asked her if she ever consciously experienced her life as some call or vocation from God. She smiled and said, "No." Wishing to probe that a bit further, I asked her if there was any sense of her life being within that great mystery-with its multiple interpretations—of "God's providence."

She smiled politely and then said, "Are you asking if I see my life within some great plan? No. I see all of life as simply a matter of making choices and each choice leads to new horizons that other choices wouldn't. I think my life, like every life, is not in any great plan but simply things happen and we are there and we have to make decisions." She went on to explain a few examples of that perspective.

"In 1956, while I was happily engaged in academic life, I was chosen to be a female member of the Japanese Delegation to the United Nations. Other women and movements had paved the way for a woman to be part of this group. Do you know how I got picked? Pure coincidence. The woman who was supposed to go to the General Assembly couldn't do it. After some looking around, those in charge asked me. So I went. It was a decision and I made it."

Then she elaborated. "Sometimes a combination of coincidences requires choices. My second child was only one year old and I had never considered leaving Japan for any length of time after I finished graduate school in the United States. So this situation presented itself. Most of life is like that. Situations present themselves and you must choose. I received a great bit of help from my parents and husband who were very supportive of me taking the position, even though it meant living in the United States in New York.

Once again, I didn't take time to reflect on this as some piece of God's call or God's will. I am a woman of action. I saw that I could act to make the world a better place with the power of this position. So, a variety of circumstances occurred and I took the job because I felt I must do that to help the neediest people, the refugees."

Our conversation then proceeded to the compassion she has shown to so many thousands of people, victims of war, of violence, of economic disasters.

Mrs. Ogata was typically quick to shift the compliment to other people who influenced her life so she eventually became a woman of compassion and strength. "I went to Sacred Heart School in Tokyo. I was very well educated there but I also was moved especially by one of my teachers with whom I stayed in contact until she died at 96 years of age. That sister is responsible for my ability to write English correctly! When that sister was an elderly nun, she went with other sisters to establish a school in a very poor area of China. When people like that touch your life, you cannot but be helped to be a better person."

I asked her about the many experiences as United Nations High Commissioner for Refugees which her book details. I referred explicitly to her final address to her staff at the UN after years of seeing terrible situations of suffering. She had told the staff to remember to have hope for the good that is being done in spite of the obvious setbacks that happen everywhere due to misused power and greed that cause oppressive suffering.

"As United Nations High Commissioner for Refugees, I of course saw terrible suffering but also I saw the incredible strength of the human spirit in its desire for life, even in the midst of unimaginable poverty and loss. That position opened my eyes and heart in new ways to what it means for us to truly be brothers and sisters to each other and to all people. It is a great challenge in our time, this being brothers and sisters to all people in need."

Then Mrs. Ogata directed me to look at a picture hanging in the president's office where we were meeting. The picture was a photo taken by a United Nations photographer that showed refugees from Bosnia-Herzegovina trying to touch Sadako as she came into the crowded mass of humanity with open arms. The camp was a mass of packed close tents.

"Notice how the people are so hopeful that somehow through me their world will be a small bit better. I was not an answer to their suffering. However the world was an answer when some nations generously sent tents and food and water for these thousands of refugees who had seen so much death. Our commission consistently begged the United Nations for more help for these people in misery, as we did for the people of Rwanda and other nations in need. We did what we could, given the limits of national responses. These wonderful people you see on this picture were so grateful for the pittance. Yet, only ten weeks after that picture was taken, over half of these people were slaughtered by those who think their personal violence gives them power. Similar patterns happened too often in my years as High Commissioner. People's eyes meet yours with hope and then they are no more. It is a terrible thing to experience over and over again."

There was a silence then as it seemed other memories were being renewed. Then we returned to the table. After a few moments I asked her about the difficulty of carrying the burden of others' suffering and how she has managed to keep hope in the midst of it.

"I simply act to do the best I can as circumstances present themselves. This job I have now presented itself when my job at the United Nations ended. So as a person of action, I looked at its possibilities and took it. Our company assists nations to be self-developing and uses the strength of people to create their own better future. We do what we can—in varieties of circumstances—to work for a long term future where life will be better for the children of these people we are assisting. That we are doing some good gives me hope in spite of the enormous and sometimes overwhelming need in our world for human dignity, justice and peace. I stay hopeful because I am doing the little I can to make possible something that would not have happened without our assistance. Anytime we can alleviate some degree of suffering that brings hope.

I am not sure how long I will be at this job since my term as president ends in a year. Whether I am asked to take another term or not, I will continue to do what I always have done. I will make choices.

Next month, I will be at a conference in Nuremberg that deals with making justice and reconciliation happen. It is a coincidence that I am going. Actually, what happened was that I was strolling through a bookstore in Berkeley, California, my former university. I picked up a book by a woman scholar on making justice and reconciliation. I eventually called the professor who wrote it and we discussed global issues. The next thing I knew, I was invited to this conference in Nuremberg. So again, it is making some choice and things happen."

As my appointment time was drawing to a close I asked Mrs. Ogata if she considered herself a "holy woman or a saint." Mrs. Ogata is a Roman Catholic so I knew the word "saint" would hold some meaning. She burst out laughing and said, "Oh I am surely no saint, as my staff would quickly tell you." I looked at the staff in the room with us and caught their eyes briefly, in spite of Japanese politeness. They smiled and mouthed, "holy woman." She frowned at them.

A final question I wanted to ask was the usual thing a professor might ask a woman of influence. Do you have any particular advice for young people who share a concern for our world and want to be peacemakers? She had no hesitation!

"Yes, I do. I would say to forget all those self-help books that make it seem like you can make out a plan to be a better person. Don't be a slave to some plan for correcting yourself and all that is wrong. Wake up to what life offers you every day and make conscious choices to do what benefits people.

Imagination is essential today when bureaucracies are becoming increasingly irrelevant. Think and act in creative ways that bring about a better future for everyone, even if bureaucracy is an obstacle. Do NOT be afraid of mistakes because we all make them and learn from them.

When I attempted to get people to "Imagine Coexistence" after wars and suffering, there was no model other than their imagination constructing what a future of peace would look like and then decide how to get there. There will be no reconciliation among peoples without justice and amnesty. This is a task for every one of us wherever we are and whatever we do. Don't be afraid of those with power because you too have power to change the world for the better. As we all use that power, the world will be a better place and our lives will have been lived meaningfully."

She was willing to continue out of Japanese politeness, but I knew our time was over so I stood and bowed politely. As we walked together to the door of her office Mrs. Ogata asked me if I thought her book about the UNHCR experience should have been more personal which is not her preference. I responded that I understood the books left by High Commissioners for the UN were to be more factual than interpretive. However, I would love to have her write her experiences as she remembers them. The memoir would be a gift to all who are concerned for human rights and the dignity of all people. She smiled and said she would like to do such memoirs about all her brothers and sisters in so many parts of the world. However, now she does not have time!

While our interview was officially over the wisdom of Mrs. Ogata is definitely not over yet. She has many more paths to create and plans that will facilitate the future which brings greater liberty and justice to all who suffer.

NOTES

[1]

[2] The reflections in this section are taken from Sadako Ogata's account, *The Turbulent Decade: Confronting the Refugee Crises of the 1990's* (NY: W.W. Norton and Co., 2005). This will be cited in future references as *Decade*.

[3] *Decade*. These reflections are a summary of the conclusions of Sadako Ogata about the UNHCR's work on 317-343. A more detailed analysis and

description of the challenges of the various countries named in this section comprise the majority of the book's content.

4   *Decade.* The full address can be found on 344-49 and additional reiteration to the Security Council which includes the addition of training and integrating former military units into a peace situation, 351-361.

5   This section is based upon a personal interview with Mrs. Sadako Ogata at her Tokyo Office of Japan International Cooperation Agency (JICA) in June, 2007. She graciously gave her permission to include the interview and my interpretations of it in this book.

15

Benedita da Silva, Brazil

The first indigenous people of Brazil arrived over 8,000 years ago. By the end of the 15th century all of Brazil was inhabited by semi-nomadic tribes who knew how to subsist on a combination of fishing, hunting and gathering. The Portuguese established a permanent colony in Brazil in 1532. The Dutch established themselves in Brazil by the 1630s but were driven out by the Portuguese in 1654. From the 16th to the 18th centuries Brazil was basically a colony of Portugal and was exploited for its brazilwood, sugarcane and rich gold supply.

During these centuries of exploitation many of the indigenous peoples were exterminated, pushed out of the way or somewhat assimilated into the conquering colonizers. Large numbers of African slaves were brought to Brazil for labor and in time would be known as the Afro Brazilians. In 1822 Brazil declared its independence from Portugal and became a constitutional monarchy after a small-scale Brazilian War of Independence which ended in 1825.

A military coup in 1889 established a new form of government for the people so the country has been nominally a democratic republic ever since except for three periods of overt dictatorship. Today Brazil is South America's largest economy, the world's ninth largest economy and the world's fifth most populous nation. In 1994 Fernando Henrique Cardoso launched a new currency backed by sound economic policies. In 2003 a former union leader Luiz Inácio Lula da Silva was elected due to his promise to put the country back on a path of economic development. Lula had some success in forging an assertive Brazilian foreign policy while grappling with the issues of inequality, public debt, comparatively high taxes and the attraction of foreign investment at home. Lula's government bettered the situation of the Brazilians who are the black minority.[1]

As in other places the darker the skin color of people in Brazil the less value that person has. In Brazil there remains a diversity of color which reflects the ethnic backgrounds. Descendants of Portuguese Africans have darker skin tones; descendants of indigenous Indian Africans have lighter skin tones; descendants of the Europeans who intermarried with both indigenous people and descendants of African slaves have lighter skin. Descendants of Europeans who married other Europeans have white skin. AfroBrazilian people are at the bottom of the hierarchy of color with AfroBrazilian women being the lowest rung of the ladder. Racism or a "whitening policy" is based on shades of skin color with the Afro or black Brazilians being treated more stringently in the legal and penal systems.[2]

Benedita da Silva is an Afro-Brazilian who experienced the racism others of her ethnic group experienced. Her work has helped to raise awareness of the need for equity and justice to the African Brazilian population and especially for African Brazilian women. Today Brazil has the highest number of African descent people living outside Africa—slightly less than the population of Nigeria. The exploitation of the colonizers that began with the Indian or indigenous population continues today.

Benedita da Silva was elected to a city council in 1982 and remained true to her campaign promises against many obstacles. In 1988 she was elected a federal deputy as a representative of the workers party in the federal congress. She was one of nine Afro Brazilians elected to the 599 roster of deputies and became one of six women senators in the federal congress.

Benedita remains an active advocate of education as a source of power for all. She has been consistent in advocacy for equality, especially equality and dignity for the most oppressed and poor people of the society.[3] Her life story details the living idealism that began in her early surroundings and continued to evolve as she became a world advocate for justice, peace and equality for all people.

An Afro-Brazilian Woman's Story of Politics and Love[4]

Benedita remembers her mother and father working hard but they were still treated so badly in their surroundings that her mother took all twelve children to Rio de Janeiro. Here Benedita's mother took in washing and all the children worked at some job. There were fifteen children but seven died from diseases left untreated because the family was poor.

Benedita's mother always wanted Benedita to be a teacher and encouraged her to go to school and stay in school. Benedita was the only person in the family who learned how to read and write. She could only go to elementary school due to the need to work, but it was sufficient for her to acquire a lifelong desire to learn. She remembers going to school wearing only one outfit every day and some secondhand shoes that were too small. She was sensitive to the laughter of the other children at her clunky shoes and one outfit, even though her mother washed the outfit daily so she would always look clean.

By age seven Benedita was already working on the streets shining shoes, selling candy, and working in the markets. She learned early that market vendors didn't want to hire girls if they could get boys. Benedita insisted she could work as hard as the boys and she did.

She remembers rising at 5am, gathering water from the well for the household and then going to work in the market from 6:30 am until noon. She went to school for the afternoon hours. After school she would collect bundles of clothes and bring them home for her mother to wash. In the evening she'd gather wood and then finally get time to study. She never had much time to play, but when she did the street children like herself made up games,

Benedita remembers how crowded their little home space was. All the children slept in one room; this included one older boy that her mother took in from the streets. At night he found it easy to rape Benedita and her cousin in the crowded arrangements. Benedita remembers that she was only seven when he first raped her. As a child she was ashamed to tell her mother. The boy realized this and continued to rape her for years.

In addition to her chores Benedita's mother cleaned houses when she could find the time. Benedita's mother was a trusting woman who believed people who told her they would pay her once they had a chance to get to the bank. Many never paid her so she took some pieces of bread or small things for soup so her children would not go hungry.

Benedita was as skilled as her mother. She knew how to be a productive domestic worker. She became a successful street vendor. She sold cosmetics. She worked in a leather belt factory, as a janitor in the school nearby and finally got a full time job in the Department of Transportation. She decided to study at home and take the high school equivalency exam.

Benedita was 40 years old when she got her high school diploma in 1980. She went on to obtain a degree in social work. Her husband was a good husband when he wasn't drinking and he encouraged her study. However, he died from a stroke at 45 years of age. After his death Benedita started to get more involved with neighborhood associations.

One of the founders of the neighborhood federation was Bola who was both a Christian and a communist. He worked with the Christian-based communities in the slums. Benedita and he had been friends for many years as they worked for the neighborhood association. In the 1980s a new political party was formed called the workers party. This party encouraged Benedita to run for office. She agreed and won by a vast majority.

On January 26, 1983, Bola and Benedita were married in a Lutheran Church. They were great companions to each other. On Christmas eve in the middle of remodeling their house they decided they should spend the holiday apart from each other. Their house was uninhabitable due to the immense remodeling project. So each went to relatives and decided they would meet on Christmas evening. Bola had a heart attack and died on Christmas Day. The death was devastating for Benedita.

Benedita decided to continue her political work even though it was a difficult time. The pain made her decide she would never marry again. However, when she left Brazil for a conference in Philadelphia one of her fellow workers Pitenga told her not to fall in love with anyone because when she returned he was going to marry her. They decided to get married in a lovely church ceremony. Benedita knew nothing but happiness.

> It's not because of the material things I've gained, but because I am loved and surrounded by such beautiful people. God always sent me an angel in my most difficult moments. And when you're surrounded by love it's a lot easier to confront the harsh realities of life.[5]

Benedita was especially influenced by the goodness of her mother who was a priestess in the Umbanda religion, which was a mix of ancient Brazilian religions with its arisha god who had many rules that the priestess interpreted. Many Afro-Brazilian religions are a mix of ancient Catholic practices and African based religious beliefs that have developed in many ways once they were inculturated within the Brazilian population. Benedita helped her mother perform the proper ceremonies in the house, and it was her mother's hope that Benedita would be the priestess after her. Why didn't Benedita follow in her mother's footsteps?

> I didn't because I ended up choosing another religion. But later in life I realized that my mother's spirituality greatly influenced my political work. I saw my mother helping people all the time

because in addition to being a priestess she was a midwife. She made food for the mothers and gave clothes to the newborns . . . The ceremonies in our house would go on and on some time until four in the morning. The first part of the ceremony was preaching and the second part was dancing, singing, and drumming. I used to help my sister sell pastries during the break in the middle . . . like any other religion Umbanda has its dogmas. Every arusha god has its rules, and as a young girl I would go crazy when my mother wouldn't allow me to do things because it went against the rules.[6]

Benedita recalls that she sometimes broke the expectations about the rules set up by the arisha god. Then she would be punished by her mother. In time, she realized some rules ought to be broken. When she was 18, she began to do community work and met other activists who were Catholics and she shared their vision about rules and goodness.

All the people I worked with were members of the progressive wing of the Catholic Church. We worked in small groups . . . Christian-based communities where people would come together to talk about the problems they faced in their everyday lives and how they could take action to solve them. These groups are part of the movement based on liberation theology which preached that the church should work with the poor to better their lives. After working with them for a few years I decided to join the Catholic Church.

Liberation theology is very different from the mainstream Catholic Church which cooperated for many centuries with a system that repressed blacks, indigenous people, and women. The church hierarchy worked hand in glove with the state especially during the military dictatorship when it was complicit with the government's gross violation of human rights . . . Liberation theology, on the other hand, defends the rights of men and women to seek happiness here on earth. It defends the right to have a piece of land to grow food and the right to a livable wage. Liberation theology is about raising people's consciousness and fighting against oppression.[7]

Benedita respected members of this more liberal wing of the Catholic Church in Brazil especially Leonardo Boff who had been consistent in challenging the status quo which made the poor poorer and the rich richer. She admired his consistency and shared his struggles to empower the poor. She was saddened when a more conservative church reprimanded him.

> With its emphasis on empowerment of the poor and social justice liberation theology fits well with my principles as a Christian and as a politician. I continue to work with the Christian-based communities because they've made a great contribution to community organizing in Brazil . . . [8]

There were many challenges that Bendita faced in her early twenties. She decided that the Assembly of God church, a branch of the evangelical Protestant church, might help her find what she needed. At this time in her life that particular community was what she needed to be introspective and move toward inner peace and tranquility. Given the social surroundings and her high hopes there was much that was out of her control. The guidance offered by this church helped her to cope with her life and to deepen faith.

> People can find this faith in any religion. Some find it in Umbanda or other Afro Brazilian religions . . . In my case it was the Evangelical Church that fulfilled my deep spiritual need. But the Evangelical Church did not fulfill my political and social needs, my desire to work with the community. It wasn't involved in these kinds of activities, so despite my conversion, I continued my social work with the Christian-based communities. [9]

People who knew Benedita wondered how she could be a member of the Assembly of God church and still be so active in politics. She simply reflected that while the evangelical church has its very conservative wing there are a few like her who think more progressively. The more conservative wing has also often been aligned with conservative and repressive governments. These people discourage church members from getting involved in politics since the focus is on the individual instead of the community.

Benedita reflects that these believers are only concerned about life after death. Her response? "Fine, it's okay to contemplate life after death, but let's not forget about life after birth."[10].

She is clear in making distinctions about what some believe and the necessity not to impose their beliefs on others of different religions. In any religion there are certain beliefs and practices to guide the people, but these are not for all people, especially those who may choose to live in a different way. In the context of Afro-Brazilian religion Benedita wonders if the ban on dancing was in origin the evangelical church's way to discriminate against Afro Brazilian cultural traditions.

Benedita has not felt her own positions on social issues compromised by what some members of her church may believe. Some habits had to be learned so she could be in conformity with the religious teaching. However, her political independence remains regardless of what others think. She is very clear that she would never use or exploit her faith to gain political support or win an election.

Benedita's life changed when she and Bola decided to marry. Bola did not want to belong to the Assembly of God. So Benedita had to separate from that religious family because members could only marry other members. Benedita contacted a pastor friend in a progressive wing of the Pentecostal church who married Benedita and Bola in his church.

> No matter what church I belong to I get my strength and religious conviction from the Bible. The Old Testament speaks of a God who fought for the oppressed and against slavery. It speaks of a God who values human beings and condemns all attempts to turn them into objects of exploitation and domination. Political issues I defend like agrarian reform have religious significance to me. God created the earth and never gave land titles to anyone. Turning the land to private property goes against the biblical concept that we all have the right to share God's bounty. The Bible also teaches us that women should be respected. Jesus defended prostitutes against that hypocritical society where they were stoned to death. Could it be that the prostitutes had sex by themselves? Or wasn't it the supposedly upright family man—the ones who are most judgmental and the very ones who created the laws condemning prostitutes—who would seek them out on the sly?[11]

For Benedita laws can only be enforced if they are respected by the people. Laws should further equality and justice and guarantee citizens their rights. They shouldn't be used to repress those who have the least. For these sentiments Benedita feels she is grounded in the Bible's approach to justice for all. To those who say she quotes the Bible too much she responds that the Bible contains a history of civilization with structures of inequality and movements toward compassionate equality that we can always learn from.

> In the Senate I deal with people who represent the interests of the big landowners. I deal with landowners who say they're Christian, but when poor peasants occupy their land to grow food for their families they use violence against them. I try to understand why these men think they need so much land. I remember a story from the Bible talks about a man who accumulated a lot of land filled the silos with food and said, "Now I can fill my soul." God answered, "You crazy fool. Tonight I will come for your soul and all your possessions will do you no good." It's true. Accumulating possessions will not make you a better person or feed your soul. We're all going to die one day, so instead of hoarding why not spend your life helping people live with dignity in a world where we all have food and a roof over our heads?[12]

The workers party works alongside more progressive members of the Catholic Church. By creating Christian-based communities and getting involved in projects to help the poor the Church and the Party can work together to have a greater impact. Like the people running Christian base communities Benedita identifies with the plight of the poorest people, lives among them and works with them to change their poor surroundings into surroundings that support a better quality of life. This includes having running water, electricity and food.

Benedita has some perceptions on divorce that are not aligned with her church but she thinks she has a better understanding from the side of poor Brazilian women. Wealthier women when they are divorced may have access to some of their former husband's assets. Poor women get nothing through divorce and remain responsible for the children. Prostitution is one way to make enough money to feed the children. There is a need for such women to claim rights from the government as well as from their husbands.

> Brazil is a country of cruel inequalities where the luxury and privilege of a small minority are sustained by the misery of the majority. The unjust social structure has its roots in laws and institutions that promote inequalities and make victims out of millions of people who don't have the basics to live a dignified

life . . . We Christians—men and women—can't isolate ourselves from social injustices and take comfort in false speeches to try to hide those injustices. We must listen to our God, a God who cures the sick, who feeds the hungry, frees the oppressed, takes care of the children and unmasks the hypocrites. This is a God who tells us to break with institutions that promote injustice.[13]

Many children still suffer and die of diseases that might be cured if the people lived elsewhere and had money to get the medicines. The mission of the Church must be to look at all these situations and make some choices to better them. Theology can choose to just have its ideas without action or it can become a liberation theology whose theories and actions may change the world's misery into a better quality of life.

For Benedita it is the socially active type of church that is the true church. The mission of Jesus was a healing and transforming one. The mission of the Christian Church is the same. Religion is not meant to be an opiate of the masses. It is meant to call people to embrace and act out the mission of Christ.

The Christian church must be a catalyst for social justice and equality of all peoples. Instead of focusing only on an afterlife and accepting the suffering of this life a church's mission is to make this life closer to the justice, equality and compassion to be known in a next life. "It is this kind of sensitive, engaged and loving church that has captured my heart."[14] Benedita's vision for justice grounds a spirituality that calls her to continue the struggle. She urges others to join her in the challenge.

In the 1960s people dreamed the impossible . . . People the world over were fighting for freedom. The order of the day was to break down barriers, to challenge prejudices, to give a voice to the voiceless, the forgotten, the oppressed . . . Somehow we have to be able to dream again.

I want to see more working people and poor people in power . . . I want to see respect for children's rights, a better distribution of wealth and jobs for all. I want to see the business community take pride in building a more equitable economic system. I want to see a society that does not separate rich and poor, black and white, men and women.

Does the society I envision already exist anywhere in the world? Not really. But that's all the more reason to keep on dreaming . . . No matter our race, nationality, religion, we are brothers and sisters if we are united by the same longing for justice.

But to transform those dreams into reality we all need to recognize our responsibility to take action. The action can take a thousand different forms—from finding housing for the homeless to stopping domestic violence to advocating for global disarmament.

I know in my own work how easy it is to feel overwhelmed by the vastness of the problems, to feel completely insignificant and defeated. It's precisely in those moments of self doubt that we have to pull ourselves up and find our inner strength . . . In my lifetime I have had the privilege of meeting thousands of inspiring women from around the world . . . These opportunities have allowed me to see the interconnectedness and the global dimensions of our work. They have given me a tremendous sense of pride to be part of this movement—a movement that values the sanctity of human life more than material possessions and places human need over human greed. I hope that each one of you feels somehow connected to this life affirming struggle.[15]

NOTES

[1] *www.wikipedia.com/wikiBrazil* This has been checked with other sources for accuracy.

[2] *Race in Contemporary Brazil*, ed. Rebecca Reichmann (University Park, PA: Pennsylvania State Univ. Press, 1998). The entire text provides chapters of examples of racism.

[3] The *Dollars and Sense* Newsletter of May 1, 1998 has the interview: "The challenges to the Brazilian left: a conversation with Benedita da Silva (interview)," and the full interview is also on www.wikipedia.org/wiki/Benedita_da_Silva.

4   This is taken from Benedita da Silva's *Benedita da Silva: An Afro Brazilian Woman's Story of Politics and Love*, as told to Medea Benjamin and Maisa Mendonca (Oakland, CA: The Institute for Food and Development Policy, 1997). Further references to this work will be cited as *Benedita*.

5   *Benedita,* 30. Summary is from 3-30.

6   *Benedita,* 86

7   *Benedita,* 87-88.

8   *Benedita,* 88.

9   *Benedita,* 89.

10   *Benedita,* 90.

11   *Benedita,* 91-92.

12   *Benedita,* 92-93.

13   *Benedita,* 99.

14   *Benedita,* 99.

15   *Benedita,* 200-01.

16

Unita Blackwell, Mississippi

Unita Blackwell was born in 1933 in Lula, Mississippi. She was the daughter of Mississippi sharecroppers who worked on a cotton plantation. Her life experiences range from plantation work to civil rights activism, to political office, to national and international actions to alleviate causes of poverty, oppression and violence. As she reflects on her long journey to freedom within herself and then as an advocate for all people she attributes any and all glory to God's use of her as an instrument of peace.

Reflections[1]

Some phrases Unita remembers from her childhood were phrases children of color picked up from the adults. The phrases were directed at her and reflected racism within her own colored community. Other children laughed at her as they chanted that if you were white, it was all right, if you were brown, you could stick around, but if you were black, you had to stand back. Her mother countered the ridicule by assuring Unita that the darker the berry the sweeter the juice.

Unita did very well all through grammar school but couldn't go to high school because it was five miles away. Since she grew up in the 1930s black children were still walking both ways to school and ten miles a day was too much to walk if chores were to get done as well as studying as well as hours in school. So she went to work, eventually married Jeremiah Blackwell, and they had a son named Jerry who was the joy of their life.

One winter when Jeremiah was working on the river Unita started hemorrhaging and was taken to the hospital. She remembers her mother saying that Unita was dead. Unita recalls that she could still hear that distant voice.

> I was transported deeper and deeper into this glorious light filled space. It was like a shekinah glory—a spectacular light that is the visible presence of God. I don't know any words strong enough to describe the feelings of tranquillity and peace and joy I experienced . . . The voice said, "Not yet. You have work to do".[2]

Unita woke up and the nurse taking care of her was shocked. The doctor came rushing in for he had already pronounced her dead! Unita never forgot the voice's message that she had work to do! Whenever her life was challenging Unita remained inspired by those words.

Civil rights activists had been coming to Mississippi since 1961. Unita and others called them *the freedom riders* because they came on buses. The people of the place paid little attention to the freedom riders and their efforts because they were too busy working to survive. In Mayersville where Unita and her family lived an 80-year-old former school teacher was having meetings with the Freedom Riders and the NAACP leaders in his house. Most other people were afraid to get too close to NAACP actions for fear the KKK would find out.

Unita eventually became aware that only 3% of black voters were registered in 1963 when her husband Jeremiah started to become more friendly with the school teacher and the causes. Events happened quickly. In 1962 James Meredith needed protection to go to "Ole Miss." Two students were killed protecting him. In 1963 the Jackson NAACP director, Medgar Evers, was murdered in front of his wife and children. The white gunman was set free. In 1964 the resurgence of the KKK caused fear among many people. They could blatantly kill civil rights workers and never come to trial. Bodies would not be found until weeks or months later. Unita decided she had to find out what the issues were that drew these workers to her state of Mississippi. Friends told Unita that she should not get mixed up with the Freedom Riders because she would be killed.

Unita got mixed up with freedom riders when they spoke at her church one Sunday. Freedom riders from Brooklyn and Virginia spoke to the people about registering to vote. The Freedom Riders were going to spend the summer in Mississippi to help register black voters since voting was one way to get better schools for their children. Voting was a peaceful way to get other things they were now being deprived of. The native population listened politely but were well aware that they would lose their jobs if they ever registered to vote to change things!

> I knew we'd be put out of work . . . I had told the Sunday school children, 'God helps those that help themselves.' I figured the time had come to put those words into practice myself . . . Jeremiah got up and I got up. I've been standing up ever since.[3]

That summer the student non-violent coordinating committee also sent representatives to Mississippi to assist the freedom riders in registering voters. Unita felt that the civil rights movement was at least part of the work the voice intended her to do. In spite of the dangers involved with this work Unita was part of grass roots leadership to keep the movement going when the freedom riders left to go back to school.

Unita went to classes and was thrilled at learning about the heritage of black Americans. She was proud to be one, and her pride increased when she met Fannie Lou Hamer and listened to her stories of being beaten in jail. Fannie Lou convinced Unita that she must work for change but never out of hatred or revenge. Anger had to be transformed into energy to make things change for the better. The two women remained friends for the rest of their lives.

Unita and Fannie Lou went to Atlanta to be trained as organizers. After their training both women offered their houses for freedom meetings and also for places for civil rights workers to stay on their visits. In Mississippi the grass roots organizers were primarily women. Black men had the titles as they did in the churches, but the workers were the women.

> We probably got away with more because white people didn't see black women as being as much of a threat . . . Black women had always kept our churches and families going, even though we weren't preachers, or deacons or head of the house . . . It was a freeing experience for us to get out in front of our own people and be acknowledged by men and women as leaders.[4]

The churches on plantations owned by white people were not open to these organizers. Many black preachers told the women that they should stop the organizing work and wait for the Lord to take charge of things. The women responded that the Lord was taking charge of things through them. Large meetings were held in as much secret as was possible. Unita knew people were very afraid and had a sense of desperation after all they had seen and endured. Yet she could inspire the people with hope.

> God has never forced anything on anybody, but you have to be willing to do something. If you make one step God will make two or three steps, but you've got to make the first one. God helps those that help themselves.[5]

Since music was such a part of the prayer of the people the meetings had lots of songs that were a mix of church and freedom songs. Much was taken away, but never the music that was part of the soul of the people. As people sang the freedom songs their hearts joined in hope for a better future in spite of the suffering it would take to get there. The old spirituals "We Shall Overcome" and "No More Auction Block for Me" were some of our favorites. Songs drew us together, reminding us of our fear and pain while also strengthening us to face it together."[6]

We did a lot of praying at those mass meetings. We prayed for guidance, for protection, for strength. "Lord binds us together so close one won't fall without the other . . . It's my prayer for all of us, black and white and red and yellow, in this nation and throughout the world. We all do have to stick together and hold one another up . . . You need the strength that comes from togetherness."[7]

In the summer of 1964 murders of civil rights workers, black and white, continued with few of the murderers ever being brought to justice. Often Unita would wind up caring for young white civil rights workers who had been beaten by other white men in Mayersville who resented their work. The white civil rights workers were not always aware that in Mississippi white and black people did not ride in the car together. When these integrated cars stopped for a light all the workers in the integrated cars were dragged out and beaten.

Those who joined in civil rights marches like the one from Selma to Montgomery were sometimes assassinated on the way back home. Some of the white storekeepers who sold food to the young civil rights workers might put arsenic in the food so they would all get sick or die. Unita remembers how difficult it was to sleep at night as they registered voters. "The Klan folks would come through and throw Molotov cocktails in my yard . . . I had crosses burned in my yard many times by the KKK . . . the incidents were not isolated incidents."[8]

Bullets were also fired through her house, but although they had been told to call the FBI when things like that happened there were so many incidents that a phone call did no good. Unita remembers one FBI man telling her to get a large gunny sack and preserve the burning cross for evidence and bullet casings as well. This advice let her know that the FBI man to whom she was speaking had no idea how terrifying life was in those days.

When Unita told the local sheriff about the shooting through her house and the cross burnings he accused the black people of setting the fires to cause trouble and did nothing about it. Unita expected to pay a price for the freedom that was coming, but at the same time a just anger played a big part in motivating her and others to keep on working. Anger can help someone keep their eyes on the prize. Of course, "sometimes all you can do is pray."[9] In July 1964, Unita helped to set up a new political party in Mississippi called the Mississippi Freedom Democratic Party (MFDP). This was the first new party formed since Strom Thurmond and others had formed the States Rights Party in 1948 as was a response to Harry Truman and others who promoted national laws that fostered civil rights as a start of equalizing opportunity. The new party (MFDP) selected Unita as one of 68 representatives to go to the National Democratic Convention in Chicago in August of 1964.

In Chicago the convention had advocates for and opposition against civil rights. The police had a challenge and brutality abounded. Inside the convention hall Fannie Lou Hamer was urging the delegates from MFDP to stand firm and demand to be seated as representatives of a legitimate legally constructed party from Mississippi. Fannie Lou Hamer was being watched by the whole nation including President Johnson in the White House.

> If the Freedom Democratic Party is not seated now I question America. Is this America, the land of the free and the home of the brave, where we have to sleep with our telephones off the hooks because our lives are threatened daily because we want to live as decent human beings?[10]

President Johnson was afraid that if he allowed the 68 representatives to be seated the other southern states including Texas would withdraw their support from him. So he sent Hubert Humphrey, the senator from Minnesota, to negotiate with the group. A committee wanted a compromise which was the group getting two seats. As Fannie Lou Hamer would later tell the watching TV audience their group of 68 had not come for just two seats. When the group would not accept the compromise many from the official Mississippi delegation left in protest. So then the MFDP delegates walked down the aisle and took the vacated seats. The sergeant at arms tried to get them to move out but no one did. Mrs. Hamer started up "We Shall Overcome" and the delegation caught the imagination of the other delegates. The group never was officially seated, but they had made their point that representation of a large segment of people was vital.

In June 1965 congress passed the Voting Rights Act. The state of Mississippi tried to use the state sovereignty act and other laws to prevent blacks from voting. The MFDP gathered together to stage a march on the capitol in Jackson to force the voting rights issue and then they hoped to register black voters. On June 14 over 600 people of all races and ages gathered to march in Jackson, but the march never progressed as far as the capitol because riot police broke in, beat many of the marchers, threw as many as they could into paddy wagons and then into garbage trucks and arrested over 1100 people.

> We had black and white women holding on to each other—we were in this together—and the police decided that gave us too much strength so they took all the white ones somewhere else . . . The police would walk us all night long . . . the guards worked in shifts to keep us awake, to harass and torture us . . . If we got too far away somebody would be standing there with a stick hitting us . . . [11]

The beatings and brutality lasted for eleven days. Unita recalls that she would never have believed anyone who said that in the United States there could be such savage and brutal beatings of people by the police, the army and others who came into the jails. "When I hear all these things that are happening now—al Qaeda terrorists, our own "war on terrorism" and the torture our own people inflicted on Iraqi prisoners—it feels so strange because black people in Mississippi went through this."[12] To see people who are innocent being beaten and brutally killed in front of your eyes is a memory whose pain does not go away.

When schools were finally desegregated in Mississippi Unita recalls that her son Jerry still had to ride the special bus for black children. There was no mixing if it was not specifically stated by law. Many black parents were saddened when their children told them how white children threw stones at them, harassed and beat them at recess. They were also made the butt of hurting jokes by teachers or school staff.

In the mid 1960s Unita became involved as a local planner of the Head Start Program. Grant money was available to set up an 8-week summer program. In the first year more than 85 such centers and programs were functioning. Unita received $80 a week for running the Mayersville programs. In the beginning the banks would not cash the payment checks from the government to protest the program for black children. Other people would not accept the government checks for rent or food as their form of protest. Eventually the district system that Unita organized made the people of Mississippi proud of their accomplishments.

In 1965 Fannie Lou Hamer invited Unita and Amzie More, another activist, to her house. The three women looked at the strides that had been made and the suffering it cost. Now it was time to look at getting some people in political office who would continue to fight for equal rights. What was needed was an ongoing education program so people could keep learning and see what their rights actually should be. That afternoon was the start of MACE, Mississippi Action for Community Education. The purpose of MACE was to help people help themselves. The group had great success over the years in training grass roots organizers, in training people for jobs, in assisting people with money management, education, focusing on realistic dreams and in general helping people use the power that was theirs. By fall of 1967 more than 180,000 black Mississippians were registered to vote. In 1968 even though Unita was one of the official delegates to the Democratic National Convention in Chicago, tensions continued over the issues of freedom and equality for all.

That same year Unita got hired by Dorothy Height to carry out a national housing program for the poor people of Mississippi. Dorothy Height was the executive director of the National Council of Negro Women (NCNW). She had met Unita during the period of the civil rights actions in Mississippi. Unita said she didn't know anything about housing or housing programs. Miss Height reminded Unita that she knew what it was like to be homeless so that was a start. Unita was trained on the job to learn how to use the loans and programs that were available for poor people to eventually own a house. This started Unita on another career direction for helping her people. She learned quickly.

In 1969 the country witnessed the assassinations of Dr. Martin Luther King, Jr. and Robert Kennedy, a potential presidential candidate. The sadness Unita felt was only lifted by her success in the new housing program. By

1970 the program was so successful that Unita had to travel more to keep up with her new job and its responsibilities. By 1971, it was clear to both Jeremiah and Unita that their marriage had ended some years before so they should simply divorce and each do what they felt called to do. Unita felt a great call to serve her people in ever larger ways while Jeremiah was content to continue living as he always had. They agreed to always remain friends

Once the marriage was over Unita felt a lot freer to do her job. "I discovered that freedom has many layers, like an onion . . . For me it is a spiritual journey which draws upon my deepest faith in the divine source and brings me closer and closer to my own spiritual core."[13]

Unita developed a friendship with Shirley MacLaine after the Democratic Conventions both attended. Shirley came to visit her in Mississippi and the two had a good time exchanging stories. Shirley and Unita were selected to go to China together in 1973 as part of a goodwill ambassador trip. President Nixon had helped pave the way with his visit in 1972. The trip was a learning experience for both of them. Many Chinese people, especially children, couldn't help staring at Unita. They had not seen black people before. Shirley MacLaine was used to cameras taking her picture but she had to get used to Unita receiving applause whenever she stepped out of the car at any public event. "I saw that a person living in China lives and loves and laughs and cries and needs friends and values family the same way we do in this country . . . people need help all over this world. That is the message I brought home."[14]

Unita has made more than 16 trips to China in addition to many other parts of the world. In spite of her global interests Unita retained a deeply felt responsibility for Mayersville where she spent most of her life. In 1976 Mayersville still lacked general water and sewer services and many streets were unpaved. So Unita decided to run for mayor and encourage the citizens to vote for incorporation. A door to door campaign explaining the benefits of incorporation was run by Unita's volunteers prior to the election. Unita won the election and served four consecutive terms, 1977-1993. She took a pause, and then served a final term from 1997-2001.

During the time Unita served as mayor she met President Jimmy Carter and Bella Abzug, who had been active in civil rights. Unita always spoke clearly among her mayoral colleagues. She soon was elected president of the black mayors. Her name came up frequently in Washington for committees. She was named to a White House Advisory Group on housing due to her experience in Mississippi. She was chosen to introduce President Jimmy Carter when he came to campaign in Mississippi for a second term. Unita was amused as she recalled herself as a cotton picker now representing Mississippi as she greeted the president of the United States.

When some women friends in China contacted Unita to return to China as part of a consulting group for American tourism she was pleased. She stopped with her party in Tibet. While in Lhasa she asked to visit the major temple of Tibetan Buddhism, Jokhang Temple. People from all over the world came to pray there so Unita wanted to pray there too.

As she was leaving the temple Tibetan women started prostrating themselves before her, apparently thinking she was a black goddess from ancient eastern tradition. Unita decided to respect the idea they had of her and simply blessed them from the van. That seemed to make the women very happy and they went back to their homes smiling. The whole experience led Unita to reflect on her own spirituality and the role of religious tolerance and diversity.

> I respect all people's religions as I respect the people themselves . . . I am troubled today when I witness the lack of tolerance among some religious people for the religious views of others and see how intolerance continues to play itself out in the politics of our country. I think fanatical conservative Christians today branding those who do not hold their views as un-American, and I remembered the Ku Klux Klan spewing hatred and inciting violence in the name of Christianity. The religious principles I know from my upbringing and from other religions as well are about compassion and love—the golden rule—and acceptance. That's what the Tibetan Buddhist women I encountered were seeking . . . I don't claim to be an expert on foreign affairs or on religion either, but I know firsthand the humiliation of having my human dignity trampled on and also the trust that comes from being accepted for who I am. And I've never found anybody anywhere in the whole wide world who feels any different.[15]

At age 50 Unita received a fellowship to the University of Massachusetts at Amherst. She was sure there was a mistake since she lacked an undergraduate degree and had attained only a high school equivalency certificate. However, her experience made her a perfect candidate for the regional planning degree. She received the Master's Degree in Regional Planning and then went to work on assisting the three-quarters of Mississippi's population who lived below the official poverty level. Her friends, James Earl Jones, the Clintons, and the Carters all helped her make new connections and then continue to accomplish great things.

Unita credits God for putting her into situations that led to new adventures and then some miracles. She continues telling the story of the past to young people of her town who look to her as a living history book. She tells them to trust and then to work together.

> Movements inspire people to rise to their best. Movements are the way ordinary people get more freedom and justice. Movements are how we keep a check on power and those who abuse it . . . We have to take responsibility for own lives. All our problems can't be solved by government . . . Too many of our people still allow their lives to be determined by the action or in-action of others because they don't believe in themselves . . . You can't sit around and wait for somebody else to carry you. Get on the road . . . Fight for the right to stay on the road . . . Pray for the strength to finish what you started. You can do it.[16]

Unita has received four honorary doctorates and numerous other awards for her work in fostering human rights. She continues to live in Mississippi and encourages all people to act for change when change is for the better. All it takes is some imagination and willingness to admit and to live as if one life can make a difference because it can.[17] She continues to believe that God can do great things through anybody who is willing to listen to the voice.

NOTES

[1] *Barefootin': Life Lessons from the Road to Freedom* by Unita Blackwell with JoAnne Prichard Morris (New York: Crown Publishers, 2006).

[2] *Barefootin'*, 56-57. The summary is from 3-56.

[3] *Barefootin'*, 75.

[4] *Barefootin'*, 85-86.

[5] *Barefootin'*, 89.

[6] *Barefootin'*, 91.

[7] *Barefootin'*, 92.

[8] *Barefootin'*, 98.

[9] *Barefootin'*, 102.

10   *Barefootin'*, 112.
11   *Barefootin'*, 138.
12   *Barefootin'*, 129.
13   *Barefootin',*. 191.
14   *Barefootin'*, 207.
15   *Barefootin'*, 228-29.
16   *Barefootin'*, 254-56.
17   *Barefootin'*, Preface, ix.

17

Coretta Scott King, Alabama

Coretta Scott King was born on April 27, 1927 on a farm in Heiberger, Alabama to Obadiah Scott and Bernice McMurray. Coretta was a middle child. Her sister Edythe was older and her brother Obie was younger. Although Coretta's family owned the farm land they lived on, the family was poor. All the Scott children had to pick cotton during the Great Depression to help the family make ends meet. Her parents protected her from the hardships of segregation by assuring her she should be proud of who she was. She was well loved.

Reflections on Her Life by Coretta Scott King[1]

Coretta never considered herself oppressed because she had to walk for miles to get to her grandfather's Sunday school at Mount Tabor. Going to church and singing and praying was a happy occasion. She sensed the harshness of segregation only when she first noticed buses carrying white children to school while passing up and splattering black children with mud as buses rattled past.

In time she noticed that she and the other black children were regarded as inferior students in school in spite of fine performances in her classes. She remembered the exact day she noticed being second place to white children even at a drug store. Black children went to the back door of the drugstore and asked for a particular flavor of ice cream and received whatever flavor the man had in excess. Coretta asked her mother why this was so. Her mother insisted that Coretta was as good and as special as anyone else; it was the way things were, but if Coretta got a good education it could change.

Coretta went to Lincoln High School, ten miles away which was one of the best schools in the area. It was started by the American Missionary Association after the Civil War when there were no secondary schools for black children. Coretta, her brother and sister boarded with families and worked because the school was too far to walk both ways and still get homework done. Coretta learned to love music and excelled in singing and playing the piano and other instruments. She was given formal voice lessons and was so accomplished at age fifteen that her church asked her to be both the choir director and pianist.

In spite of the joy from these new discoveries there was also sadness at the racism she experienced. White teenagers from Lincoln would try to knock her and her friends off the sidewalk and call them dirty niggers. During her time at Lincoln her father's small sawmill business was burned down one day and the family home was burned down the next day. The authorities wouldn't put out the flames because they claimed the mill and house were not quite in the city limits. Some white people came forward and said they would ask for an investigation because her father was well liked. Everyone knew there would be no investigation.

Yet Coretta's father assured her there were good white people as well as biased ones. He wanted her to remember that hatred and revenge should not be part of Christian life. She attributed her own spirituality of reconciliation and forgiveness to her father's example. After Coretta graduated from Lincoln as valedictorian in 1945 she went to Antioch College where she and two white women students shared a room. The three learned much about each other's particularities and became friends in the process. The total Antioch experience deepened the values of courage, love and hope that were part of Coretta's heritage from her parents. The world famous baritone Paul Robeson encouraged her to continue her voice studies.

Antioch College consistently reinforced the Christian spirit of giving and sharing. Often the students heard the line that they should be ashamed to die if they had not won some victory for humanity.

> Antioch gave me an increased understanding of my own personal worth. I was no longer haunted by a feeling of inadequacy just because I was an African-American. I enjoyed a new self assurance that encouraged me in competition with all people of all racial, ethnic and cultural backgrounds . . . The total experience of Antioch was an important element in preparing me for the role I was to play as the wife of Martin Luther King Jr. and for my part in the movement he led.[2]

After graduating from Antioch Coretta received a small grant to study at the New England Conservatory of Music in Boston. Her father could help her with the train fare to Boston and an additional $15. Coretta had been told to look a Mrs. Bartol, a friend of Antioch College, who lived in Boston on Beacon Hill. Coretta was invited to work for Mrs. Bartol and to live there while she went to the Conservatory. Two Irish maids of Mrs. Bartol's taught Coretta how to do things she hadn't done before, like scrubbing floors on hands and knees.

Coretta loved the Conservatory and did well with her classes. She was always watching her expenses. One day she received some monetary help from the state of Alabama, as other African Americans did who were doing professional study. Since state schools were still segregated and Alabama did not want blacks getting professional training in the Alabama colleges with whites the state decided to pay a small sum to keep African Americans out of Alabama colleges by paying them to study elsewhere.

Coretta did so well at the conservatory that she won additional scholarships. She was focused on a career so was not really too interested when a friend insisted she meet Martin Luther King, Jr. Mary and other young women had been taken with Martin's charm and intelligence. He was studying to be a Baptist minister. Coretta had been brought up in the African Methodist Episcopal church and was not interested in meeting a Baptist minister.

> I was deeply religious but I was growing away from fundamentalism . . . I wanted to identify myself with a church or religious body that was more liberal than the kind I was brought up in . . . I was, in fact, dissatisfied with organized religion as I knew it and sought to find a faith with which I could identify totally. For this and other reasons I did not attend church regularly when I first went to Boston . . . I said, 'I can worship in my room'[3].

Coretta finally agreed to a short meeting with Martin. After that they agreed to meet again and soon Martin was talking of marriage. This frightened Coretta who wanted to pursue the career she was training for. At the same time she was impressed by the depth and breadth of Martin's learning, his spirituality, his dreams and the humor the two of them shared. They laughed easily when they were together. Coretta recalls that she was being pursued but also that she was not running away very fast.

In June 1953 Coretta and Martin married. They agreed that they would go back to Boston and both would finish their doctorates. They talked often about their dreams, their faith and their hopes for their future together. Both Coretta and Martin strongly believed in an intimate and infinite God whose presence was within all people. As they both were finishing their educational work Martin was invited to go to Montgomery to replace a pastor of a small Baptist church. Coretta did not want them to go to Alabama because she remembered the racism and segregation that were part of her childhood their. She knew there would be little opportunity for her to pursue her own career in Alabama in spite of what Martin could do. She agreed to accompany him to the Sunday "trial" to meet the congregation. Martin preached and then invited Coretta to address the congregation. After the service the congregation said to both of them that they wanted this vibrant young couple to be their leaders as permanent pastor and wife.

The community's words led both Martin and Coretta to consider whether this place at the time was just what they should do as a step toward wherever God would lead them in the future. While both Coretta and Martin were preparing for graduation in spring 1954 the movement toward desegregation was also happening. That same year the Supreme Court declared that the former "separate but equal" clause regarding segregated education was no longer valid and passed a clear desegregation law to be enacted as soon as possible in 1955. There was violent opposition to this in the South and the Ku Klux Klan went into action again.[4]

The Kings went to Montgomery where Martin became pastor of Dexter Avenue Baptist Church. In March of 1955 fifteen-year-old Claudette Colvin refused to give up her bus seat to a white passenger. She was handcuffed and taken to jail. On December 1, 1955, Rosa Parks was sitting in the front part of the colored section on the bus. More white passengers came on and she was told to get up and move back. She refused because she was too tired to move. Rosa was arrested and had to be bailed out of jail after she finally had a trial which cost her $10 plus additional expenses. This blatant discrimination initiated the movement for a bus boycott in Montgomery.

During the Montgomery bus boycott the King's house was bombed and many of their sympathetic white and black friends were also victimized. Martin encouraged people to fight the growing violence and distrust with love and non-violence and not to stoop to hatred. During these days of challenges and fears Coretta came to a deep sense of God's wisdom. For some reason God seemed to want Martin and her to be here at this time in this city of Montgomery which was a place she had never wanted to live!

> I felt that a larger force was working within me and that I was not alone . . . I was able to draw strength from my religious faith that if you are doing what God wants you to do you will be successful and filled in the process. That does not mean that it will be easy . . . but you will be given the strength to do what must be done.[5]

Soon the movement that began so simply became a national movement and Martin was called upon to travel to many cities while Coretta stayed in Montgomery. In November 1956 after threats and sufferings to many people the Supreme Court declared that Alabama's bus segregation was unconstitutional. In Montgomery while many people were ready for equality for all there were some extremists who continued to drag African Americans off busses, beat them, shoot them, verbally abuse them or shame them in other ways.

In 1957 Martin and Coretta were invited by Nkruma of Accra, the leader of Ghana, to come for the handing over of power from Britain to Ghana at the parliament session. Nkruma had compared the colonialism the Ghanaians experienced under British rule to the segregation African Americans experienced in the US. The Kings were moved by the ceremonial taking down of the flag of Britain and the raising of the flag of free and independent Ghana. There were close to 50,000 people witnessing the event that marked the first of the African nations to achieve independence. Others would follow.

Things were relatively calm until 1958. While in Harlem after Martin's first book was published a woman stabbed him. He had the presence of mind to tell those close by to leave the knife in until a doctor could remove it the right way. Had he not done that he could have been dead before the ambulance arrived. When Coretta saw him in the hospital she remembers that both she and Martin knew it was not the time for him to die, but it was a clear sign from God that someday a greater trial would come

> We felt that we were being prepared for a much larger work; that in order to endure the persecution and suffering ahead, we would have to rededicate ourselves to nonviolence and to the cause of bringing freedom and human dignity to all people . . . victory in Montgomery had been only one small step forward. The south was still almost completely segregated.[6]

In 1959 it seemed that moving to Atlanta would provide a better center for the many civil rights actions that now became part of life, so Martin, Coretta and the children moved to Atlanta. The people in Montgomery gave Martin and his family a wonderful send-off but agreed that he could do more with a position in Atlanta, Georgia. Martin now assisted his father at Ebenezer Baptist Church in Atlanta, Georgia, to the delight of the congregation.

In the 1960s freedom marches were led by Martin and ministers of many faiths. College students joined in as did many other people. Marchers were often taken to jail for their efforts. Prayer vigils accompanied the movement and these vigils became a vital force for keeping the movement alive in the midst of suffering. President John Kennedy and his brother Robert were supporters of civil rights and had become friends of Martin. In 1962 while the movement was meeting opposition and violence in the south Coretta was invited to go to Geneva to address an international meeting on world peace.

Coretta and the women representing the United States went to the meeting with Arthur Dean from the state department who clearly regarded the women as incapable of speaking about peace and non-violence; he openly ridiculed their ideas about stopping wars. How could war cease when the Russians were so obstinate? He told them to go talk to the Russian delegation if they were so sure everyone wanted peace.

So Coretta and the other women set up an appointment with the Russian delegation and the meeting was very cordial. The Russian men treated the women with much greater respect than the male delegates from the United States led by Dean! The Russians even gave the women a final party to honor their perspectives on the future of peace. They had been more successful than the men in setting a peace agenda.

In 1963 Martin was put in jail in Birmingham, Alabama for leading a civil rights march. Coretta was worried about the treatment he would get in jail so she called President Kennedy, but he was with his ill father. Robert Kennedy came to the phone and said he would do what he could. The next day President Kennedy called her to say the FBI had been sent to Birmingham and that Martin was all right. Within ten minutes after that call Martin called to say he was being treated all right, but for the first time in three days he had just been let out of his cell for exercise. Coretta told him about her conversation with the president. In 1964 a civil rights bill was finally passed by congress that gave equal rights to all.[7]

When President. Kennedy was assassinated in November 1963 the Kings joined the nation in grieving. The following year Martin won the Nobel Peace Prize which he received on December 10, 1964. He was formally received at the White House a week later. In January 1965 marching and demonstrations for voting rights in Selma began and wound up in violence. The Selma March would go down in history as Bloody Sunday.

More than sixty state troopers and some cavalry ordered the marchers to stop near a bridge which they did. At the end of less than a minute the troopers put on gas masks. Major John Cloud shouted to them to go forward and the troopers began swinging clubs and whips that tore into the people. Tear gas grenades were thrown into the crowd. The men on horses rode into the dispersing group with their whips slashing those who fell or couldn't run fast enough. People who were helplessly lying in the streets were ridden over by the troopers. Much of this was caught on television and the country was horrified.

Coretta was sickened at the suffering and violence. She had a sense that the degree of hatred and opposition in the hearts of some of the people might play itself out in Martin's future. She tried to protect their children as best she could, but they were aware of television reports, and the children at school were telling them all sorts of things about Martin, both good and bad. Coretta did what she could to make the children proud of themselves and of Martin's work as she continued her work for equality. Coretta, Rosa Parks and others joined in a third march in Selma in spite of the opposition. This time Martin gave a speech that enlivened the crowd to hope.[8] At the same time Coretta sensed a deep fear for what might happen to the family.

She knew somehow that her own courage needed to grow. It was clear that a day would come when a bigger sacrifice would be asked of her. She now sensed God's presence in a deeper way and knew that she would be able to go wherever life's journey took her.

> I had to prepare for the days ahead because I did not know what they would bring . . . I believe God is working. We are coworkers with God trying to bring about the kingdom of love and peace . . . when you decide to give yourself to a great cause you must arrive at the point where no sacrifice is too great.[9]

In spring 1968 Martin went to Memphis and led the march of garbage collectors on March 28. During the march some teenagers broke ranks and began throwing rocks, and the response was quick. Police arrested more than

200 people and at least 62 others were injured. Another march in Memphis had been set for April 8.

The night before the march there was a rally at the Mason Street Temple. This was the night that Martin eloquently uttered the "I have a dream" speech. The applause of the people was deafening. Ralph Abernathy was in the room when Martin stepped out on the balcony to exchange a few words with Jesse Jackson who was below the window. A shot rang out and struck Martin in the neck. Quickly Ralph came to his side, and others gathered trying to stop the bleeding. An ambulance was called, but the onlookers knew Martin had already died.

When Coretta answered the phone in Atlanta she heard Jesse Jackson say that Dr. King had been shot, and she should get on a plane and come to Memphis as soon as she could. As soon as she heard the message Coretta sensed that Martin was dead. Within moments after the call Ivan Allen, the mayor of Atlanta, contacted Coretta and said he would make the plane reservation and escort her to the airport. While he waited with her for the flight to Memphis, Dora McDonals, a close personal friend of Coretta's and personal secretary to Dr. King, rushed to the airport. She was supposed to tell Coretta that Dr. King was dead, but Coretta already knew the truth. With great dignity Coretta told Dora and Ivan that she would go back home to tell the children. She would claim her husband's body the next day in Memphis.

When Robert Kennedy heard the news he called Coretta to say that he would send a plane for her and her friends to claim Martin's body in Memphis. The next morning Coretta and some friends boarded the plane for Memphis. Ralph Abernathy had chosen a temporary casket for use in Memphis. He and some workers and friends had an early morning memorial service there before going to the airport to meet Mrs. King. Between civil rights workers and Memphis people who were appreciative of Dr. King there was a two-mile procession of cars honoring Dr. King as the casket made the journey to the Memphis airport. Here Coretta met the casket and wept softly as it was lifted onto the plane. Then with great dignity she went back on the plane.

By the time Coretta's plane arrived at 1:30pm in Atlanta, a large crowd had already gathered at the airport— a mixture of whites and African-Americans, people from all professions, politicians, ministers, civil rights advocates and sympathetic Atlantans. Coretta with her children stood at the door of the plane and watched Martin's casket being placed into the waiting hearse. Coretta was already a dignified widow who knew that this was part of the destiny that she and Martin expected to happen. It was clear that the funeral would draw thousands to Atlanta, so Coretta turned over the planning to one of Martin's organizers. Meanwhile, Harry Belafonte and his wife, Julie, stayed with Coretta during the long preparation period to help in any way they could.

Coretta knew that one of Martin's greatest concerns was that there might be violent retaliation if he died violently. To honor him and to dissuade those who might use violence, Coretta held a press conference during the days of mourning before the funeral. She reminded people that Martin faced the possibility of death with no bitterness. He spent his life to save society from the violence and racism that was destroying it. She asked the people to honor Dr. King's spirit by not using violence as a way of avenging Martin's death.

Meanwhile, to honor Martin in her own way Coretta flew to Memphis to lead the march that her husband had agreed to lead before he was killed. The turnout was gratifying, and the march was peaceful as Martin would have wanted. Then she flew back to Atlanta for the funeral the next day.

Martin's funeral on April 9 was the largest funeral a private citizen had ever had in the United States. More than 150,000 people attended some part of the three part service. The streets were lined for miles. The first part of the service was at Ebenezer Baptist Church where Martin had served as pastor. The second part of the service was a five-mile march from Ebenezer Church to Morehouse College. The third part was a larger public service at Morehouse where special friends were invited for the post funeral condolences and memories to be shared. During the six-hour service Mrs. King and the children were dignified and courageous. When Mrs. John Kennedy approached Coretta at their post funeral gathering no words were necessary. As soon as the women were alone they embraced each other for a long time needing no words to convey the deep love and union they each shared with the other.[10]

Coretta did not let her grief deter her own work for justice in the world and also her effort to secure land and monies for the Martin Luther King, Jr. Center which would combine history and research. It would also house the remains of Martin and in time the remains of Coretta. The King Center officially opened in 1982. The National Park Service continues to operate a visitor center across the street where more than 600,000 people visit each year.

Coretta received many invitations to speak around the world. She strongly opposed the expenditures of war that were depriving children and poor people of health care, adequate education, and other social services. She organized protests against apartheid outside the South African Embassy in Washington, D.C. She visited Soweto and met with Mrs. Mandela and Desmond Tutu while visiting the squatter camps enforced by apartheid in South Africa. Nelson Mandela invited her to be at his side after he was released from prison and elected as President of South Africa. Coretta received honors from around the world as well as from home. At age 75 she responded to students at Bennet College asking her about the meaning of her life.

> I would like to think that my years of working for peace, human rights, and a society free of racism, sexism, homophobia and all forms of bigotry have helped to make life a little better for your generation.[11]

Coretta Scott King died in her sleep at an alternative medical clinic in Mexico on January 30, 2006. Coretta was the first woman to be honored by lying in state at the rotunda of the Georgia Capitol. Georgia State Patrol officers carried the casket into the rotunda. On February 4, 2006 more than 42,000 people stood in rain and sleet to walk past the casket in tribute. On February 6 and 7 another 170,000 people paid their respects at public viewings at Ebenezer Baptist Church and New Birth Baptist Church.

The funeral on February 7 was a six-hour celebration of Coretta's life. Dignitaries included past presidents, current presidents or prime ministers and a host of entertainers and admirers. More than 10,000 people tried to fit into New Birth Baptist Church where Coretta's daughter Berenice was an assistant pastor. The tribute by President George Bush acknowledged that he and Mrs. King did not always agree. However, he said, "She worked to make the nation whole . . . Coretta Scott King proved that a person of conviction and strength can also be a beautiful soul."[12] Coretta has been laid next to Martin at the King center.[13]

NOTES

[1]   A close friend of Coretta's who worked with her has also written a biography for older readers. Octavia Vivian, *Coretta: the Story of Coretta Scott King* (Minneapolis: Fortress, 2006. Coretta's personal reflections used in this text

  are from her work, *My Life With Martin Luther King, Jr.* (NY: Penguin Puffin Bk, 1995).

2 Coretta Scott King, *My Life With Martin Luther King, Jr.* This work will be cited in future references as *My Life*. The section is a summary of 1-43. The quotation is from 43

3 *My Life*, 50.

4 *My Life*. Summary of 51-101.

5 *My Life*, 125.

6 *My Life*, 158. Summary of 102-158.

7 *My Life*. Summary of 159-216.

8 *My Life*, Summary of 215-251.

9 *Coretta*, 73.

10 *Coretta*. The section from 81-100 details the assassination and the aftermath.

11 *Coretta*, 124.

12 *Coretta*, 4.

13 *Coretta*, 1-6. Videos/DVD's that detail one or more dimensions of the Civil Rights Movement are many. Some examples include *Long Walk Home, Ruby Bridges, Separate But Equal, Mississippi Burning*. Many made for TV dramas also explore the period.

18

Elise Boulding, Norway/U.S.

Elise Boulding was born in Oslo, Norway in 1920 to Birgit Marianne and Josef Biorn Hansen. Elise grew up outside Newark, New Jersey in an immigrant Scandinavian community. They came to the United States in 1923 when Norway was experiencing an economic depression. Her father was an engineer; her mother was an outgoing person who was always politically active.

Few people in this Norwegian community ever attended the Lutheran Church that was close by but they were happy to have a church in their community. Everyone knew the evening service was in Norwegian, but that wasn't enough to draw the people of Elise's community. The fierce individualism of the people was manifest in a strong desire for a privatized spirituality, rather than one shared in community.[1]

Birgit was an accomplished pianist who had studied at Oslo Conservatory. However, the financial challenges of the times influenced Birgit's decision to train as both a nurse and a masseuse. Josef was an engineer.

While living in Oslo Birgit refused to use servants to assist her with the children and housework because she was strongly opposed to the operative class system in Norway. Rather than spending time hiring and supervising servants Birgit organized clubs and activities for women factory workers. This activity made Birgit disapproved of in the 'better circles' which included some members of her own family. Josef did not mind his wife's avid views of equality.

Because of the depression in Norway in 1923 Josef and Birgit decided to come to America. Elise was then three years old, and her parents wanted a better life for her. Once in America, Birgit insisted that Elise learn the language and traditions of the Norwegian people and respect the culture that formed her. At the same time Elise was learning American ways from her friends. The family spoke Norwegian at home until Sylvia and Vera were born in 1929 and 1931, respectively.[2] Then they switched to English.

Elise recalls that while the family did not go to any church, her father had a family bible that he read from often. Every family had a bible that was prayed even if no one went to the nearby church. The Scandinavian community celebrated Christmas and Easter with great festivities. Church was not a part of the festivities because the home itself was considered to be the center of spiritual formation of children and adults. Here Elise sensed a Presence of God.

> My mother and father never talked about God, never used petitionary prayer and only read the Bible once a year on Christmas Eve. Yet God was present . . . Father became an engineer and poured out his love for God and his wife and children in the ways that shy people can: through a thousand affectionate deeds . . . my parents were giving me in the only way they knew something from the very depths of their being . . . Listening to God is one of my clearest childhood memories. There was always a quiet inner space I could go into, a listening place . . . the sense of God's presence was often with me.[3]

At age nine Elise decided to attend a church now and then to learn something about the God whose presence she felt. Elise recalls that she enjoyed just sitting in a church and feeling a sense of God with her. Then she decided it would be interesting to go to Sunday school as well as church. In Sunday school, she began to learn of different images of God and Jesus. Mrs. Northwood, the minister's wife, sensed Elise's deep spirituality and often invited her to tea to talk about life and its meaning. Elise always remembered this gracious and holy woman as one of the major mentors in her life.[4] The lessons at Sunday school and her own intelligence that interpreted and applied them led her to form her own images about God and Jesus.

> I came to understand that while God is present across an unmeasurable far awayness Jesus is present in the nearness of a friend; while God teaches through being Jesus teaches through speaking and doing . . . Many years later, very unexpectedly, I came to experience Jesus in an inward way as a teaching Presence.[5]

As she matured it became important for Elise to remember how close she felt to the Sacred Presence as a child because she stopped experiencing the closeness of God. She later attributed this to a mix of her intellectual arrogance and the extreme busyness of college life.

> The inner listening place I developed so early has always been there for me in a very conscious way . . . As an adult I lost the feeling of the immanence of God's presence. I only remembered the space. All children are listeners, but some stop listening and remembering sooner than others.[6]

Elise won a scholarship to the New Jersey College for women which is now part of Rutgers University. The influence of her mother became very obvious during the time Elise was in college, Often Birgit would say to the girls that they were not just any immigrants; they were Norwegian immigrants. That meant they had to work hard so they could be the best. Birgit's vision of a classless society was also something that Elise found shaping her spirituality through her college and post college years. Elise imbibed Birgit's strong equality perspective. Birgit felt that intelligent and self-sufficient girls like Elise should never be given privileges especially when Elise could accomplish her goals without the privilege. In time the event opened Elise's eyes to see the number of times a social system favors those who do not need favors and ignores the needs of those who do need favors sometimes just to survive.[7]

Elise was both intelligent and highly motivated. She finished college in three years with a major in English. She had continued her cello practice during these years and was accomplished enough to play with trios and quartets in college to earn extra money. After graduating from Rutgers Elise moved to New York City to work for a publishing house. Soon another publisher coaxed her to work with them as a writer of high school textbooks which initially was a good learning experience, but soon she found it boring. She was expected to attend the many office parties where she found the small talk meaningless.

The only good thing that happened at one of these parties was her meeting a young man who invited her to join him in his volunteer work at a Catholic Worker hospitality house. At that time those who worked in the Catholic Worker movement were considered radicals and anarchists because they opposed war and violence of any kind. They worked among the poor and marginalized people of the city. The movement had been started in New York City by Dorothy Day whose works Elise soon devoured. Elise was inspired by her activism and her inner spirituality that reached out to the poorest people.

Some of the Catholic Workers sensed Elise's commitment to peace and her willingness to work for equality for all people. They invited Elise to meet Catherine de Hueck, a Russian immigrant from Russia's upper class, who was also working with the poor in a New York slum where Elise volunteered. Elise and many others who worked with Catherine were impressed with her dignity and graciousness. Among themselves they referred to Catherine as the Baroness Catherine. Elise remembered the surprise she felt the first day she went to see the operation and the work of the Baroness.

> To find in that sordid city (New York seemed very sordid to me though I also loved it) a place where people very frankly and openly loved God and fiercely worked with and on behalf of Negroes was like being lost in the dark and suddenly finding home—though the home was so different from anything I had known that I could not be totally at ease there. I had lived among ethnics all my life, both North and South European, but never among blacks.[8]

Catherine directed a place in Harlem where Elise's friends worked with some Quakers who came now and then; when she could Elise also helped there. Elise was sure that Catherine had no idea the effect her life had on Elise and the other young people. This woman had forsaken her wealth and upper class comfort to live among the poorest people in New York City. Elise wrote to her parents that Catherine's life taught social justice and love for others as a core spiritual reality. The strength and dedication of Catherine who was humble enough to get on her knees every evening and pray continued to inspire Elise for years.

In young adulthood Elise was delighted to find people her age who could work in such loving kindness for the good of other people with no expectation of reward. For Elise this was the first time she worked side by side with African Americans because she had always been with Scandinavian American communities when she was growing up. She told her parents about this wonderful experience. Although her parents did not approve of her living and working in such a situation she continued to do it.

In 1939 and 1940 Elise became involved formally in a variety of social movements so she decided to locate a Quaker community that she could be part of and who would support her efforts. She moved back to Syracuse where her family had relocated. Here she rediscovered her inner space and appreciated the purpose of Quaker worship—to be silent and listen with a discerning heart to discover what God was saying. At the same time she sought out a local Catholic church where she liked to sit and think.

Elise met her future husband Kenneth Bolding while he was visiting Syracuse and speaking to a quarterly meeting of Quakers. Kenneth had emigrated from England, taught at the University of Edinburgh and was already well established as a scholar. Elise was 21; Kenneth was 31. Kenneth's deep spirituality was so evident that it touched Elise in a way that freed her to acknowledge her own depth of inner spirituality. Each quickly saw the goodness in the other, and they fell in love.

The Quaker community with whom they prayed realized that these two had a special bond with each other and suspected that they would do great things together. Kenneth and Elise announced their engagement three weeks after they first met with the affirmation of their Quaker community. They were married in August 1941 under the care of the Quaker Syracuse meeting.[9]

> The different ways in which we experience the world were the very spice of our life together. The differences came together in our love of creation, the creator, and each other. They also came together in a passionate conviction that the world needs mending and that what we do, whether in family, community, or the world itself, matters.[10]

Kenneth and Elise were delighted in each other's company. Together they decided to have their home be like a "colony of heaven," a place where all would be welcome and where tranquillity and love would be for all who were in need. They also wanted their home to be a peaceful and loving place for their five children so they could listen and hear their own inner voice of God. Elise recalls, "I found God in the midst of the mundane tasks like changing a messy diaper. It seemed to me that it was in those tasks that God's love shone most clearly. This was the meaning of incarnation."[11]

The Quaker community was a source of great support for Elise, Kenneth and the children. The peace activism that was becoming more and more a part of Elise's life was strongly supported by the Quaker community. All in the community were active and at the same time dedicated to making the family center a place of love and support for the children. Each family was supportive of the children of each other and the bond made the families like one extended group. In the busyness Elise felt that God was never absent—just ignored.

Kenneth's academic appointments took him to Princeton in 1941, Nashville in 1942, Ames in 1944. Elise went to the University of Iowa in Ames and completed her MA in Sociology in 1949. The family moved back to Ann Arbor where Kenneth took another academic position. Elise and Kenneth and other Quaker families always took their children to peace activities as part of the children's spiritual formation.

Elise was a well known peace activist in the 1950s and 60s, so she was asked to write a peace curriculum for the Ann Arbor school district. Elise was also writing and speaking for the Society of Friends and began to work with the Women's International League for Peace and Freedom (WILPF). Elise considered herself primarily a homemaker during this time, but she was gaining recognition internationally as a sociologist of peace.[12] Kenneth and she remained active in Quaker efforts for peace.

Spirituality and Leadership in Peace Activities

In 1961 Elise and Kenneth founded the Friends Lake Community on an eighty-acre property of woods outside Ann Arbor where families could come for family renewal. People of diverse cultural backgrounds and religious beliefs came to share with each other. There were seminars that trained the adults to deal with conflict resolution and principles of ongoing dialogue. The vast difference in ideologies across different groups made it imperative that there be ongoing dialogues as well as a sense of how to foster this instead of some version of war. The common hope was that the people who came would then be a trained group who would assist others to try reconciliation instead of war.[13]

As the five Boulding children were growing up their family experiences were recorded by Elise and then published as *Friends Testimonies in the Home*.[14] Elise and Kenneth hoped their children's spirituality would be nourished in solitude just as their respective spiritualities were nourished in childhood by prayerful and respectful parents.

The inner listening place I developed so early has always been there for me

> . . . When our own children came I was very conscious of their need for listening . . . It makes me sad when I hear discussions about not introducing children to "God" until they are old enough to understand. I grew into the Lord's prayer and am still growing into it. All religious language, all devotional books, and

particularly the Bible provide growing room for young minds and spirits.[15]

In 1963 her work with the Women's International League for Peace and Freedom brought Elise to Moscow, Russia. Members of the Soviet Pedagogical Institute wanted to talk with her to try to understand her peace curricula for children. She then traveled to London to talk about the important role education plays in promoting world peace. She thought that children should be taught loyalty to the world so that demonizing other cultures and people stops. Elise even communicated with Mrs. Khrushev about the necessity of children learning to care for more than their own country and ideology.[16]

In fall of 1965 Elise received a Danforth Scholarship for doctoral study at Hanover. She had been an adjunct professor at Ann Arbor where many colleagues encouraged her to run for the second district congressional seat while studying for a doctorate. Elise was hesitant at first, but then decided that campaigning would give her a platform for talking about peace during the turbulent Viet Nam era. She had a strong platform that urged an end to war in Viet Nam and a long term program for peaceful settling of existing tensions. She also had a plan to abolish poverty and discrimination in the US. Her activity in the international peace community increased.[17]

In 1967 Kenneth accepted a position in Boulder, Colorado and the family moved again. Elise was awarded a PhD in Sociology in 1969 and began to teach courses pertinent to family life and religion and religion and culture. Student evaluations from these classes indicate how popular Elise was as an inspirational scholar. She became chairperson of the Consortium on Peace, Research, Education and Development in 1970 and guided it until her resignation in 1974.

Although she was a scholar whose research was admired by many in her field of sociology she also was very pragmatic in translating research ideas into workable programs. She continued to maintain her lifelong perception that peace was first and best learned in the family.

In the early 1970s another conversion of heart happened as Elise went to India in her position as chairperson of the Women's International League for Peace and Freedom. Her lectures on peace and reconciliation and ways to resolve conflicts and move hearts toward peace were discussed and appreciated. She stayed at the home of the Director of the Ghandi Museum and his wife who lived very simply and not in accord with their distinguished class.

> In the very modest unheated apartment of my friend, who chose
> voluntarily to live at a level of simplicity considerably more austere
> than that of most Indians of "their class," I discovered the human
> condition through the very ordinary experience of being terribly
> cold day after day! It was January with temperatures well below
> freezing every night, and each morning I would read in the paper
> about the number of Indians who had frozen to death the night
> before in the streets . . . (I) thought of all the extra shelter and
> warmth spread in wanton abundance across suburbia USA.[18]

In 1974 Elise's efforts for peace education, her many lectures to the larger
Quaker community and her academic work with all its extra international
activities contributed to a feeling close to "burnout." She had also been
concerned about the affluence that she and Kenneth had even though they
shared so many things with so many people. She decided to spend some
renewal time in a Roman Catholic monastery. She felt the silence of a praying
community would be a perfect context for her to get in touch again with
her inner self. She wondered if her intelligence would be a block to this
journey for peace but decided that God can use intelligence and any other
gift to effect whatever change of heart is necessary.

Elise went to a small Benedictine Monastery in Cold Spring on the
Hudson to revive her spirit. She was delighted at the richness that the
liturgical life of Catholicism added to her Quaker silence and inner light.

> In my own religious tradition of Quakerism the fear of
> participating in artificial reconstructions led to a witness against
> all sacraments and all celebrations. We were to live every moment
> as a sacramental moment and every day as a celebration. What
> has happened, of course, is that we have lost the sense of the
> sacramental and have forgotten how to celebrate. Yet the Quaker
> testimony points to a real problem. The inward cycles of our souls
> do not correspond to the great cycles of the church . . . my own
> calling has increasingly been toward solitude.[19]

Elise continued living an active academic life and also publishing for the
Society of Friends and numerous academic journals and books. She began
to experience the tensions in her desire to be quiet and grow inwardly in the
Presence of God and the invitations to be more professionally involved as
her invitations to speak and write increased. She talked with Kenneth and

they decided to build a hermitage where Elise could reflect and pray and do her writing in a way that renewed her. It was built behind the family cabin in the Rockies close to Boulder. She loved Kenneth for his support and understanding of her own spiritual journey into solitude. "The wisdom of solitude is not easy to translate into the world . . . There is a way—and it is my task this year to learn it—to be present both to God and to the world."[20]

In between periods for solitude Elise continued to hold leadership positions and influence policies in the American Sociological Association, the Board of Directors for the Institute for World Order, consultative work with the University of the United Nations-a peace endeavor—and UNESCO. President Jimmy Carter appointed her to the Congressional Commission on Proposals for the National Academy of Peace and Conflict Resolution (now called the US Institute for Peace).

Elise's reputation continued to spread as a thoughtful and inspiring peace activist. She became a visiting professor in areas of peace and international understanding, always delving into her own deep-seated Quaker roots of inward listening to God that directed outer action. In the early 1990s Kenneth became ill, and Elise cared for him until he died in 1993. It was years after his death before she could speak his name without tears.

Elise continued her academic and lecturing life. In 1995 and 1996 as a representative from the Quaker tradition at dialogues sponsored by the Interfaith Peace Council she spoke of and became more convinced that peace will come only out of a deep spirituality. "Where is the love going to come from to transform human violence into peaceful societies if not from a more developed human spirituality?"[21] In 2000 Elise decided to move into North Hill Retirement Community in Needham, Massachusetts. She now chooses how much speaking she will do and when. All activity she believes is really only a drop of love that she hopes God sees in her own life and that of others. "I had a sense of God looking at that one drop. And suddenly I knew that in the eyes of God it was enough!"[22]

NOTES

[1] Mary Lee Morrison, *Elise Boulding: A Life in the Cause of Peace* (Jefferson, NC: McFarland and Co., 2005). This comprehensive biography includes contributions Elise continues to make to peace as described on 202-208. The work will be cited as *Elise*.

2   *Elise*, 1-29.

3   *Freedom in Christ*, a Tulane Catholic Center Publication, republished electronically, is the source of this quotation. The particular chapter by Elise is called "Born Into Remembering." The citations are from the electronic pages on the website. *Www.pendlehill.org/pendle_hill_pamphlets.html* 4; also see 39 of *Elise*.

4   *Elise*, 33-34.

5   *Freedom in Christ*, 7.

6   *Freedom in Christ*, 5,6.

7   *Elise*, 30-31.

8   *Freedom in Christ*, 10

9   *Elise*, 42-43.

10 *Elise*, 37-48; the citation is from 48.

11 *Freedom in Christ*, 13.

12 *Elise*, 65-72.

13 *Elise*, 76-79.

14 Elise Boulding, *Friends Testimonies in the Home* (Philadelphia: Religious Education Committee of the Friends General Conference, 1953). Cited on 222 of *Elise*.

15 *Freedom in Christ*, 7

16 *Elise*, 73.

17 *Elise*, 81-86.

18 *Freedom in Christ*, 15.

19 *Freedom in Christ*, 25.

20 *Freedom in Christ*, 30.

21 *Elise*, 202.

22 Excerpted from *Concentrating on Essence, an Interview with Elise Boulding*, by Alan Atkisson, reprinted with permission from In Context #26-What Is Enough?, Summer 1990, copyright © 1990, 1997 by Context Institute, *www.context.org*.

19

Judy Mayotte, American in South Africa[1]

> In the depths are the violence and terror of which psychology has warned us. But if you ride these monsters down, if you drop with them farther over the world's rim, you find what our sciences cannot locate or name, the substrate, the ocean or matrix or either which buoys the rest, which gives goodness its power for good, and evil its power for evil, the unified field: our complex and inexplicable caring for each other and for our life together here. This is given. It is not learned.[2]

These remarkable words of Annie Dillard ring true for me. I have traveled long and far, deep and wide, willing to embrace that which is foreign and unfamiliar physically and spiritually. Radical change has remained a constant. In the course of a ten-year period, I became an ex-nun, wife, Ph.D., widow, and changed my career from teaching to television producing. Following my stint in television producing, I became a nun and a former nun again, worked with and wrote a book about refugees, became a refugee advocate, a government appointee in the first Clinton administration, a university professor at four separate universities, and a volunteer for the newly created Desmond Tutu Peace Centre. I made the longest residence change of my life, moving from Milwaukee to Cape Town. To this day, I rarely feel rooted. In fact, my sisters once called me "the bag lady." They gave me a place to hang my hat and store my computer whenever I was in this country during the research phase of my book, *Disposable People?: The Plight of Refugees*.[3]

Events that led to that book were linked to my husband Jack Mayotte. He was a father of six, four of whom were retarded, when I first met him. Jack was a successful business man—an international vice-president of Square D Electric Company, then a large multinational company. We fell in love and were married for three short but exquisitely beautiful years. Jack died of cancer all too soon—only six weeks from the day he was diagnosed. I always consider it a privilege and joy to have been married to him, and I cherish the love he gave me—love that enabled me to love and believe in myself in a way I never had before. Jack died in my arms at home in early September 1975 in the fall of the year, a season he loved. Our life together and his love now sent me forward to another phase of my life.

WTTW, Chicago's Public Television station, was creating a position of Director of Research for News and Public Affairs. Ira Miskin, Executive Director, agreed to interview me for the job, mainly out of respect for my husband. Less than twenty-four hours later Ira called and offered me the job. Four years later when Ira was asked to be Executive Producer of Ted Turner's new five year series *Portrait of America* he asked Marty Kileen and me to join him as the senior executives of the series. It was wonderfully exciting to be paid to travel to every state in the Union to portray the strengths of this nation. We and the series won many top awards, including the Peabody.

As exciting as television producing was something else was tugging at my heart, a calling to live again in a faith community and to work among the poor in the developing world. In 1984 I completed the production of the "Washington State" segment for which my co-producer/director and I subsequently won an Emmy. I left Turner Broadcasting to become a Maryknoll Sister with the intent of working among the poor in developing countries. During my preparatory year at the Maryknoll Sisters Center in New York and prior to my going overseas I worked among Cambodian refugees who had gained asylum in the United States and now lived in the Bronx.

I worked with Dominican Sister Jean Marshall who met newly arrived Cambodians who had lived through the killing fields of the Khmer Rouge and refugee camps along the Thai-Cambodian border. Sister Jean ascertained the specific needs of the Cambodians and asked the pastor of St. Rita's Catholic Church to provide minimal space for her to open St. Rita's Asian Center. By the time I began working with Sister Jean the center was thriving. Educational programs benefitted both women and children. Legal experts contributed their knowledge of immigration matters and helped newly arrived Cambodians advance through the maze of legal papers and actions required for them to gain refugee benefits and US citizenship. Volunteers offered their assistance in tackling the varied housing difficulties the Cambodians faced. Building superintendents were almost impossible to track down especially when I wanted them to replace broken windows, repair broken pipes and address other problems.

Unscrupulous people preyed on the Cambodians, many accessing their telephone accounts and billing long distance calls to them. I frequently just sat and listened to the stories these beleaguered people needed to tell. More often than not the refugee would begin her or his agonizing tale with the phrase, "In Pol Pot time . . ." while simultaneously moving the index finger across the throat, indicating the torture and death so many experienced during the reign of the Khmer Rouge. Work with the newly settled Cambodian refugees fueled a new desire to go to Somalia to work among refugees with other Maryknoll Sisters.

However, it was then that I was thwarted by a heart condition that prevented me from going overseas for the intended five-year period. How then was I to work among refugees?

A path opened to work with refugees two years after my former colleague and friend John Callaway, Director of the William Benton Fellowships Program in Broadcast Journalism at the University of Chicago, asked me to become Associate Director. When he left I served as Acting Director until I was blessed with a substantial grant from the John D. and Catherine T. MacArthur Foundation to write a book on long-term refugees. The MacArthur grant started me on a three-year odyssey through the refugee camps and homelands of the Cambodians in Thailand, the Eritreans and internally displaced Sudanese in Sudan, and the Afghans in Pakistan. I worked to document their lives and the conditions that have forced so many of the world's peoples into refugee status. That odyssey resulted in my book, *Disposable People?: the Plight of Refugees.* The experiences that led up to that book changed my life.

I had now entered a world where the most horrible atrocities against humanity occurred. I went to war zones and refugee camps the world over where people have fled to find safety anywhere they could. In the ruins of towns and villages people once called home, I held children almost dead from starvation, saw people freshly blown up by land mines, and conversed with women and children left alone, exploited and abused in their search for food. Among the ruins of a number of war torn nations, I became tangibly aware of the centuries it takes to build a culture and a nation and the few months or years it takes to obliterate the land and split apart the people who gave spirit and life to that particular culture and nation. The appalling devastation was all because people would not acknowledge their human bonding as brothers and sisters.

Each step of my life to that time led me to my work among and on behalf of the then approximately 20 million refugees and more than 25 to 30 million internally displaced civilians in our world—80% of whom were then and still are women and children.

During the research and writing of my book, I lived with the Maryknoll Sisters in Ossining, New York. I also became quite involved with three organizations dedicated to refugee advocacy and humanitarian relief. I became Board Chairwoman of the Women's Commission for Refugee Women and Children and served on the board of Refugees International. Both are well known advocacy organizations that took me to the field to assess refugee crises and repatriation issues. When I returned from the field, I spoke before a variety of audiences, appeared on radio and television programs, wrote articles and op-ed pieces, testified before Congressional Committees, and met with government officials and UNHCR personnel. I did whatever I could to advocate on behalf of those who are voiceless, uprooted, and forced to flee from their homes to survive. I also served on the board of the International Rescue Committee (IRC) which is one of the largest US non-sectarian refugee relief organizations.

It has been one of the greatest privileges of my life to have walked with so many refugees and internally displaced civilians as well as with those returning to their homelands in places as far flung as Bosnia/Herzegovina, Mozambique, Eritrea, Ethiopia, southern Sudan, Somalia, Cambodia, Thailand, Laos, Vietnam, Pakistan, Hong Kong, Malawi, and more. It has also been a privilege to walk with many great humanitarians, among them Leo Cherne and Carel Sternberg of the International Rescue Committee. When Leo asked actress Liv Ullmann, a cofounder of the Women's Commission, to participate in a trip to refugee camps on the Thai-Cambodian border on behalf of the IRC, Liv asked Leo how long the trip would take. Leo responded, "It well may take the rest of your life." Carel Sternberg, who as a young man twice fled the Gestapo and in 1940 hooked up with the nascent IRC in Marseilles, once said, "The refugee condition, once experienced, does not wash off."

What both men expressed resonated with me and drew me into a world I never dreamed of. I walked that road for almost a decade and saw millions of uprooted people—people one by one—just like you and me except their lives have been turned upside down and their roots torn asunder. In flight they have left behind homes, traditions, histories, pots and pans, and pictures. They have sought safety in a strange land or hidden somewhere within their own borders away from a government bent on destroying them.

It saddens me that so many of the post-Cold War civil conflicts exploit racial, ethnic, tribal, religious, and linguistic differences. Genocide and ethnic cleansing such as we saw in Rwanda, Bosnia/Herzegovina, and southern Sudan and still see in Darfur and other places fly in the face of the celebration of diversity as does the growing xenophobia in the United States and other Western countries.

As I walked among refugee populations, in war zones, and past too many human skeletal remains, I became convinced that it is imperative that we as a human race must do something about the refugee crisis, discern and prevent the causes of flight, and work toward creating peace and stability in our world. It seems to me that if we do not want to witness one humanitarian crisis after another, each more brutal than the one before, we are compelled to be bold in setting new priorities and principles and finding new, nonviolent ways to respond to conflict as did Gandhi and Martin Luther King, Jr.

We have lived long in a war and weapons mentality. While we know our past is past and that we cannot change it—cannot disinvent the weapons we have made, disavow the wars we have fought, deny the disharmony in so many parts of the world—we can shape and create the future we dream of. But we must change the way we think about and act with each other. I found as I traversed war-torn nations that one of our greatest contemporary challenges is to work for reconciliation between warring parties and among citizens caught in conflicts and help others find ways to settle their differences apart from killing and destruction. The world over I have witnessed how people who return home have to find ways to live again in peace and trust with their neighbors, often in situations where massive genocide, rape used as a weapon of war, and other brutalities have broken hearts and bodies.

Underlying most conflict situations, particularly civil conflicts in which nations and peoples have been embroiled, are deep wounds both ancient and new. At conflict's end, transformation through reconciliation and healing are needed, but they do not take place in a moment, a month, a year, or even sometimes a generation. No returnee returns home the same, nor will the nation to which he or she returns ever be the same. Every person and every place is altered radically by the experience of war, exile, and the decimation of structures and land. War-torn nations are as much in need of reconciliation within broken societies as they are of rebuilding infrastructure.

It is imperative that we address the root causes of ongoing conflicts and find ways to prevent others from erupting in order to staunch and prevent further displacement of people. We must go further than conflict resolution and crisis prevention to deal with the political, social, developmental, environmental, and economic situations that compel people to leave their homes. As I moved forward in my thinking and actions, I wanted to be a part of this tremendous opportunity for change and growth in the international community and in reshaping foreign policy. How I was going to manage this was not yet clear, but I did know a door would open.

It was September 8, 1993—a day that I and those around me thought I would not survive. I was critically injured during a relief food air drop in the remote war-torn village of Ayod in southern Sudan. The plane dropping the bags of grain veered totally off course and flew directly toward a group of us standing far off to the side of the drop site. Even though World Food Program people in charge on the ground called for the pilot to abort the drop, he did not. We all ran for our lives as 100+ pound bags of sorghum rained down around us tumbling at a speed of 120 m.p.h. One of the bags hit my right leg. I came close to bleeding to death, but the small plane we had traveled on to Ayod was waiting for us. Fortunately and quite by accident, a doctor had come with us that morning to check on the village feeding center. Had physician Bernadette Kumar not been with us, I would not be alive today. I was flown first to Lokichokio, the relief base on the Kenya border with Sudan. In a tool shed converted to a mini-operating theater, ICRC doctors staunched the bleeding. A large C130 was recalled from another relief drop to fly me at life-saving speed to Nairobi where I underwent nine hours of surgery. The Kenyan doctor saved my life, but not my leg, which was amputated below the knee at Mayo Clinic.

Just as the death of my husband and my inability to go with Maryknoll to work full-time overseas were life-altering situations, so, too, was the loss of my leg. However, had Jack lived, my life would have been quite different—wonderful I am certain, but different. Had I been able to go overseas, would I have ever written the book and immersed myself in the work of advocacy? Would I have worked at building a more peaceable, secure, and habitable world?

What I do know is that the people with whom and on whose behalf I have walked and who I hold in my heart deserve a better world. They are treasures in my life. In Bosnia, Muslim women confided, "We have lost the picture of ourselves. We have lost the picture of ourselves." Why? Because they were victims of rape, used as a weapon of war to terrorize and cause

Bosnian Muslims to flee. When I met with them, they were trying to regain the picture of themselves. The children born of rape in Bosnia are now teenagers. Will they perpetuate the cycles of violence or will they become intent on building a culture of peace?

Once in southern Sudan, I asked a group of midwives what message they would have me take back to the United States. One woman spoke for all victims of war. "We are tired of running—running from bombardments, massacres, and starvation. We gather our children and try to find a hiding place of silence. Sometimes we stay in the bush for months. We look for water and try to stay awhile. But guns break the silence and we have to run again." These midwives wove a beautiful bark cloth mat for me when they learned of my accident. Because the withholding of food and medical supplies was used by the government of Sudan as a brutal weapon of war, these midwives, at the time I met with them, did not even have clean razor blades with which to cut the umbilical cord in the birthing process. Yet, they thought of me.

Commander Elijah, who was in charge at Ayod when my accident happened and who had seen family members starve to death and had watched his village burn, went into seclusion and fasting for three days following the accident because of what happened to me, a stranger in his village. If we have the moral and political will, I believe we can create a better, more equitable world for the millions displaced by war, civil conflict and persecution. But we can do this only if we envision and believe that we do belong to one another and we are willing to "sing a song of peace . . . with a great shout," as did Yitzhak Rabin, and see that in the words of poet Archibald MacLeish, "we are brothers [and sisters], riders on the earth together."[4]

The Gem of *Ubuntu*

My life took a new and unexpected turn in 1994 when the first Clinton administration asked me to become a Special Adviser on refugee issues and policy in the US Department of State, Bureau for Population, Refugees, and Migration. Being there opened another door. Dr. Grace Goodell of Johns Hopkins University's School of Advanced International Studies (SAIS) invited Le Xuan Khoa and me to teach a course on refugee issues and policy. In 1975 Khoa was a professor at the University of Saigon. Two days before the North Vietnamese entered the city, Khoa and his family, bereft of all their possessions, escaped only with their lives. In the US he became prominent in Southeast Asian affairs as President of the Southeast Asia Resource Action

Center (SEARAC) in Washington, D.C. I knew I could teach the course Dr. Goodell had in mind. I finally became a professor.

A few years later at Seattle University, a Jesuit university, Tom Taylor, then chair in the history department, encouraged me to create several courses and I did—"Modern Civilization Through a Refugee Lens," "Sub-Saharan African History," and "The Evolution and Theory of Human Rights." None had been taught before at Seattle University. I was also asked to design and implement the International Development Internship Program that to this day sends students out to developing countries in Africa, Asia, and Latin America for a quarter of the academic year. Students receive university credit for the work they do. In turn they have the opportunity to grow as responsible global citizens.

Ron Slye, a good friend and a professor in Seattle University's School of Law, had served for a year as a consultant to South Africa's Truth and Reconciliation Commission. It was he who proposed Seattle U invite Archbishop Desmond Tutu to receive an honorary degree. I had never ceased asking the questions: How do we get upstream from wars? How do we prevent them from happening? How might the people in decimated lands, who have been pulled apart from one another, create a culture of peace? Little did I dream that the visit of Archbishop Tutu to Seattle University would offer me the opportunity to move more surely in the direction I dreamed and hoped for. Archbishop and Leah Tutu established a trust whereby a peace centre would be established. Chris Ahrends, Anglican priest and former chaplain to Archbishop Tutu, traveled to Seattle with the Archbishop. Chris was now executive director of the nascent Desmond Tutu Peace Centre. He asked to see Ron and me and invited us to become involved in some way with the Peace Centre. I became a member of the Board of the Desmond Tutu Peace Foundation which was founded to support the work and raise funds for building the Peace Centre in Cape Town, South Africa.

In 2001 I returned to Marquette University as Professor and Women's Chair in Humanistic Studies. I had come home to the theology department from which I had earned my Ph.D. years earlier. Although I came for a year, I remained there happily for four once I was invited to set up an international service learning program for Marquette students. The format for this program was quite different from the program at Seattle University. I found great joy in creating the South Africa Service Learning Program (SASLP) due to the incredible support I had from the Marquette team who worked in making this program become a reality. The SASLP is affiliated with the Desmond Tutu Peace Centre and the University of the Western

Cape in Cape Town, South Africa. Students immerse themselves in the culture and customs of South Africa through their studies and working two days a week in a grassroots, community based organization. Students who engage in service oriented, culturally participative, international programs are challenged to open their interior doors and windows to a world crying out for the celebration of diversity and peace. The marvel is that as they open doors and windows in their house of life, they will encounter, receive, and embrace ever more of our increasingly interdependent world and its peoples. What I hope is that new worlds will open for them. I hope that what is strange will become familiar; that they will see their fellow humans in new and wondrous ways. I believe that through concrete knowledge of others, rather than abstract images, each individual can more surely understand our common humanity and embrace that commonality in diversity rather than demonize, categorize, or belittle that which is other and unfamiliar. Concrete knowledge of the other breaks down barriers we create in our minds and builds bridges that will transform our engagement in the world.

South Africa, long a country of closed doors and windows, serves as a beacon of hope for multitudes across the African continent and the world. It is here that I have chosen to spend my retirement years volunteering for the Desmond Tutu Peace Centre. I believe South Africa is a gift to the world, and I am grateful to be a part of the Desmond Tutu Peace Centre and the gift it can be to the world. For more than 350 years, South Africa traveled along a destructive path of wars, colonialism, and apartheid. Apartheid was the most inhumane manifestation of this violent past, dehumanizing all it touched. This legalized separation of the races was first theologized and then implemented by a white Christian minority. Finally, both leaders and ordinary citizens became exhausted under the specter of apartheid and looked for ways to resolve the separation and hate that divided so many who call South Africa home. Thousands of peace workers went out to build bridges throughout all regions of South Africa and at all levels of society, helping antagonists of different color hues and tongue to discover each other's humanity. People learned new ways to respond to conflict and differences. Hearts and mind of people began to be transformed.

Two leaders among them were paramount—Nelson Mandela and Desmond Tutu. Both men led South Africans to opt for restorative rather than retributive justice and for reconciliation rather than revenge. On May 10, 1994, as genocide raged in Rwanda, newly elected President Nelson Mandela stepped forward to give his inaugural address. He pledged a Covenant with the peoples of the new South Africa saying: "We enter into a covenant that we shall build a society in which all South Africans, both black and white, will be able to walk tall, without any fear in their hearts, assured of their inalienable right to human dignity—a rainbow nation at peace with itself and the world."[5]

To advance the peace of this rainbow nation and create a culture of reconciliation, President Mandela wisely appointed Archbishop Desmond Tutu to chair the South African Truth and Reconciliation Commission. Both understood that transfiguring peace requires reconciliation; reconciliation requires forgiveness; forgiveness requires confession; confession requires contrition, contrition requires reparation which leads to restoration.[6]

Both Nelson Mandela and Desmond Tutu's lives and actions have been influenced by the African notion of *ubuntu* wherein a person is a person only in relation to other persons. *Ubuntu* means "I am human because you are human. Your humanity affirms my humanity, my humanity affirms yours." This world view values affirmation and acceptance of the other, interdependence, participation, openness, and concern for the common good. To live in a world of ubuntu assumes forgiveness, reconciliation, and rehabilitation. Desmond Tutu, in his book *No Future Without Forgiveness*, says: "Our humanity is caught up in that of all others. We are human because we belong. We are made for community, for togetherness, for family, to exist in a delicate network of interdependence."[7]

South Africa and the world are now ten years beyond the opening of the Truth and Reconciliation Commission (TRC). The Desmond Tutu Peace Centre as it opens its doors and windows to all who search for peace might in some manner consider the TRC to be the Centre's pivot point—looking back from it into both the recent and more distant past to what brought about both the TRC and the transition to democracy in South Africa and looking forward not only to finishing the business of the TRC but also to making the rights delineated in the new, liberal, and inclusive constitution operative for all. The TRC opened the door to reconciliation and the opportunity for South Africans to find new ways of being human together. But achieving true reconciliation in this brutalized land will, as I have learned, take more than one generation.

I have grown to understand more certainly as well that creating a culture of peace and reconciliation, whether in South Africa or anywhere else in the world, has a very practical cast to it. True reconciliation kindles transformation and quickens the spirit of *ubuntu* with its sense of human solidarity—of a common humanity in all its diverse manifestations—and a relational responsibility for the well being and realization of each individual's human potential. To foster transformation through reconciliation and the spirit of *ubuntu* requires a new mind set, a new way of thinking, acting, walking in the world. It encompasses the political, economic, social, and religious life of the peoples of South Africa who today live in a global world.

Within South Africa's borders I live among peoples who recognize eleven different languages. This beautiful country is a rainbow mixture of races, cultures, and traditions, adherents to a variety of the world's religions, and residents and visitors from around the world. Here, too, within South Africa's borders exists one of the highest crime rates in the world, an ever widening gap between privileged wealth and life-threatening poverty, the scourge of HIV/Aids, unequal access to housing, education, clean water, adequate sanitation, health care, and employment, racism, and more. At the Desmond Tutu Peace Centre we are poised to address these issues locally and globally. Those of us whose lives are caught up in the work of creating a culture of peace will do well to take inspiration from Joan Chittister's reminder: "Change is a dynamic that builds a coherent future out of a chaotic present. Change, if it is real, takes us where we have not been before and could never have imagined that we'd go. It takes the courage of an explorer, the fancy of a dreamer."[8]

The Spirit Spirals

At age 70, I am crossing over into the end time of my journey. Looking back, I see now how my spiritual life unfolded, stumbling often, while continuing the upward spiral. I have witnessed the depths of human brutality and the heights of human love and compassion. "Celebrate diversity" includes race, culture, tradition, tribes, gender, nations, politics, economic systems and ecosystems. This is clear whenever Archbishop Tutu speaks to an audience and extends his arms wide bringing them to form a circle as he says, "All, all, all belong." This is the mystery of life.

For me the people in my life have given me life, even my family in its own way. The sisters, my friends, colleagues, students, refugees—all, all, all have enriched my life and enabled me to grow. One of the greatest gifts has been the gift of *ubuntu*. Another great gift was my marriage to Jack Mayotte. He loved me deeply just because I was me. Through Jack's love, I was finally able to know that I was included in the ancient Genesis text which reads, "God saw everything that he (she) had made and behold it was very good."[9]

NOTES

[1]   The reflections in this chapter were graciously submitted by Judy Mayotte.

[2]   Annie C. Dillard, "Teaching a Stone to Talk" as cited in Parker Palmer, "Leading from Within," *Insights on Leadership: Service, Stewardship, Spirit, and Servant Leadership*, ed. Larry C. Spears (NY: John Wiley and Sons, 1998) 102.

[3]   Judy Mayotte, *Disposable People?: The Plight of Refugees* (Maryknoll, NY: Orbis, 1993).

[4]   Archibald MacLeish, *Riders on the Earth* (Boston: Houghton-Mifflin, 1978) xiii-xiv.

[5]   Anthony Sampson, *Mandela: the Authorized Biography* (NY: Alfred A. Knopf and Sons, 1999) 485-86.

[6]   Informal reflection by Rev. Christopher Ahrends, based on material from Desmond Tutu's *God Has a Dream: A Vision of Hope for Our Time* (NY: Doubleday, 2004) 52 ff.

[7]   Desmond Tutu, *No Future Without Forgiveness (NY: Doubleday, 1999) 196.*

[8]   Joan Chittister, OSB, *The Way We Were: A Story of Conversion and Renewal* (Maryknoll, NY: Orbis, 2005) 14.

[9]   Genesis 1:31. *The Oxford Annotated Bible.* Revised Standard Version (NY: Oxford Univ. Press,1965) 3.

Edwards Brothers,Inc!
Thorofare, NJ 08086
24 June, 2010
BA2010175